Contact the author at: **Art_Hellyer@yahoo.com**

To order your free bonus 72-minute documentary DVD
"Wake Up, Chicago! The Art Hellyer Story,"
send a check or money order for $7 (shipping/processing)
to: Art Hellyer Productions
    P. O. Box 6012
    Naperville, IL 60567–6012
(Available in the United States only.)

THE HELLYER SAY

Autobiographical Essays by
Chicago Radio and Television Legend
Art Hellyer

The Hellyer Say

Autobiographical Essays by
Chicago Radio and Television Legend
Art Hellyer

Copyright © 2008 by Art Hellyer

Printed by Lulu Publishing (Lulu.com)

Library of Congress Cataloging-in-Publication data is available.

ISBN: 978-0-6152-4337-5

10 9 8 7 6 5 4 3 2 1j3

Cover design and book layout by Jeff Hellyer.

Printed in the United States of America.

TO MY WONDERFUL LITTLE SISTER,
WITH ALL MY LOVE —
FOR THE GOOD TIMES,

8-22-08.

Acknowledgments

The author wishes to acknowledge the invaluable assistance of the following people: my mom and dad who produced me, and thanks to the youngest of our five wonderful children, Jeffrey, who with his wife-partner, Leny, in their most successful business Edit House Chicago, not only designed and created the fantastic cover for this book, but also somehow found time in their twenty-hour workdays to publish this volume. And to our other children Larry, Mike, Debbie and Vickie, who not only suggested and encouraged me to write this book, but also solved and taught me how to approach each and every frustrating battle I've had for over four years with the computer.

Thanks must also go to all the fine instructors and advisors who taught me the rudiments of broadcasting back in 1946 at "The Radio Institute of Chicago." Two of those instructors, WBBM-CBS chief announcer Bob Cunningham and Paul Barnes, "The Man of a Thousand Voices," after six months told me to not waste anymore time in school, but instead "get out in the field."

Thanks to Manager Jack Gelder at WKNA, Charleston, W.Va., who gave me my first job New Year's Day 1947, and WCFL program director Bob Platt for being the first person to hire me in Chicago in May 1950. Talent agents Mary Dooling, Shirley Hamilton, Sabie, and Amelia Lorance, and advertising Agency men Walter Schwimmer, J. Walter Thompson, Leo

i

Burnett, Charlie Temkin, Sandor Rodkin, Ray Freedman, Mike Barkas and so many others who employed me over the years. Music czar James Caesar Petrillo, and his son Lee, who made it possible for the magnificent Lenny Kratoska, my "Dr. K," to light up the airwaves with me.

And thanks also to former students of mine at Columbia College and the University of St. Francis, whose success makes me so proud of them: Dan Merkle, ABC-TV News, New York; Roz Varon, ABC-TV News, Chicago; Lane Closure and Leslie Keiling, WGN-Radio News, Chicago; Marty Lennartz, WXRT-FM, Chicago; and so many others.

And I must thank Dr. Richard Guzman at North Central College in Naperville, Illinois, for his very insightful, helpful critiques. And without the prostate-cancer surgery skills of Dr. Jeffrey Feinstein and Dr. Robert Baskind, Hinsdale Illinois Hospital, and the multiple skin cancer surgeries of Dr. Renuka Bhatt, St. Joseph's Hospital, Joliet, Illinois, I would not be on this mortal coil to author this book.

My thanks go also to these fine doctors who keep me ticking 365 days each year: Richard J. Steslow, Paul Lyon, Byron Tabbutt and James Mamminga.

And a special tip of the hat to eight-time Emmy Award-winner Ben Hollis and Andrea Raila for their inestimable contribution.

Many, many thanks also to the millions of people who over the years tuned in to my spot on the dial.

And last, but most important of all, thanks to the Lovely Elaine, my incredible wife and partner through this odyssey for 51 years.

The Essays

Foreword

By Chuck Schaden—
America's Foremost Authority
on the Golden Age of Radio

Art Hellyer was king of Chicago radio and I was one of his willing subjects. No matter when he was on, no matter what station he was on, I followed Art eagerly, just to hear what he would say or do. And I was never disappointed. His programs were original, creative, imaginative, funny and always in good taste.

He cracked me up when, speaking for an automotive dealer, he would say, "This car comes fully equipped with radio, Gabriel Heater and asthmatic. Plus two doors cleverly hinged on each side." Or, "It's a Club Coupe, complete with a club, and a seat so you don't fall through to the street."

I loved it when he would kid the station manager about something, perhaps a newly imposed station rule, often getting him in trouble. Station management would post a memo on the bulletin board—or send a special inter-office memorandum directly to Art—saying that there should be more music and less talk on the station.

Art would read the memo on the air. He would say something like, "Well, I guess management knows what you want and if you want me to stop talking and play more music, so be it." Then he would stop talking and simply play music. Listeners would be up in arms that Art was being stifled and would respond with irate letters to the station complaining about the new rule, and telling management they wanted more Hellyer, less music and less management.

Naturally, management wouldn't like this and would tell Art he should not have read the memo on the air. Art, feigning amazement at the listener response, said he was only letting his audience know why they wouldn't be hearing him say much anymore. Occasionally, in view of listener response, management would back off and tell Art to carry on as usual, but more often—to sooth their own bruised egos—they simply yanked him off the air and fired him from the station.

That's when we loyal listeners would follow him to another station where his great show continued to pile up huge ratings, leaving his former station to wonder whatever happened to the audience they used to have.

Art continued in great form, with his wonderful humorous style and great comedy, novelty and pop records, time checks and weather reports. Plus his original use of those "wild lines" from nowhere:

"There's no light in the men's room."

"Get a nickel back on every bottle, Jim!"

Those lines knocked me out and I still remember them-and use them-fondly.

They were the result of the made-in-heaven collaboration between Art and his record turner Lenny Kaye, whom Art referred to as "Dr. K." These two were somehow joined at the funny bone. Art would make some comment about something—anything—or read a commercial, and Dr. K would somehow find an appropriate line from a comedy record and slip it in instantly.

ART: "Do you know where you can get the best deal on a

mattress?"

RECORD LINE: "I don't as a rule." (Wild line from a comedy record by Billy DeWolfe and Hermione Gingold.)

Cracked me up every time.

Over the years listeners really got to know Art. He told us everything about himself, his cars, his family, and his wife, "the Lovely Elaine." We knew what he liked and didn't like. When his neighborhood and home in Skokie were flooded by heavy rains, he told us he lived in "Soakie."

He could remember exact dates. We knew the date he entered military service and the date he was discharged. We knew the date of his first-ever radio broadcast (January 1, 1947), and the dates he left his last four radio stations. And we loved every moment of it. We loved every moment with Art Hellyer. This book adds to that treasured time.

THE HELLYER SAY

THE LOVELY ELAINE

* Essay 1 *

The first time ever I saw the lovely lady who would be my wonderful wife for over fifty-one years was in the halls of York Community High School, in our hometown, Elmhurst, Illinois.

She was rapidly threading her way through the throngs of chattering and laughing students who would always congregate within the hallowed ivy covered walls between class bells. Some would swiftly traverse the halls to the next class, others would seem to be slowly moving in varied-sized clumps. Some of the clumps were made up of boys turning into men, others would be clumps of girls turning into women. Some were mixed clumps, and then there was me, the mixed-up clump. I was a member of the minority clump group. I was a lone clump. The best thing about being a lone clump was not having to carry on a meaningless conversation with other clumps. As a loner I could have undivided thoughts.

And the first time I saw the Lovely Elaine she was clutching a big batch of books to her chest. Elaine loved books. She read books. She quoted from great books. Elaine was a bookworm, and she was a wordsmith, and she was beautiful. Elaine Lydia Miller lived in a modest home at 270 May Street, Elmhurst, Illinois, a western suburb of the city of Chicago which in 1940 had no zip code. In fact, no city had a zip code in 1940, and first class postal stamps were three cents.

I lived at 189 S. Kenilworth, approximately a mile from Elaine's home, and I had no idea when I first saw her in the York High hallway, I would make that walk hundreds of times a few years later.

My friend Jim Roorda, grew up to become a very famous medical doctor, and would have an-depth article written about him in Reader's Digest. He and I would often shoot baskets at his home which Elaine Miller would pass each day on her long walk to and from high school. I often saw her passing by Jim's parents home carrying many pounds of her beloved books

Jim had a basketball hoop attached to his folks' garage and we passed many happy hours there shooting baskets, speculating about our futures, and watching pretty girls walk by. Dumbbell me was never aware that when Elaine Miller saw me at Jim's house, she always crossed the street, which was a bit out of the way. It wasn't until years after we were married she told me why she took that circuitous route. One of her girlfriends, which one she never did reveal, had told her Art Hellyer was a lunatic, so she avoided me.

Was it Doris Gestland whom I had inadvertently stood up on a date one Saturday night? I showed up the following Saturday night, with flowers yet, and her mom told me Doris was out on a date. Then her mom told me my date was the previous Saturday night. I still feel badly about that oversight, because I would never intentionally do that to anyone.

Was it Dr. French's daughter Katie? I never had a date with her. But I had my first ever dental appointments with Dr. French, and I can recall vividly the heat I felt in my mouth as the good dentist pedaled his treadle dental drill ever so slowly into my decaying molars.

This was a great advancement over earlier dentistry when the teeth were never saved. Instead the patient would be given a slug of rotgut, then held down by two bouncer types and the dentist would pry, rip and pull until the bloody tooth came out. If the terrified patient was a teetotaler, the only other choice was to be knocked into unconsciousness by a crude baseball bat. I was always pleased to be in the capable hands of Doc French, who practiced modern up-to-date dentistry.

Perhaps it was one of the Chant girls whom I never dated. My brother Dick dated one of Doug Chant's daughters. Somehow she escaped Dick's clutches, and her sister ended up married to Georges Papandreou, the Prime Minister of Greece. These things just don't happen only in fairy tales you know.

It couldn't have been Elaine's best friend, who lived directly across the street from her, Shirley Grover. I knew Shirley slightly, and liked her enough to ask her if she'd be my date one night, Christmas week 1945, when Elaine Miller was going to the Marine Dining Room of The Edgewater Beach Hotel with another of my closest friends, Ralph Hartsing.

She agreed and Ralph picked me up in his dad's beautiful 1938 Packard limousine with the famous spare tire side mounts. Then we drove across town to Elaine's house, and Ralph went to her door to walk her to the car. As they came out the front door of 270 May Street, I was struck by the beauty of this girl I had never before seen without a stack of books hiding most of the upper part of her body. It was a chilly December night, and Elaine was wearing a cloth coat with a little fur collar wrapped around her throat. She was gorgeous! Then as she got into the car she smiled, the original Julia Roberts smile at me, and I was a dead duck.

Ralph then drove across the street to Shirley's driveway, and it was like docking the Queen Mary. I had forgotten how really large that limo was. Somehow, I pinned Shirley's corsage on her without damaging her, and got her into the back seat, at least a mile behind Ralph and the dazzling woman who had captured my heart.

THE HELLYER SAY

Young people today spend a date screaming and hollering, and snorting and smoking awful things while five or six tramps, wearing too-tight blue jeans, undershirts and baseball caps turned sideways destroy their hearing apparatus, thumping guitars and shouting filthy words they can't understand. And they call that music.

When Ralph drove the Packard into the curved entryway to The Edgewater Beach Hotel, the car's doors were opened for us by men in tuxedos. And as we climbed the stairs to the main entrance our ladies were beautifully gowned and Ralph and I were wearing blue suits and white shirts and ties with Windsor knots.

We were both home on furlough, Ralph from the Navy, I from the Air Force, the war was many months over, and we were wearing civvies for the first time in over three years. This was a wonderful evening!!!!!

I've always remembered that night as though it were yesterday. It was the most important night of my life. How could I forget it? After checking our coats, we walked on beautiful red carpet to the entrance of The Marine Dining Room. As we opened the doors, the lovely room was awash in the soft music of "Russ Morgan, His Trombone and His Orchestra," to quote the words I myself, unbelievably, would be speaking as I introduced him on the ABC Radio Network, coast to coast just seven years in the future. But that was years ahead, and tonight I was in another world. What a pleasure to listen to this lovely music played by sixteen professional musicians, all dressed in tailored blue suits, white shirts and matching dark blue ties.

I was enchanted by Elaine and thrilled when I, the world's worst dancer, lumbered around the dance floor once that evening with Elaine in my quivering arms. Poor dear Shirley had to suffer with my size twelve gunboats smashing her tiny toes all evening long.

The Lovely Elaine

I just now for the first time had this thought, Shirley Grover must have been thrilled when on the way back to Elmhurst that night, I announced to her, in our seat a mile behind Elaine and Ralph, "I'm going to marry Elaine."

As long as I live I will remember that magic night of nights.

As I write this on May 12, 2006, the eighth anniversary of the day our wonderful family lost our treasured Elaine, I am deeply saddened, but also so thankful I was the most fortunate man who ever lived, for I did indeed marry the Lovely Elaine, on March 14, 1947.

It is impossible for me to believe the rapidity with which those fifty-one years passed, and the millions of memories our family made. And today, the Lovely Elaine has been gone from our lives eight years...EIGHT YEARS!! And I shall never get over that terrible loss for me, our five super-wonderful children, Larry, Mike, Debbie, Vickie, and Jeff; our seven truly fine grandchildren, Gina, Ricky, Michael, Matthew, Jeremy, Jocelyn, and Jessica; and the world.

And I probably would have made little, if nothing, of my life without this great lady. Elaine inspired me, she put the polish on my speech, AND she was so much more intelligent and learned than I. I learned so much from her. Elaine loved life and for her the glass was always half-full, not half-empty. Each time I was fired she'd say, "Don't worry Hon, we'll get along just fine. We always have before and we will now." She'd bolster my ego by saying at these times, "Art, you're a legend in your own time. Please don't worry; you'll be on the air again. Just relax. We'll be fine." And we always were, as long as she was here.

Anything I might have become, I owe to this remarkable lady. And I miss her terribly. I still believe she will walk through the front door! And she'll smile at me, and say, "Hon...let's go to Burger King and get OUR USUAL, and sit in the car at the curve in the river, and have another one of 'Our mini-picnics' listening to our favorite classical music on WFMT."

The Elmhurst, in which we grew up, was a beautifully groomed, tree-lined community. Most of its male inhabitants were employed in Chicago. And they, like my dad, traveled to and from work on the two commuter railroads, the Chicago and North Western steam railroad, and the Chicago Aurora and Elgin electric railroad.

The few brave souls who drove to and from the loop each day had no expressways until 1957. My dad drove to his loop office only when business meetings forced him to do so, and it was an hour-plus adventure each way. East on St. Charles Road into the morning sun, then South on Mannheim Road to Washington Boulevard, then East another fifteen miles with the sun blasting into the drivers' eyes. The trip home each afternoon was once again into the sun. More than once dad said to me, "Son, each time I drive to work I wish I'd bought a home in a northern or southern suburb." I agreed.

Traffic was so heavy, a driver was constantly shifting the gear box up and down hundreds of times (I once counted my manual shifts from WOPA's studios on Oak Park Avenue to the Loop—over four hundred in eight miles). And the automobile companies had only two options drivers could add for a nominal charge to the cars' four-hundred- to eight-hundred-dollar base price: a heater and an AM radio.

Listening in the car to Norman Ross Sr.'s fine shows on WMAQ (Chicago's great NBC radio station we all loved, now gone forever, replaced by a sports station with unknowns, most of whom couldn't carry the jockstraps of the magnificent broadcasters who formerly graced that frequency on the dial), for the Northwestern Railroad and Simoniz, and the "News with Alex Dreier" made the drive almost pleasant.

The few females who worked in those days did so as clerks

or secretaries, or waitresses in the banks, stores and restaurants in downtown Elmhurst: Walgreens, Ollswang's Department Store, Phil Soukup's Hardware Store, The Elm Store, Woolworth's, The A&P, The Elmhurst National Bank, Max Borger's Rexall Drugstore, Mannebach's Meat Market, Cooper-Pollack Ford Agency, Stevens Restaurant, The York Theatre, Pfund and Clint Florists, Harold Cruger's *Elmhurst Press*, and Rabe's Dairy with its adjacent baseball field where one of my favorite sluggers of the nineteen-forties, a slip of a girl named Polly Rebec would pound out three-hundred-foot home runs. And many of the working ladies taught in the grade schools and York High School, but they had to be unmarried to do so. Even when Beaver was in grade school in the nineteen-fifties, his teacher was not married. Remember Beaver always saying, "Yes, MISS Landers?"

The only two women I was aware of working daily in the loop were Greenie and Brownie, so named by us because that was the color of their clothing as they walked past my folks home to and from the steam trains. We later heard, when one passed away, they were sisters and both were attorneys.

The great majority of Elmhurst women stayed home, cleaning their houses, preparing three meals a day, doing the wash, first on a scrub board in a tub, and then with the modern-marvel--the wringer-washer. My sister Irene, as a little girl, had beautiful long ringlets of hair that one day in the nineteen-thirties almost cost her her life. She leaned too close to the wringer, and got her hair caught in with the clothing as it slowly moved up the slanted platform toward the device. My dear mom heard Irene scream, and was close enough to turn the cruncher off before it made mince meat of Irene.

When the Japanese sneak-attacked the United States naval base at Pearl Harbor on December 7, 1941, they actually did two things of the greatest consequence: they forced us to become an active participant in World War Two, and they freed American women forever from eight hours plus of daily household drudgery.

The men went off to war, and the women went to work in defense plants or allied industries. When Elaine graduated from York High School in 1942 she went to work almost immediately, as a secretary in the purchasing department at Commonwealth Edison on West Adams Street in the loop. And she made a few extra dollars over her four years there appearing as a model in their newspaper ads. Our youngest daughter Victoria Elaine Hellyer-Siegel, and eldest son, Larry, sent this e-mail to our family on May 9th, Mother's Day 2004, three days before the 6th anniversary of the day we lost Elaine:

"Thanks, Lar, for sending this out. It was very nice of you to do on Mother's Day. I remember seeing this in something for the Congregational Church, I believe(?). I'd forgotten that she wrote it on mom and dad's 50th anniversary. I thought it had been written longer ago. Thanks. Reading mom's words does help make it feel a bit like Mother's Day. And Happy Mother's Day to Deb and Sheila!
Vickie"

At 08:01 PM 5/9/2004, Larry wrote:

"While I do not agree with all of mom's conclusions, I thought I'd send out something she wrote because it seems like a good idea for Mother's Day. And some words from our mother might be of interest to everyone.

"'DO NOT WORRY. Therefore do not worry about tomorrow, for tomorrow will worry about itself. Each day has enough trouble of its own. Matthew 6:34'

'Who of you by worrying can add a single hour to his life? Since you cannot do this very little thing, why do you worry about the rest? Luke 12:25-26'

"As a champion worrier, I am hard put at times to keep the above passages in mind. My mother was a worrier, too. And my husband, Art is a world's-champion worrier. All our worrying, however, never changed a single thing. Sleepless nights and digestive disturbances and moodiness and crankiness were all that resulted. Big worries and little worries came and went, and life went on as usual. I can't even remember most of the worries. Health and money were the main ones, of course, and fears about the family are still present.

"I am aware, too, that much worrying is self-centered and can disappear when challenged by the greater burdens and needs of others. This can be a tremendous help in putting problems into proper perspective.

"I have found that there is a solution, though, to excessive worrying. And that is prayer. The harder I pray and more I ask for the Lord's guidance, the lighter the burden becomes. And prayer coupled with learning is an unbeatable combination. Especially when it comes to family. For instance, if children are taught what to do in case of fire, accident, illness, or any other emergency, worries can be lessened all around. And if your faith sets an example for them, so much the better. Their faith might get stronger and rule their actions, which will help alleviate much worrying.

"Today is Art's and my 50th wedding anniversary. We are grateful for these years together and for our wonderful family. A lot of worrying went on, but prayers won out and we have been truly blessed. Thanks be to God!

"Thank You, Lord for Your love and care,
    Every moment, everywhere,
    To be forever worry-free,
    All we need is faith in Thee.
    Amen.
Elaine Hellyer, Naperville, Illinois"

Elaine Miller Hellyer was murdered by the horrors of

breast cancer, which metastasized to her liver. This shy, gentle, kind lady, this lovely wordsmith-poet, suffered through many agonizing surgeries and procedures, multiple hospitalizations, and chemotherapies, and a multitude of errors that were made by the hospital staff, doctors and nurses.

Yet not once did she complain, and, no matter how terrible the pain, she always had a smile, and a "thank you." And her husband, wonderful children, and her grandchildren were buoyed by her to the end.

Elaine continued with her treatments, and each time she returned from the hospital she went back to her job of twenty-six years as church secretary at the Naperville Congregational Church, where she worked for several outstanding ministers (including Dr. Edwin Briggs, who was featured in a 1941 *Life Magazine* article, in conjunction with the Fredric March movie "One Foot in Heaven" as "typifying the best in Protestant ministry," and the young, dynamic Reverend Donald Limmer).

Her last Mother's Day (1998), as she lay in the hospital bed in our home, son Jeffrey played the guitar and daughter Vickie played the Steinway piano I gave Elaine on our Fifth Wedding Anniversary, March 14, 1952. It took me five years to pay it off at Lyon & Healy, but the happiness it brought our family over the years certainly made it so worthwhile. And this last Hellyer family concert, just a day before Elaine died, made it all worthwhile.

Daughter Debbie and her husband Rick, their daughter Gina, and two of their three fine sons, Mike and Matt, were here. The wonderful man Vickie would marry, and we all believe Elaine was aware of that, Jon Siegel, stood alongside our other two sons, Larry and Mike. Larry's wife Sheila and Mike's wife Patty also were here all day raising their beautiful voices in song.

(Jeffrey would not meet the splendid woman, Leny, who is

now his wife, until after we lost Elaine. It's so sad, because Leny and Elaine would have loved each other.)

This musical family of Elaine's sang everything from Cole Porter to The Beatles to grand opera, and the Lovely Elaine was so happy. There has never been a finer family than the one the Lovely Elaine left to care for me.

And when she left us, and the world so much richer for having known her, she left, in an envelope, a letter to her family. This will tell you better than I ever could, the fine person we lost forever on May 12, 1998.....

"MY WONDERFUL, BELOVED, ADORED FAMILY
When it's time:
1. Please call the Episcopal priest. St. John's number is 355-0467. (Father Jeffrey Liddy is currently the rector.)
2. Request a prayer when he arrives (you don't have to stay in the room if you'd prefer not to)
3. Funeral home is to be called---cremation as soon as possible.
   Beidelman-Kunsch, 117 W. Van Buren Ave., 355-0264
   (I suggest this one because I got acquainted with John Kunsch through the church, and he's nice and very helpful and pleasant.)
4. No visitation (wake) or funeral service.
5. Please have a prayer offered during the following Sunday's worship at St. John's.
6. After worship service, a private committal service to be held at church's memorial garden (attendance not obligatory). (It is my wish that the urn remain with the priest until the committal service.)
7. Please request a prayer each at the other two churches:
   The Naperville Congregational Church, 357-4092. Current pastor is the Rev. Joseph M. Cimbora, Jr.
   Big Woods Congregational Church, 898-0451. Current

pastor is Dr. David W. Nasgowitz.

8. A while ago, the only time I checked, the total cost was $540.84 at a funeral home for all services and permits, etc. The cost is higher now, I'm sure, but reasonable enough. The church charges nothing for burial in the little garden, but please offer the priest a gratuity and give the church a little donation in my name (my requests, not the church's)

9. Always remember:

I LOVE YOU!!!

10. And now.....Please go out to dinner, and carry on with your lives as before they were so rudely interrupted.

Whether I'm in the hospital or at home, no extraordinary measures are to be taken to keep me breathing.

Elaine M. Hellyer

4-7-94"

CHILDHOOD

* Essay 2 *

**"ARTHUR L. HELLYER, JR., Winner,
City of Chicago, Central States Fair.**
*Better Babies Conference
Conducted by State of Illinois,
Len Small, Governor. Aug. 30–Sept. 7, 1924"*

"Arthur is a dear little boy in school."
*Mrs. Rathbun, Kindergarten teacher
Washington School, Glen Ellyn, Illinois*

I was born in my parents' apartment (it was so much nicer than arriving in stirrups in a hospital) at 7942 S. Harvard Avenue in Chicago, Illinois on August 7, 1923. My dad, president of his law class at Chicago Law School the following June, was so excited with the arrival of his and my mom's first born, he ran to the bathroom, shaved, and then grabbing for the aftershave, splashed himself liberally with turpentine, which might or might not explain my turbulent approach to life.

Dad grew up on a farm outside Poughkeepsie, New York, and my mom was born and raised on the south side of Chicago. Dad went to Tusculum College in Greenville,

Tennessee, and became close friends with a young man from the Great Smoky Mountains, named Dale (Moose) Alexander.

In 1932, the same Dale Alexander led the American League in hitting, and during one of the series he played at Comiskey Park he phoned my dad at his office in the loop and arranged for dad to pick him up after the game that day. Ballparks had no lights at that time, so dad met Dale at the park at 35th and Shields around Five-Thirty PM, and brought him to our home at 714 Grant Street in Hinsdale, Illinois. There the hitting star of the Detroit Tigers/Boston Red Sox could find a refuge from the huge city he so detested.

On May 30, 1933, Dale Alexander suffered a terrible leg burn while being treated with diathermy by the Red Sox trainer, and returned to the Smokies never to play major league ball again. I remember him as a large man, well over six feet tall, who spoke few words, and when he did, he had that heavy southern Smoky Mountain drawl.

My dad's serial number in World War One was 3891. This meant he was one of the very first Americans to enlist before we entered the war in April of 1917, and shortly thereafter he found himself in France.

Dad fought in the trenches in the seven major battles of that "war to end all wars," and Marshal Ferdinand Foch, the brilliant French, Supreme Commander in Chief of the Allied Armies, pinned the Croix de Guerre on dad's tunic for "gallantry in action."

Dad was felled by the dreaded mustard gas in the second Battle of the Marne (July 15–August 4, 1918), the definitive battle that forced Germany to surrender, and brought to an end my dad's active service.

Somehow dad had survived the terrible war that had cost over ten million lives. And he also survived what must have been an agonizing steamship trip across the Atlantic Ocean to New York City, where for some unexplained reason, this resident of New York State was shipped by railroad to a hospital on the south side of Chicago.

It was here the fates brought a fulltime telegrapher at the Pullman Company and part-time volunteer Gray Lady named Irene Connery into his life. She was walking between hospital rooms one day when she saw a telephone fly into the hall and drop with a crash to the hall floor. The patient in the room had, in desperation, pulled the phone out of the wall, and thrown it as an attention-getting cry for help. Gray Lady Irene Connery answered Private Arthur Lawrence Hellyer's cry for help. On August 15, 1921, Irene Marie Connery married Arthur L. Hellyer, and I arrived on August 7, 1923.

Times were tough as a depression era child. I grew up, as most in that time, moving from place to place. I went to kindergarten and first grade at the Washington School in Glen Ellyn, Illinois where my dad had a beautiful large old stucco home at 725 Euclid Avenue. It had a porch that wrapped around three sides, and a wonderful fruit-tree-filled two acres orchard. One time my right leg slipped into a tree hole in the orchard, and it took the local fire department to dig me out of the ground. I am looking at a photo of the house and my mom wrote this note on the back, "Everything is beautiful now—the snow stays white much longer here than in Chicago." And she dated it...December 1928.

It was while living there my dad decided my mom should learn to drive a car. My grandma, Catherine Connery, was staying with us and she and I witnessed the beginning and end of mom's only attempt to master "the machine," as grandma always called it.

Mom left the driveway in dad's 1927 Dodge, that to me, a small child, seemed to stand thirty feet high. Mom looked good at the wheel as she slowly drove out of the driveway into Euclid Avenue, the instructor in the right front seat waving at us, and the car soon disappeared from our sight. The great adventure had started. My mom was on her way to getting a driver's permit.

Well, about twenty minutes later the great adventure ended forever. With herky-jerky motions, the big black Dodge lurched into our driveway and started toward the garage about sixty feet away. Grandma Connery stood watching with me, holding my small hand, as the car seemed to be picking up speed, with mom now, seemingly welded to the steering wheel. We could see the instructor wildly waving his arms as the car, still gaining speed roared into the garage, and without the single brake light ever lighting, the car, now a raging bull, roared through the back wall, with boards and two-by-fours splintering and flying in every direction as grandma and I looked on in horror. Dear sweet mom climbed unscathed out of the car which now rested in back of the collapsed garage and sweetly said to her mom, "Well, I tried, didn't I?" My mom never drove again.

Grandma Connery, my mom and I, hand-in-hand, witnessed another famous "transportation first." The Graf zeppelin floated slowly over Euclid Avenue on its twenty-five-thousand-mile flight around the world in 1929. Today, every American would have a video camera filming the great event. All we had then was our eyes, and our memories to record the awesome moment. After the Wall Street crash of October 29, 1929, dad, sadly, lost this beautiful home, and the now-rebuilt garage.

I was a skinny little boy and the bigger boys beat me up frequently. I remember one day in particular when we all made paper kites and I was skipping merrily home, flying mine. It would go about ten feet in the air and then crash, but I was six years old and for me it was a great adventure. Then two or three bullies tackled me on the concrete street about eight blocks from home and tore my pretty red kite into little pieces and left me bleeding and crying. I limped the rest of the way home.

I still have a report card from Washington School. My teacher, Mrs. Rathbun graded me E for excellence in Reading, Conduct and Effort, and D in Writing. Under "Remarks" she has written, "It is difficult for Arthur to write. Please have him do things with his hands at home. Drawing and cutting would be a great deal of help. He is a very dear little boy in school." Wow!!

My handwriting has always been dreadful. Many, many years later, when I was a junior at York Community High School in Elmhurst, Illinois, I stood one day in Physics class to read a paper I had written. That was all I did...I stood. Finally the instructor, Mr. Olson asked me what my problem was. The class roared with laughter when I said, "I'm sorry Mister Olson. I can't read my writing." Perhaps I should have done more "drawing and cutting at home" when I was in the first grade.

Over the years my extremely poor handwriting would continue to haunt me. At ABC-TV in the early eighties at a reception for Jimmy Carter at The Blackstone Hotel, I wrote the directions to Ch.7's studios so he could be my guest on the late night news. To this day he has never shown up. I believe I know why. And in the 1980s, at The Satellite Music Network I continued to answer every piece of mail I received, but apparently not everyone could decipher it. A doctor's wife in the Seattle, Washington area, who assumed I was at KIXI in Seattle, when in reality I was broadcasting from our studios in Mokena, Illinois, wrote me at KIXI to thank me for answering her letter.

"My dear Mr. Hellyer. I continue to enjoy your shows so very much, in spite of your terrible handwriting. Or was this written by your four-year-old granddaughter? Sincerely, Mrs. Patricia Downing."

Christmas day of 1927, Santa Claus left me a small metal

model of my first hero's airplane. It was "Lucky Lindy's Spirit of St. Louis." The Ryan Company of San Diego built the REAL one for him. Charles Augustus Lindbergh barely got the overloaded-with-gas-flying-bomb over the telephone wires and into the air at Roosevelt Field, Long Island, New York, as he started his successful solo flight to Paris, France.

I have since read and reread his books about that first-ever solo flight: thirty-three and-a-half hours later he was the world's first civilian air hero. I was running with the little model plane and zooming it up and down over the dining room table when I tripped and fell headfirst on the metal propeller. It imbedded itself in my left forehead just above the eye. The doctor who sutured me back together told my folks "another inch and Junior would have lost that eye." Like Lindy, I too was lucky.

I hated that name "Junior," which unfortunately stayed with me well through grade school, and resulted in my being involved defending myself in many fist fights as the assailants would taunt me. "Show us your girl's underpants, Junior!" .....Fun.......yeah!!!

Our third home was a third floor walkup at 81st and Bishop in Chicago. While living there I took my beatings from the toughs at the Fort Dearborn School. Next stop was 714 Grant Street in Hinsdale, Illinois. I remember one day when I was being beaten up on the long walk home from the Madison School, my little sister Irene came running down the hill on Grant Street shouting, "You leave my brother alone." And bless her she fought off the assailants before they damaged me anymore. Thanks to Irene I lived to get beaten up another day.

Some days I would walk home from school with my next door neighbor Kenny Williams and he would invite me in for an after school snack, Ken'l Ration Dog Biscuits. He would smear them with Welch's concord grape jelly and wolf them down like a delicacy. I NEVER EVER tried one.

Childhood

Hot summer days, Irene, Kenny and I would run down the street chasing the ice wagon until the driver saw a house with a sign in the window. If you don't remember those signs—my mom used hers at least once a week in the thirties—the signs had the number 100 printed on top, 75 and 50 on the sides, and 25 on the bottom. Mom would put the number of pounds of ice she needed on top in the front window. Usually to save a few pennies she would put up the number 75. The ice man would stop his horse drawn cart, go to the rear, and using his eyeballs as his scale he would chop off what appeared to him to be 75 pounds, hoist it up with his tongs and rest it on the leather pad covering his shoulders, and then head for the back door of the house. As he disappeared, we'd lean into the ice wagon and scoop up as many ice chips as we could. Then we'd run away, sit on a curb or a back porch and suck on those heavenly, cool chunks. This was as close as we got to air-conditioning in the nineteen-thirties.

Another thing we loved to do on a very hot day was sit on the curb, and with a small twig pull up the hot melting tar, and chew it. Believe it or not it had a wonderful taste to it. Would I recommend kids do that today? No way!

I carry with me so many wonderful memories of the nineteen-thirties. Things were so much slower and quieter then. We didn't have any of the "conveniences" of today and we lived just fine without them.

I tell my grandchildren about waiting on hot July and August afternoons for the horse-drawn Good Humor wagon to arrive. This was a daily neighborhood social event that involved all the kids and ALL the moms.

Back then mom didn't go to work. DAD WENT TO WORK, PERIOD. And the country would be so much better today if someone would be home each afternoon when the children arrive after their day in school. I have no objection whatsoever to women working. I just want an adult in the home after school hours.

One of the kids would be the very first to sight the horse as it turned the corner at Sixth and Grant Streets and slowly started up the hill towing the Good Humor wagon, as we jumped up and down, hardly able to contain ourselves. Ice cream cones were five cents, so I knew I must be certain of my choice. My dad always said to us "Money doesn't grow on trees, and five cents is a lot of money, so spend it wisely."

So, would it be vanilla, chocolate or strawberry? Three out of five times my choice would be vanilla, and it still is today. There is something cool, soft and creamy about vanilla, the other two flavors just don't have.

As the horse came closer we could hear it whinny and snort, and one of the moms would say, "Poor thing. Clarence, how would you like to be pulling that heavy wagon full of ice cream up a hill in the hot summer sun?" Then one of the little girls, sometimes my sisters Irene and/or Loretta, would run to the hose stretched on the lawn like a long green garden snake, and get some water for the struggling beast of burden.

One or two of us would always stroke the old boy (we all assumed it was a "he"), and give him just a short snort of cooling water. It was guaranteed one of the moms would say, "Junior, don't give him too much water."

While we kids were standing in line discussing ice cream flavors, the moms would be excitedly talking about the big sale on electric fans at Walgreens. One mom would say, "Isn't two dollars and ninety-five cents too expensive for an electric fan?"

I remember one "old lady" who was probably all of thirty years old, saying, "They can charge those high prices because the weather's so hot, and we need fans to keep cool." And another one saying, "I heard Charles Walgreen has one of those fancy Sheridan Road apartments facing Lake Michigan, and it's so cool he doesn't even need a fan. He just opens his windows and lets the lake breezes cool him. It sure must be nice to be rich. When you're rich you don't have to buy expensive fans at Walgreens."

All this small talk under the hot summer sun was interesting for a kid of ten, and helped fill the time I was standing in line anticipating that first of thirty licks of vanilla. Then it was my turn. I looked up at the back of the wagon with its stacks of dry ice wrapped in straw encasing the three heavenly tubs of frozen delights, and I said, "One scoop of vanilla, please." "That will be five cents young man," said the purveyor with the handlebar mustache. I, of course, in the frenzied excitement of the moment, dropped my buffalo-head nickel, and had to suffer childish ridicule as I crawled among the horse-apples beneath the wagon to retrieve my precious coin. Having finally done so, I paid for my beautiful, by now not so-frozen, melting vanilla cone.

I put it to my lips for that first succulent, cooling taste of nectar, when the kid behind me bumped me, and the ball of vanilla plopped to the sizzling August asphalt. My dear mom softly said to me, "That's alright, Junior. Tomorrow's another day."

It was in Hinsdale and Elmhurst our family got to know the county nurse, a lady who would stride to the door dressed in black men's-clothing complete with a black felt, snap-brim fedora, and tack contagious-disease signs on our front door. The first one was "WHOOPING COUGH" and the last was a double-header. We had two diseases at the same time, so the door was plastered with "MEASLES" and "CHICKEN POX" signs. When those signs were posted, dad had to stay at his office. Times have changed. I don't believe I've seen those signs since the nineteen-forties. I suppose some groups marched in the streets protesting that the signs were an invasion of their privacy, or maybe the children don't catch those diseases anymore, or maybe a Dr. Salk-type found how to eradicate them. I sure hope so, because I don't recommend anyone having measles and chicken pox at the same time as I did.

Back in the nineteen-thirties, I idolized many, many broadcasters and of course dreamed of some day being one myself. I probably heard more radio shows than the average child because I was home sick at least half the years I was in grammar school. Flat on my back in bed with a thermometer sticking out of my mouth, and a steamer running full blast keeping my chest and nasal passages open so I could breathe. How I ever passed every grade, without flunking and repeating a semester or two I don't know. The teachers must have felt sorry for me because even when I was in the classroom I was usually shaking with chills. The world had not yet heard of Woody Allen so there was no one to compare me to or with. The scholastic world is lucky Woody was born in New York and I in Chicago, because if we'd been schooled together, many, many teachers would have ended up in mental institutions.

Listening to radio, as a child in the 1930s, was for me escape and pure magic. And even today in 2008, I fall asleep every night listening to the nation's foremost old-time radio guru, and my dear friend for over forty years, Chuck Schaden, and his "When Radio Was" program. Then during the night, when I get up at nature's urging, I turn on my Father's Day Gift of two years ago from son Michael, my XM satellite radio, and I keep it tuned all-night to the old-time radio channel. A gentleman named Greg Bell does a nice job hosting the shows I still love to hear. Just last night he played my favorite Lux Radio Theater presentation "Stella Dallas" which starred the beautiful lady I have loved all my life since I first saw her as Stella in the movie version in 1937, Barbara Stanwyck. When all my boyhood friends were frothing at the mouth over Lana Turner, Rita Hayworth, and Betty Grable, I was, and still am, in love with Miss Stanwyck. I have always had an extremely vivid imagination (which would be used extensively some years later as Dr. K and I did our ad-lib on-the-air skits) and I would envision in my mind what was being portrayed through the loud speaker.

Example? "Vic and Sade," my all-time favorite comedy radio program. I would see the small house in Crooper, Illinois, where the Victor Gook family lived, as announcer Ed Roberts (who would with his wonderful announcer brother Howie Roberts become dear friends of mine in those many magic years later I never dreamed would or could happen) would tell us was "halfway up the next block."

Vic would often walk home for lunch from Plant Number Fourteen of the Consolidated Kitchenware Company where he was employed as a bookkeeper. He would always come into the kitchen which was alive with the sound of "beef punkles" sizzling happily in the pan as his wife Sade and their adopted son Rush would be involved in small talk about a phone conversation Sade just had with her closest friend Ruthie Stembottom which invariably involved concern for Ruthie's husband Ted's latest knee problems.

Often Sade's flaky Uncle Fletcher would join them, regaling them with a story about Rishigan Fishigan of Sishigan, Michigan, and the woman he married, Jane Bane of Pane, Maine. I, being a lifetime railroad fan, enjoyed most Uncle Fletcher's description of the terror at the Bright Kentucky Hotel as the speeding Wabash Cannonball came roaring out of the night, headlight boring into the rooms, straight at the hotel only to veer at the last moment and race around the building, whistle screaming as it disappeared into the darkness on its mad dash to St. Louis. And I would scream with laughter as Uncle Fletcher, who never heard or paid any attention to what anyone else said, would say "fine."

Uncle Fletcher would tell his stories about Robert and

Slobert Hink who were twin brothers, and he would talk of obscure people who were born in Dixon, Illinois, and for some never-explained reason at age 38 moved to Dismal Seepage, Ohio, or Sweet Esther, Wisconsin.

Vic would always come in the back door but one time he came in the front door and Sade really laid into him for that indiscretion. He used the front door that one time because he was in a hurry to change into a white shirt for a luncheon he had been invited to attend with his two bosses and a very important executive from the main plant in Iowa.

I still laugh as I recall this event of over seventy years ago. This was a last-minute get-together and when his boss, Mr. Buller, called for a reservation at The Little Tiny Petite Pheasant Feather Tearoom, the only table available was for only three people, next to a window. So Vic solved the problem of where he would sit by announcing he would place a ladder outside the window in the alley and lean forward through the window. When Vic tells Sade and Rush they are aghast, and she then gives us one of the greatest moments in radio history, you must hear it to appreciate it.

Mr. Buller even phoned Vic while he was at home changing his shirt to make sure Vic really wanted to sit there. Vic assured him it would be "fine" and as Vic was going out the back door the show ended with Rush very slowly saying, "Vic, it's starting to rain." Hilarious fun written by a genius, Paul Rhymer, who never, NEVER in his lifetime received proper credit for this best of all daytime radio shows.

Each weekday morning at 11:15, announcer Dan Seymour (these announcers were, along with baseball players Lou Gehrig, Hank Greenberg, Luke Appling, Joe DiMaggio and Ted Williams, footballers Sid Luckman and Bill Osmanski, and flyer Charles Augustus Lindbergh, my boyhood idols) would introduce "Aunt Jennie's True Life Stories," where following the story each day we'd hear Aunt Jennie's "golden thought for the day."

After ruminating over this daily bit of homespun philosophy through the network system cue and local commercials I would anxiously await the rich baritone voice of Fielden Farrington as he spoke the magic words, "Time now for 'The Romance of Helen Trent'...who when life mocks her, breaks her hopes, and dashes her against the rocks of despair, fights back bravely to prove that because a woman is 35 and more, romance in life need not be over, that the romance of youth can extend into middle life, and even beyond."

All this being said as a 5-string banjo plunked in the background and we heard the song "Juanita" being softly hummed further in the background. To this day, I often find myself softly humming "Juanita."

"The Romance of Helen Trent" hit the airwaves in 1933 when I was nine years old, and ran until the final day radio soap operas were on the air....June 24, 1960, at which time I was 36 years old and Helen was 60-plus, and still finding romance. In fact, Gil Whitney, the man in her life all those years, in an apparent attempt to keep interest in the show alive, frequently would compliment Helen on her gorgeous legs. Pretty racy stuff for radio soap operas.

But even that couldn't save "The Romance of Helen Trent." Fade in banjo, fade in hummers......fade out "The Romance of Helen Trent"!!!!!!!! Fade out radio soaps!!!!!! Radio soaps were all washed up.

When I wasn't ill, my mom and dad, if our homework was done, would invite my brother and two sisters to join them in the 1930s entertainment center, the parlor. We would gather around the modern 1934 Zenith 12 tube console radio with dual speakers and "Shadow Graph Tuning." Neighbors, hoping they could twist the tuning device, would actually stop in to listen to the number one rated show of that time, "The

Maxwell House Showboat" starring Charles Winninger as "Captain Henry." We would use our imaginations to see the radio shows, and I can still remember actually seeing "The Showboat" as I listened.

My favorite radio comedians were Jack Benny, Fred Allen, Fibber McGee and Molly, Lum 'n' Abner, Red Skelton, and George Burns and Gracie Allen. Each show was marvelously written, and every actor was a master of the craft.

Dialect comedy was very rare on radio. Freeman Gosden and Charles Correll were, for over a decade, the number one radio show in the ratings services of that day. They played all the characters on "Amos 'n Andy," and to this day one of the most beautiful and heartwarming radio shows of all-time was their annual Christmas program. All my years on radio, I would play it every Christmas Day as part of my nationally syndicated Christmas show, and on my local radio show, too.

Mr. Kitzel (Artie Auerbach) would appear in a street scene on "The Jack Benny Show," but most comedic shows did not inject dialect. Then "Life with Luigi" hit the airwaves in 1948, and it was all Italian dialect. Three great character actors headed the cast, J. Carrol Naish, Alan Reed (whom I interviewed years later when he was the voice of Fred Flintstone) and Hans Conried. The setting was Taylor Street in Chicago, "Little Italy," and for five years the entire country laughed at this pioneer show. Then, just as rapidly as it had appeared, it disappeared in 1953. I can still hear Naish, as Luigi closing the show, "So long, Mama-Mia. This is your lovin' son, Luigi Basko, the little immigrant."

After Chuck Schaden's midnight old-time radio show, my "XM" satellite receiver stays on all night, every night. It's super hearing Fibber McGee and Molly, Jack Benny, Fred Allen, Bob Hope and Red Skelton again, but my best nights are the ones the radio detective shows of the thirties and forties are playing. How wonderful to once again hear superstar movie actor/singer Dick Powell portraying "Richard Diamond, Private Detective." His pretty-boy singer movie image in the 1930s changed when he played Philip Marlowe in the movie "Murder, My Sweet" in 1944.

Howard Duff's background was primarily as a war correspondent with the Armed Forces Radio Service in World War Two, and his great voice and amateur acting experience found him winning radio show roles. He was heard by "Suspense's" director, William Spier, who was looking for a lead for an about to be produced new radio show, "The Adventures of Sam Spade." It was as though Duff had been born Sam Spade. No one could have played the role better.

In high school I read all the Nero Wolfe novels by Rex Stout available in the Elmhurst, Illinois, library. When the show came to radio in 1943 I was beside myself with joy. In the early days a great radio actor Santos Ortega played the massive, orchid-sniffing detective, and Elliott Lewis was Archie who did all of Nero Wolfe's legwork. Lewis also played hundreds of other supporting roles on radio, including Phil Harris's and Jack Benny's goofy guitarist, Frankie Remley. Later, in 1950, the role of Nero Wolfe was portrayed by one of Hollywood's greatest actors, Sydney Greenstreet. I would listen to the show just to hear Greenstreet's rolling laugh.

Rounding out my top-five detective radio shows, which I am still hearing frequently, thank goodness, are "Broadway Is My Beat," which was directed by Elliott Lewis, who must have worked 24 hours a day for over 30 years, and "Yours Truly, Johnny Dollar," an unusual PI who, at the end of each episode, accounted for every penny he spent on each case.

Two shows that scared the daylights out of me at 11:30PM to Midnight were "Suspense" and "Lights Out." A "Lights Out" episode written by Arch Oboler that had the master sound-effects crew working overtime was a show that still haunts me. All the people on earth suddenly had their bodies turned inside-out, and they oozed, and dripped, and splashed and squished as they walked.

For years people visiting our house after Elaine and I were married, would find me, as today, probably not watching television, but reading a book. Reading, I do what I did listening to radio, when it was REAL radio: I see every scene in my mind.

My dad must have realized early on his goofy eldest progeny just might end up on the radio, so he surprised me one day with a 5-watt public address system he had purchased from one of his law clients, Sam and Abe Poncher's, Newark Electric on Madison Street, in the heart of Chicago's loop. Well ten-year-old me and my seven-year-old brother Dick decided, why waste our talents inside the walls of our house, when we could bring enjoyment and entertainment to all within reach of our mighty 5-watt broadcasting station.

We put the speaker outside a window on the second floor roof, and placed our favorite recording artist Bing Crosby's 78rpm Decca recording "I'm an Old Cowhand" on the single speed, of course, turntable. I say that because back in the thirties, LPs, 45s, tape, and all the rest had not yet been invented, much less heard of.

Well, it wasn't too long before the village constabulary arrived and shut down our first venture in broadcasting. That quickly shot down the other wonderful plan we had—to sell commercials to the local merchants.

It was then that brother Dick came up with a great alternative plan: We would leave the speaker on the roof, but we would camouflage it and we would hide back of the chimney, and boom out comments to passers-by.

Among the first of these lucky people was the parish priest in his somber black Buick four-door sedan. In a voice as deep as a ten year old could muster, I delivered some made-up scripture, and at mass the very next Sunday, the good father spoke to the congregation in hushed reverential tones. He told us that while driving in his car that very week he thought he had heard the "Voice of God Himself" speaking to him from heaven. Only Dick and I did not start clicking our beads, or "praising God."

As home radio sets became art-deco and their circuitry more sophisticated in the mid-nineteen-thirties, people started throwing in the trash their late nineteen-twenties and early nineteen-thirties "superheterodyne" receivers. So, I would pull my "Radio-Flyer" wagon behind me and fill it with four or five of these dinosaurs.

Then I would strip them of their multitude of tubes, capacitors, resistors, and tuners, and assemble one that actually would work. My folks had to put up with fifty foot strands of copper antennae wire strung between the trees with an insulator at each end, and a lead-in wire that I fastened to a clip on the back of the receiver so I could pull radio stations out of the Kennelly-Heaviside layer of the ionosphere. Next, I would "ground" the set. This was done by pounding a four-foot rod of steel from Soukup's hardware into the earth. Next I would solder a length of doorbell wire to it, and then attach the other end of the wire to the "grounding post" on my receiver.

I would use this antennae-ground equipment on the crystal sets I also built. A crystal set was a simple device, needing no batteries, or electricity as did the superheterodyne. I could purchase for thirty-nine cents a Philmore crystal set all ready to hook up, or I could build one.

I did both, and I sure wish I had them to display today. A crystal set consisted of a small base to which was affixed a little metal pot with a piece of galena ore in it, a "Cat's whisker" (the primitive tuning-device), and clips for the antennae, ground, and earphones.

People in the early nineteen-twenties when radio stations

KDKA, Pittsburgh, and KYW, Chicago (KYW moved to Philadelphia in 1934), started broadcasting, had only crystal sets to listen to the new miracle of "hearing music coming through the air."

I would listen to the radio every chance I could, and I worshipped the announcers at WLS where I loved "The National Barndance" on Saturday nights. I would listen closely to Jack Holden, the announcer and host, and I would repeat after him, every pronunciation and enunciation.

"Arkie" (Luther Ossiebrink), "The Arkansas Wood-chopper" (Red Foley), "LuluBelle and Scotty" (Myrtle Cooper and Scott Wiseman), Louise Massey and The Westerners and her brother, Bing Crosby-like Curt Massey; cute little Patsy Montana and The Prairie Ramblers, the comedy and singing of thirteen-year-old native-Chicagoan George Gobel, whose guests we would be exactly twenty years later at his home in the San Fernando Valley, the fantastic yodeling of the DeZurik Sisters, and the solos and duets by Grace Wilson and Henry Burr.

Twenty years later when I broadcast my daily morning show on WCFL, one of the big thrills of my lifetime was receiving a fan letter from LuluBelle and Scotty. I, of course invited them on my show. They told me they grew up in North Carolina 40 miles apart and then met on "The National Barndance" in Chicago, fell in love and married. What a lovely story and what lovely people they were. I am still so proud I got to meet them. Had I not been on radio, I never would have.

Through his job in the 1930s, as DuPage County, Illinois, Treasurer, my dad knew the legendary WLS Program Director Art Page, whose home was in the city of Wheaton, Illinois, which is the county seat. One day when they were talking, Mr. Page invited dad to stop in the WLS studios and meet some of the performers.

Childhood

Needless to say I HAD TO GO WITH HIM. I JUST HAD TO!!!!

And so it was that our entire family was seated in the front row of the audience studio at WLS watching Art Page host his daily noon program, "The Dinner Bell Hour," and we got to meet two of my favorite WLS stars, Red Foley and—swoon, swoon—Patsy Montana.

WLS was founded by Sears Roebuck and Co., and the call letters meant "World's Largest Store." The fifty-thousand-watt powerhouse was the favorite station of millions of farmers throughout the Midwestern states.

And why was a show at noon daily called "The Dinner Bell Hour?" Well, I worked on a farm one summer as a kid and I can answer that question: because that's when farm families had their dinner. They called the evening repast "supper."

If I learned one thing my summer on the Ralph Hartsing farm outside Wheaton, Illinois, it was how much I looked forward to dinner each day.

Monday through Saturday, we were up at 4:30AM. We started our chores at 5AM in the barn. It goes without saying we would milk the cows, and feed and water the cows, and horses. Then we would clean the barn areas, and get the motive equipment (tractor, reaper, hay-bailer, thresher, etc.) ready for our day in the fields. We would move around during the summer months, from one farm to another, helping other farmers work their land too. And of course, they would reciprocate.

Since that long ago summer I have had a soft spot in my heart for farmers and their families. They lead very, very hard lives. And I only worked in the summertime. I can just imagine how tough that life is, as Merle Haggard sings "Deep in December." At six in the morning, the ladies of the farm family would have a HUGE breakfast prepared, and we'd line up at a side table and fill our plates. And what a selection of food from which to choose. There were platters of eggs, fried, hard-boiled, poached and scrambled, bacon, sausages, toast, home-made jams and jellies, and coffee and tea, for everyone but me. I've had a very dangerous lifetime allergy to caffeine, so I'd always pour myself a cool glass of fresh milk right off the farm. Udderly delicious!

7AM until the dinner bell sounded exactly at noon we would WORK! By noon I was pooped! Farm work is hard, it is rigorous, it is severe. Oh! Man!! It was all I could do to stagger, exhausted, into the farmhouse and tackle dinner. AND WHAT A DINNER!!! Breakfast was just an appetizer compared to this spread.

Platters were stacked high with fried chicken, pork and roast beef. And you haven't seen bowls of potatoes until you've eaten on a farm. They were glorious, fluffy, hot-buttered mountains of spuds. And the biscuits and hot gravy! Oh! My! There is nothing like a farm dinner. How I ever got back in the fields for four more hours each day I can only attribute to my youth. Even then, I was in my bunk every night and sound asleep at 8PM.

If I had the opportunity to be young again, would I spend a summer, knowing what I know now, working on a farm? You bet I would!!! Everyone should work one summer on a farm.

As I grew older the kids beating me to a pulp sort of turned around. For a while, I held my own with the bullies and then I started to win some of the battles. By eighth grade I was beating off the attackers. And in high school where I captained the community American Legion baseball team the only fights I was involved in were my fault, usually for sliding into second base, spikes flashing a la Tyrus Raymond Cobb. That was when I quickly learned how to dodge bean balls. And at my next school, St. Isaac Jogues in Hinsdale, Illinois, I learned how to dodge erasers thrown by the sweet nuns.

May 1st, 1935, dad bought a house at 189 S. Kenilworth

Childhood

Ave., Elmhurst, Illinois, for twelve thousand dollars. Someone else living in it in 1999 sold that same house for six hundred eighty-nine thousand dollars. I'm glad my late dad doesn't know that.

It was in this large old home with the oilskin covered walls, and ball-and-tube electrical wiring that would spring to life with lightning bolts racing around the perimeters of the walls during heavy thunderstorms, and its coal-fired Holland Furnace, which always seemed to go out on the coldest winter night, I began my communications-journalism career the summer of 1937.

At age 13, I founded a DAILY newspaper, *"The Hellyer Gazette."* My staff consisted of my three siblings. Irene, age 10, I appointed, "Society Editor." Her duties were to first cover the daily social events in our home, and there were many, after which she would cover the community social life. Our father, who at that time was not in heaven, was in his third year as the duly-elected, by 13 votes, plus a recount that showed his plurality to be 784 votes, DuPage County, Illinois Treasurer. To this day dad is the only person ever elected on the Democratic ticket to a four-year term office in this extremely Republican county.

Dad took us to the county courthouse in Wheaton one day to watch the recount, but the only thing I remember is the Illinois National Guardsmen with their 1927 Thompson submachine guns, patrolling the area.

I have always been a moderate-independent voter who selects the person I feel is most qualified for the job, whether Democrat or Republican. I was merely following in the footsteps of my father who was also an independent voter.

In the summer of 1934, my dad was drafted by the DuPage County Democrats, led by Pete Meidel of Lisle and Hinsdale's Tom Green, to be their candidate for County Treasurer. I have not checked recently, but I will soon, to see if the burghers of

DuPage County, Illinois, have yet filled the blanks at the county court house where dad's name should be engraved.

I have another not-too-pleasant memory of life as one of the children of a Democratic public servant in DuPage County in the nineteen-thirties. My folks had a death-threat warning, and for the four years dad was in office it was feared one of us would be kidnapped. So we could only leave our house to go to and from school each day, and we were required to play only in specific friends' yards near our home.

As we walked to and from school, we were followed by a Model A Ford at first, then the latter years a Ford V8, with a Secret Service agent at the wheel. As we played after school and weekends, an agent was always watching us closely. These four years and the period in 1938 when dad was the Democratic candidate for DuPage County Probate Judge were strange years indeed for the Hellyer family. I remember mom saying to us when dad lost in 1938, "I'm glad your dad lost. Now we can go back to a normal life like everyone else."

Has DuPage County changed? Well, in 1964, son Michael, expressing his opinion, placed a Lyndon Johnson sign in his front bedroom window. Our house was almost immediately splattered with eggs and had to be washed and repainted. And I've noticed in September of 2004, as I write this, the Bush-Cheney signs remain on neighbors' lawns, but the Kerry ones disappear.

My position with *"The Hellyer Gazette"* was Publisher, Editor and Sports Editor. My folks had an old Royal typewriter, and using one finger as I still do today, I would type out the world news, the national news, and the sports news on white 8 by 11 inch paper, with plenty of carbons. The carbons were responsible for the demise of our daily journalistic effort. Youngest sister Loretta was our distributor. It was her job to take the awful looking, crinkly, sloppy, smeared carbons door to door in the immediate area and sell them to the housewives for a penny each. We thought we were doing great because Loretta would sell every copy of the paper. You would have bought one too, for a penny, if a tiny, pretty, shy girl with a slight lisp came to your door. But people soon tired of each day buying, even if for only a penny, a messy carbon-copy newspaper they could barely read.

Irene would take her notes at my dear, long-suffering mom's luncheons for Democratic ladies. Eight or ten brave women would run the Republican gauntlet to 189 South Kenilworth Avenue fearing for their very lives.

On the other hand, my brother Dick—who was born on the very day my first hero, Charles Augustus Lindbergh, was taking off for Paris, France, on his 33½-hour flight into the history books, May 20, 1927—was our automotive, aviation and railroad editor. This 10-year-old kid would write highly knowledgeable articles on the methods of transportation of the nineteen-thirties. He covered everything from the Baker Electric that drove by the house every day with a little old lady at the tiller, its two cut-glass containers filled daily with freshly cut flowers, to Mr. Brazelton's glorious black Lincoln Zephyr. Mr. B owned the Elmhurst Airport, and among his planes was a stunning Stinson Gullwing that our young Transportation editor gave a wonderful review. I've never asked Dick about this, but his articles were so in depth even at that tender age, I'm sure he sneaked a test flight in the Stinson, and I know he rode many times in the Brazeltons' Zephyr.

It was while I was editor of *"The Hellyer Gazette"* I became a published author for the first time. A poem I had written appeared in the March 2, 1938, *Chicago Daily News* column "The Voice of the Grandstand." Mr. Lloyd Lewis, an ardent Cubs fan, wrote the daily column, and he printed my "poem" reluctantly because it put his beloved Cubs in a bad light. I was fourteen years old.

For my effort I received a free ticket to a Cubs-White Sox

exhibition game which was rained-out and never played. Story of my life early on, huh? I guess I don't embarrass easily or I wouldn't be printing this early writing effort in a book that will be read by sophisticated, scholarly folks.

"Dear Mr. Lewis. I am a loyal White Sox fan.
  I am submitting a poem I wrote and I hope you will
  publish it in your column.
I
Hurrah for the White Sox
And a lot of boos to the Cubs
When it comes to playing baseball
The Cubs act like Scrubs.
II
Take a look at the spring series
Of which the Cubs have won few
The Cubs fans are bleary
When they see what the Sox can do.
III
It's too bad about Stratton
But the Cubs feel relieved
For when it comes to battin'
He could hit them off Lee.
IV
At second base there's Jackie Hayes
Who can field smooth as a church sermon
He leaves the Cubs in a daze
And especially Billy Herman.
V
At third base there's Marv Owen
And owin' to this fact
He could run circles
Around Stanley Hack.
VI

Childhood

At shortstop there's Appling,
Who fields mighty well
He makes the Cubs look silly
With their newly acquired Bartell.
VII
In the White Sox outer garden
There's Radcliff, Steinbacher and Walker
To get by these fellows
You have to be a good talker.
VIII
And in conclusion
This I must say
The Sox are a better team
You can see that any day.

ART HELLYER, JR.,
189 S. KENILWORTH AVE.,
ELMHURST, Illinois"

"Dear Mr. Hellyer: Your poem arrived in the same mail with a sonnet to the late Dempster MacMurphy, who in his times as conductor of 'The Voice from the Grandstand' took great pleasure in the poetry that fell out of envelopes as he opened them. He could write very good verse himself and he certainly would have published yours, too."

My dear mom was born in Chicago, Illinois, September 23, 1898, and my dad first saw the light of day less than thirty days later at Poughkeepsie, New York, on October 12, 1898.

Dad's father Max, who had owned and raced Hambletonian ponies, had at one time been quite wealthy, but when I first met him, he and my paternal grandmother Esther lived in a rented third floor walk up apartment two stories above the small butcher shop they operated on the first floor of the building. I recall the building as being on Market Street. Were

41

grandpa's horses winners? I have no idea, but I do know he and my Grandmother were very poor when I first met them in 1935.

When our eldest, Larry, first heard our Poughkeepsie grandparents' last name he was ecstatic. His favorite author is the creator of "Tarzan of the Apes," Edgar Rice Burroughs, and he assumed my grandparents having the same last name, were related to the great author. His elation rapidly diminished when I spelled their last name for him, Burros. We were not related to the famous writer, but rather we were related to a jackass.

The Hudson River flowed within a few blocks of the meat market, and I loved to walk down to the shore and watch the riverboats puff their way up-and-down-river to romantic sounding places like Hyde Park, home of the president, Franklin Delano Roosevelt, and the Vanderbilts; and to the south of Poughkeepsie, the fortress on the Hudson—West Point, where Lee, Grant, Sheridan, Pershing, Sherman, Eisenhower, MacArthur, Marshall, Patton and my granddaughter Joci had studied; and Croton-on-Hudson, and Tarrytown and Ichabod Crane flying through the night. Many times each day, I would stand in awe and gaze in wonderment at the mighty New York Central Railroad passenger trains just out of Grand Central Station, New York City, stopping briefly at Poughkeepsie on their way up the gloriously beautiful Hudson River to the state capital at Albany, where they would end their northern pursuit and swing to the west to the shores of Lake Erie, and then the Queen of the New York Central fleet "The Twentieth Century Limited" would begin its daily race with the pride of the Pennsylvania Railroad, "The Broadway Limited," to see which one could arrive in Chicago sooner.

When I was older I would drive to the stations at 63rd and Englewood on Chicago's south side, and await the late afternoon arrival of these two giant racers. And more than once I boarded one or the other for the short run into the city, just to get the feel of "The Century" or the "Broadway." I'd catch an "El" back to 63rd and Englewood, pick up my car and reflect on what I had just done. From the ridiculous to the sublime. From "The Century" or "The Broadway" to the "El."

People have always considered me strange, and weird. I don't disagree with them. I've always marched to that "different drummer" to whom Henry David Thoreau paraded. Elaine and I even walked out from Concord, Massachusetts to Walden Pond, where Thoreau hid from humanity and cogitated, ruminated and meditated. Until I saw it, I always thought of the pond as being terribly remote. Actually it was just a short walk from Concord. Hmmm!

I had my very first-ever corned beef sandwich in my paternal grandparents' little shop, and to this day I look forward to ordering "a corned beef sandwich—slice it very, very thin please." How thin? "So I can read a newspaper through it, please."

Our trip east in 1935 was marred by tragedy. Dad bought a brand new Blue Oldsmobile 8-cylinder, four-door sedan with an extended trunk. Back in the thirties, Olds was General Motors' test car, so while most all other cars that year continued to have roofs constructed of wooden stringers covered by fabric, or leather, the 1935 Olds had a STEEL ROOF. They called it, in their advertising, "A Turret Top," and Oldsmobile also pointed out they now had "tempered safety glass." These two features alone would help to save our entire family's lives.

Dad was at the wheel, my younger brother Dick was in the middle and I was in the right front seat READING my Tom Mix Big-Little Book. Mom was in the back seat, with the youngest member of the family, little sister Loretta, in the rear middle seat. Second-eldest Irene was seated in the rear, directly behind me.

Our first stop was just two blocks from our house at the Immaculate Conception Catholic Church. Father William J. Plunkett, resplendent in his ceremonial robes, sprinkled the sparkling new blue car with holy water. Approximately three hundred miles into our trip this special car bath would pay off.

Dad was driving, of course. Mom gave up her driving career, as documented in this treatise, and the rest of us were far too young to sit behind the wheel. We were eastbound on US6-US20…just east of Painesville (what an appropriate name), Ohio, on an S-curve that would take us under a New York Central Railroad overpass, when suddenly a 1935 Ford Coupe was hurtling toward us on OUR side of the road. Dad, a highly decorated World War One veteran took immediate evasive action, swinging the larger brand-new Oldsmobile, with THE TURRET TOP and SAFETY-GLASS, to the RIGHT.

Dad and the car, and as Father Plunkett and the nuns would later say, "The Holy Water" saved our lives. The smaller Ford struck the larger Olds "amidship" just behind dad's left front door. The big car did a complete roll as it was "totaled." We, with seat belts as yet unheard of, bounced all over INSIDE the car, and as the MIGHTY one-hundred-twenty-one-inch wheelbase OLDSMOBILE rolled back onto its four wheels, we were all miraculously alive, albeit looking and feeling like smashed potatoes.

Mom and dad had been seriously injured. My sister Irene suffered a fractured skull and Dick suffered an injury that caused fainting spells at unexpected times for many, many years. Baby sister Loretta had head and eye injuries that still plague her. I, who had been reading, struck the windshields SAFETY GLASS, and lost my vision. Was I blinded forever? No. I suffered a severe injury to the optic nerve, the blindness lasted five or six weeks, and then my eyesight, which had been

20/20, had a new and permanent reading of 20/600. I remember asking Dr. Herbert Nash, our family ophthalmologist, when he came to the house what that meant, and he told me, "That means you can see at 20 feet what a normal eye sees at 600 feet."

When it was deemed safe for our entire family to travel, dad with a seriously injured back, and six taped broken ribs, suffered from striking the steering wheel as he fought to save our lives, mom in a hospital bed and the rest of us walking wounded, rode the New York Central's crack train, "The Twentieth Century Limited" back to Chicago. Ambulances then took us from the loop to our home at 189 S. Kenilworth Avenue in Elmhurst, 15 miles west of the city of Chicago.

Do I remember all this clearly? No, the very last thing I remember is people running toward us, and the wife of the man whose car struck us, SITTING IN THE RIGHT FRONT SEAT OF THE FORD READING THE NEWSPAPER!!!!!!! For years afterward dad talked of her callousness, and also of 8-year-old Dick who ran to the driver who had struck us and screamed, "You ruined our beautiful new car." From then on I remember nothing, not even the train trip home.

I do know dad's brand new Oldsmobile with The TURRET TOP and THE SAFETY GLASS, the Right Car at The Right Time, was declared a "Total" by the insurance company, and dad went to the Olds plant at Columbus, Ohio to pick up another brand new 1935 Oldsmobile. Dad told us many times it was the last 1935 Olds built, and he showed us the serial number, which was one hundred twenty thousand something. Our FIRST 1935 Oldsmobile remains my favorite car of all time because along with Dad's skillful maneuvering, it saved all of our lives.

My dad had another major scare twenty-one years later. The Headline of the *Chicago Daily News* (cost: 10 cents), Saturday, September 1, 1956, proclaimed...

"HERE'S HOW IT FEELS TO BE STRUCK BY LIGHTNING"

Then a sub-headline: "Like stab from Giant Pin." Then the story:

"What's it like to be struck by lightning?

"'I felt as though somebody had shoved a giant pin through my head,' said Arthur L. Hellyer, Sr., Democratic candidate for state treasurer. 'There was a terrific roar. The whole world seemed to light up.' Hellyer was hit Wednesday night while making a phone call from a gas station in El Paso, Illinois, about 30 miles east of Peoria. Hellyer said, 'The bolt came out of the phone. It was an old-fashioned phone on the wall. I knew at once it was lightning and I thought about death.' He said he had no feeling of electric shock, just a deep burning feeling throughout his body. 'I wasn't knocked out,' Hellyer said. 'Things grew black for a moment. Somebody led me to a chair.' He recovered and was driven to Springfield where a doctor told him, 'God was with you.' Hellyer said he believes this.

"His left hand and arm were left slightly paralyzed by the lightning, but doctors have told him the paralysis will last only a few days. He is now undergoing treatment in his home in Elmhurst. Hellyer, 56, is the father of four. He said his wife Irene was stunned by the news at first, but then uttered, 'the words we all felt, thank God I survived.'

"He could make jokes about his experience: 'I'm glad it was my left arm and hand. I'll still be able to shake hands during my campaigning.' He said he expects to rest up over the long holiday weekend in his home and then again hit the campaign road.

"Illinois Bell Telephone company officials said that such accidents are extremely rare. Telephone lines, they explained, are protected by two fuses which blow when subjected to any heavy electrical charge."

Childhood

This might be a good spot to mention why I have always had a quirky personality. From the time I was a very young boy my dad never let up on me. I suffered many, many childhood beatings from dad's belt. Many were vicious beatings I can never forget. But it was statements dad frequently said to me from early childhood right up to the day I was married that stayed with me and haunted me most: "Take that smile off your face son, we weren't put on this earth to have fun," "There are only three things I will allow my eldest son to be when you are grown-up, son. My first choice is priest, secondly a doctor, and third a lawyer. You will be one of the three, I know." "You must never associate with anyone whose father is below a vice-presidency." Well, I didn't become any one of dad's choices, and dad refused to listen to my radio and TV shows because "a radio announcer is well below our station in life." And the beat goes on.

I was not struck by lightning, but I too had a political career. It lasted one week, in June of 1939, when I was one of two lucky boys selected by Elmhurst, Illinois, American Legion Post THB 187 to attend Premier Boys State and participate in the State of Illinois legislative process. The Governor himself, The Honorable Henry Horner, welcomed us and the Secretary of State, The Honorable John Stelle, and his staff guided us through our selection of candidates for state office at our very own convention. Then there were campaigns by the candidates, including a number of speeches, and finally we performed the actual duties of the offices we'd won.

I have in front of me my official "Legislative and Judicial Districts, Premier Boys State Certificate of Election" stating, "This is to Certify that at a general election held in Premier Boys State on the 27th day of June, A.D. 1939, ART HELLYER was duly elected as REPRESENTATIVE in and for the 3rd District.

In witness, Whereof I have hereunto set my hand and seal

this 27th day of June, A.D. 1939.

CHARLES CARROLL, Secretary of State

And there is yet another official document here at my hand these 67 years later. This one states "For Election Officials and Appointive offices, Certificate Of Appointment, Premier Boys State. By virtue of the authority vested in me by the constitution of Premier Boys State and the statutes in such cases made and provided, and reposing full confidence in his ability and integrity, I do hereby appoint ART HELLYER as Sergeant at Arms in and for the House of Representatives of Premier Boys State.

In witness Whereof, I have hereunto set my hand and seal this 30th day of June, A.D., 1939. CHARLES CARROLL Secretary of State

Pretty heady stuff for a fifteen-year-old, but thanks to that very special week I probably learned more about our government by actually DOING, than I could have learned from two to four years of BOOK study. It was a wonderful education that has stayed with me all my life. I think it also taught me, because I actually was involved in the caucuses, the campaigning for office, writing and delivering speeches, and the election process itself, and then governing, to always vote for the best-qualified candidate and to not just follow one party line. Living closely with my fellow party members and my opponents I found they each had their virtues and their vices. I found we are all just human beings with our frailties, and that a straight party line does not always get the best people. I learned we must study each candidate, no matter his or her party, and then vote for the one, no matter the ticket, whom we feel can most help the people. I have always had a warm spot for those wonderful members of the American Legion who made that highlight experience possible for a youngster. I humbly thank them for caring enough for our beloved country and for me.

Childhood

Have you ever tried to get a 400-page book published? It is not easy. Back when I was Art Hellyer I would have mentioned one time on any of my shows I was looking for a publisher and I would have been flooded with phone calls. Now, as I write this is in early 2007, I am nobody and the few offers I've had have been ones to self-publish.

Good friends and excellent authors Chuck Schaden and John Russell Ghrist have been most helpful to me, as has old listener-friend Dan McGuire, by telling me much about the roads they traveled in publishing successfully.

My son Larry, always generous to a fault, wanted to bankroll the publishing for me, but I know financially he is in no better shape to do it than I. All the wonderful children "The Lovely Elaine" left me with have offered to chip in, but I just can't allow them to jeopardize themselves financially. After we lost the Lovely Elaine to the horrors of breast cancer and bad medical personnel (EXCEPT FOR THE ONCOLOGY NURSES), I could not have made it this far without our children's and grandchildren's visits, emails and phone calls. Living alone, after 51 years of being in Elaine's company, love and care, is hell.

One of the few good things that has happened as a result of finding myself still composing this tome is finding old newspaper articles like this in the attic: From the column "Random Ramblings" in the Downers Grove, Illinois, REPORTER January 7, 1937......(Writer not identified) "We had the pleasure last week to be entertained in the home of Arthur Hellyer...Who is the treasurer of DuPage County...At his home in Elmhurst...Along with a few other congenial people...The evening was different....The Hellyers are strictly home folks...Having their interest in their children...They neither play cards nor dance...Which is, in this day, almost something to write home about...As there are few people as young as they who haven't one of these vices...or virtues...Depending on the point of view...Personally we do both, the one indifferently well; the other not so good according to the rules of Work, or one of the other sharps...But we derive real pleasure from both pastimes...What we started to say was that the Hellyer children demonstrate that their parents have raised them in the right manner...They are polite, well-behaved, intelligent and have the most marvelous electric railroad to play with we have ever seen...We questioned Mr. Hellyer whether the road was for the pleasure of his children or himself...He was honest in his answer that originally (it has been collected for 12 years) it was for his pleasure but now the boys get the greatest kick out of it...Electric switches which work...Semaphores which stop a train before it can get into the next block...Things like this will give you an idea of what the road is like...And the boys have at least three complete trains to play with....From the President's Special to the utilitarian freight."

My brother Dick and I still have those wonderful 1920s and 1930s wide-gauge American Flyer trains. Dick today has an N-gauge empire and I have a running Lionel-MTH O-gauge railroad. We still love playing with trains, thanks to our dad.

My dear friend Ralph Hartsing's parents owned a 1937 Packard V-12 Touring Limousine which had a HUGE 136 inch wheelbase, and cost the Hartsings an outlandish twenty-five-hundred dollars, complete with side mounts, and a separate chauffeur's compartment.

One glorious summer's day in 1940, when the world smelled so young, Ralph Hartsing dressed himself in a chauffeur's uniform and picked up our closest friends starting with Paul Albert whose grandparents were the Pentecost Fish Company, Pentecosts. Their mansion was at the southeast corner of Cottage Hill and Church Streets, in Elmhurst, and every week I would HAND mow their very large lawn for ten cents an hour and Mrs. Pentecost would at the hottest time of the day bring me a glass of her famous homemade lemonade, and some butter cookies. So good, and so nice of her.

I often noticed a man, in very old clothing, tending their shrubs, flowers and plants, and I assumed he was the gardener. Quite recently Paul Albert informed me that that was his Grandfather Pentecost, Fish Merchant to the World, home early from his office at the Fulton Fish Market.

The next friend Ralph picked up that day in the Packard Limo was the scion of a very well-to-do family, Frank Sturges. For years Frank and I and Jimmy Anderson would build rubber-band powered model airplanes and fly them from the third floor balcony of the Sturges' mansion. The circular driveway three floors below us, that had in earlier times seen the cream of ELMHURST society arriving in horse drawn carriages, was SUPPOSED to be our landing field, but it rarely was.

Most every flight seemed to find its way beyond the friendly confines of the Sturges property, and land in Cottage Hill Avenue where the fruits of our many hours of labor would quickly end in one loud, pathetic crunch of balsa wood stringers and banana-oiled paper, as a Packard or Ford or Terraplane or Studebaker would run over the little plane and continue down the street, the driver oblivious to the destruction he had wrought.

How did we enjoy this day of days? Ralph Hartsing drove us all the way to Evanston and back. We leaned back in the gloriously comfortable upholstery, smokers puffed on cigarettes and cigars, we whistled at pretty girls, stopped to fill up with gas, had hamburgers and "One in a Millions" at a Prince Castle, drove through the beautiful campus of Northwestern University, along the shore of Lake Michigan, and then Chauffeur Ralph drove us back to our homes in Elmhurst. Just five young men, still in high school, on a beautiful summer's day, with a war, that we all soon would be involved in, going full blast in Europe, enjoying a harmless day of good clean, simple fun. That special day not one of us had any idea it would be many, many years before we would see that kind of a day again.

And a sidebar at this point. Ralph Hartsing survived many naval battles and came out of the Navy, a full Commander. And Paul Albert was right in the middle of D-Day, June 6, 1944, landing at Iowa Beach and somehow surviving the terrible fighting that eventually led to Germany's surrender.

As I write this in the year 2007, the massive and ugly sprawl of shopping malls across our nation has not beautified, but rather cluttered our national landscape.

Back in the nineteen-thirties, we who were born and raised in the shadow of the Wrigley Building, Tribune Tower and the Board of Trade Building enjoyed our neighborhood shopping areas, but we went to the loop for major purchases. You have to have lived in that time, as I did, to appreciate how much nicer it was then.

From my parents' apartments on the far south side of Chicago, it was a trip to the loop, and Michigan Avenue on the Illinois Central, and/or the Rock Island Railroad. The "El" was equally as rapid transit. And when we moved to the western suburbs we would journey to and from the loop on the Chicago Aurora and Elgin electric railroad, or the Chicago and Northwestern steam railroad.

Once in the loop (the area bounded by the "El"), we could spend a full day on State Street, "That Great Street." With my mom leading us we would visit Marshall Field's, Carson, Pirie, Scott and Company, Mandel Brothers, Charles A. Stevens, Wieboldt's, Goldblatt's, J.C.Penney's, Sears and Roebuck, and The Fair Store, where the lady I would marry years later, the Lovely Elaine, would purchase her wedding gown in 1947.

Childhood

As I write this in 2007 the last of the great State Street stores has closed. "Carson Pirie Scott AND Company," as I would say, years later, on their commercials has vacated the great Louis Sullivan building they occupied for over one hundred years. Berghoff's wonderful restaurant is gone and so is the Binyon family restaurant. Both great eateries in the loop since the 1890s. I have not been in the loop since 1984 and I shall never be again. And that is a sad commentary.

We often had lunch in the "lower level" restaurant at Walgreens on the northeast corner of State and Randolph, or, if mom had a few extra dollars, we'd lunch in The Walnut Room on the Seventh Floor of Marshall Fields, now Macy's I am sorry to report, across the street. If we had to grab a quick lunch, we had our choice at the counter of one of the two Woolworth's stores located on State Street, and Elfman's had a wonderful deli, with corned beef sandwiches six inches high, next door to the Chicago Theatre. Within a few feet of State Street were my three favorite loop restaurants, Berghoff's, Binyon's, and Elaine's and my "courting restaurant," the Italian Village. She and I always ended our evenings in the loop with "The World's Greatest Strawberry Shortcake"...35 cents each at Toffanetti's. This of course was in 1946.

Movies and stage shows ran all day and evening at the many Balaban and Katz "movie palaces" on, or adjacent to State Street. The Oriental Theater, The Roosevelt, the United Artists, and the State Lake Theatre, where years later I would host the opening of "Mary Poppins" and "Around the World in Eighty Days," and I'd introduce and interview on the stage Julie Andrews, David Niven, and Victor Young, who won an "Oscar" for the title song. Eddy Seguin, the public relations director for Balaban & Katz, listened to my morning shows and often hired me to host movies on "Premiere Nights." God....how I miss those great days.....

The Chicago Theater had the best stage shows, in my

opinion, because they featured all the name "Big Bands." On stage, to name a few, I saw, when I was a teen-ager, LIVE…the great Big Bands of Glenn Miller (I can still see the lighted trombones glistening in the darkened theatre), Tommy Dorsey with a skinny kid named Frank Sinatra singing *"I'll Never Smile Again,"* Benny Goodman and Artie Shaw playing their fabulous clarinets, with Peggy Lee, Helen O'Connell, and Bob Eberle as the vocalists, and Helen Forrest causing me to nearly faint as she sang with the great trumpeter Harry James and his orchestra, *"It's Been A Long, Long Time,"* and so many, many others.

My generation was so fortunate. We listened to real musicians who dressed in fine suits and beautiful gowns, and singers who presented songs with clean lyrics. And they enunciated so we could understand each and every word.

Yes, back then Chicago's loop was our ONE AND ONLY major shopping and entertainment center. THERE WERE NO SHOPPING MALLS!!!!!! And I sure wish they'd never appeared on the scene.

In downtown Elmhurst, we had the only Walgreens in town, and we had Soukup's the one hardware store in town, and we had The A&P (The Great Atlantic and Pacific Store), for our major grocery needs, and we had the one movie screen in town, The York Theatre, and Keeler's Ice Cream Shoppe, and "The Greeks" as my dad called the excellent "Stevens Restaurant" across from the Chicago and Northwestern Railroad station.

For our occasional Chinese fare, the Moy family with all the cute little kids, had an excellent Oriental restaurant. There was also Mannebach's fine meat market, a Shell Gasoline Station, a Texaco Gas station, a large Sears, Roebuck store, Pfund and Clint Florist (to whom I had paid off over seven years the nine dollar and ninety five cent charge for Elaine's corsage for our wedding), and the Cooper-Pollack Ford

Childhood

Agency, where Elaine and I, though penniless, managed to help, with a small bank loan we procured, my father-in-law purchase a brand new green 1953 Ford Mainliner for $1695.00, including the only two options available, an AM radio (FM in cars was eight years down the road), and a heater.

From my folks' house in Elmhurst, I would walk the twelve blocks each way every day to and from the York Street Chicago Aurora and Elgin railroad station to journey east to Oak Park to attend Fenwick High School.

"Attend" is not the correct word, because in my freshman year at Fenwick I had a mild case of polio, measles and chickenpox (at the same time), pneumonia, and an appendectomy.

My final three years and TWO MONTHS of high school were spent at Elmhurst's York Community High School, where I had a two-mile walk each way, but no railroad trip, and I was restored to good health. And in the wintertime I would lace on my Nester-Johnson ice skates and skate down the middle of the streets, with hardly a car visible, to York High School. What a wonderful way to start the school day.

The extra TWO MONTHS of high school were required to make up the credits I missed my first year as I battled everything but the bubonic plague.

Also, because of the health problems of my frosh year at Fenwick I did not qualify to cross the graduation stage with my fellow students of the class of 1941. Principal George Letts did not hand me my diploma, but the United States postman did a few months later, because I made up my one deficient credit in summer school.

It was during the period I was writing this book, I had lunch one day with my good friend Pat Carson. In the course of conversation she said, "Art do you remember the old credit cards that had a metal band around them?" Well, I sure did, and the next thing I knew I was recalling Ollswang's Department Store in downtown Elmhurst, and my days there as Santa Claus.

Ollswang's was an upscale family-owned, cut-above-the-average clothing store with a cross-section of name brands. The people who owned it and the people who worked there were knowledgeable and dedicated. The manager of the Men's Department, 37 year-old Vern Carman, was very interesting in my seventeen-year-old eyes. He had worked at Ollswang's all his adult life during which time he had amassed two degrees at Elmhurst College, and was well on his way to studying every course the school had in its curriculum. And Ollswang's was the only store in Elmhurst that had a State Street store feature…the overhead pneumatic-vacuum lines that magically whooshed our checks and invoices to the accounting office upstairs, and then whooshed the papers stamped "Paid" or whatever, and our change, if any, back across the store and down to the clerk, who would open the round container, take out the papers, and complete our transaction.

In the fall of 1939 I was sixteen years old, a junior at York Community High School, when I received a phone call from Mr. Levinson, Ollswang's store manager. He had talked to my folks, who regularly shopped at Ollswang's, and the three of them agreed I would make a "jolly and friendly" Ollswang's Santa Claus.

So for the two weeks of Christmas vacation 1939, I had my regular part-time job for Postmaster James Grogan at the Elmhurst post office delivering mail twice daily to the southwest side of Elmhurst, and I would be "jolly and friendly" six nights weekly, for two weeks, at Ollswang's.

The mail was delivered at 9AM and 3PM, Monday through Saturday, and once on Sunday at Christmas time. I was the youngest part-timer so I was assigned the far southwest side of Elmhurst, which was a long, long roundtrip walk. All mail delivery men walked their entire route in those days, and on snowy days I would tow my Flexible Flyer sled, loaded with holiday greetings the length of my route. It was invigorating and good exercise. Seinfeld's "Newman" would have quit the first day.

My appointed route was a six-mile roundtrip twice daily, followed by four hours of Santa-Clausing. The first night went fine, although, until you've done it, you have no idea how stressful it is. Little kids, and some not so little, sitting on your front-side, becomes numbing after awhile, in a very sensitive area. And all kids are not nice sweet kids. And some kids can be very nasty kids. It is really a very unattractive, hot, sweaty job. Smartass kids would pull at my beard which was attached by spirit gum and a long rubber band. Many times I would be looking at the ugly thing a foot in front of my face waiting for the horrible moment when the kid would release it, and it would sail back at me, stinging the daylights out of my always sensitive epidermis.

I did not like being "jolly and friendly" to bratty kids, so when a smiling mommy would be quite close to me with her brat, on my midsection, asking me for a Lionel train or a Shirley Temple doll, I'd say, "HOHOHO!!! Of course Santa will bring you a nice new Lionel train...And HOHOHO Santa will bring you a Flexible Flyer sled, and I promise you Benjamin, I will bring you a new Philco Radio, and Chicago roller skates, and Nestor Johnson ice skates, and a brand new Wilson baseball glove, and a Louisville Slugger baseball bat. And, etc.," The kid would be bedazzled, practically peeing his pants, and mommy would be ashen faced thinking of the huge bill Jolly old Saint Nick was running up.

Soon mommies started calling Mr. Ollswang and Mr. Levinson and soon Ollswang's had a new Santa Claus, and I had been fired for the FIRST time, but not the LAST time, in my life. And I was thrilled.

My mother and father were not thrilled. My dad was going to speak to Mr. Levinson to make sure it did not go on my "job record," and mom told me to never tell anyone I'd been "FIRED." If it ever comes up, just say two jobs were too much for you." Years later I played Santa Claus often for the two Chicago Veterans hospitals, but that was a labor of love.

My college days were spent in the city of Chicago, at Central YMCA College, now Roosevelt University, where I was thrown out of school for eating a sandwich while dissecting a frog. I guess they didn't care about that at Loyola University where I was accepted the same semester for the wartime accelerated study program.

And then on December 12, 1942—the last day for college students to enlist in the services—the entire Loyola student body reported at 5AM to the Insurance Exchange Building in Chicago to sign up for one of the service branches. I was refused early in the morning by my first choice The United States Marine Corp. Mid-morning saw me refused by the United States Navy, by 3PM the United States Army Air Corps decided they didn't want a man with 20/600 vision possibly bombing and strafing his own troops, so it was after 9PM, I was accepted by the Infantry, where in all probability I would be used as cannon-fodder.

But something good happened at Camp Grant when I reported there for active duty in April of 1943. After I had taken all the tests, and had viewed through horror-stricken eyes, the dreadfully graphic VD movies, I was transferred to the Air Corps to study to become a meteorologist, at which job I helped win the war figuring adiabatic lapse rates and drawing isobars on thousands of weather maps.

MILITARY SERVICE
12-12-42 TO 2-18-45

* Essay 3 *

Fred McGuire
327 So. LaSalle Street
CHICAGO
March 31, 1943
Sgt. Robert Carpenter
Camp Grant, Illinois

Dear Bob:
    The bearer of this letter Art Hellyer has signed up with good ole "Uncle Sam" and will report to Camp Grant.
    I have known Art and his parents for many years and he is very much interested in baseball. He has played around the prairies, and with a little help from you may be able to make your team, at least I hope so.
    Will you kindly take him under your wing and who knows that when this Worlds Series across the pond is over, that Art will be a teammate of yours with the Giants.
    With best wishes, I am
Cordially yours,
Fred McGuire
(Scout, New York Giants Baseball Club)

On December 12, 1942, the last day for college-deferment

enlistments in World War Two, almost the entire student body of Loyola University of Chicago reported to the Army Recruiting office in the Insurance Exchange Building at 175 W. Jackson in the Loop.

I caught the first eastbound Chicago Aurora and Elgin electric train that day at York Road in Elmhurst, jumped off the rocket at Quincy and Wells, the CA&E loop terminal, and I ran the few blocks to the Army center, arriving promptly at 5AM. Even then, before I had any idea I'd spend the majority of my life on radio-TV's split second schedules I was living by the second hand. I sat down at the end of a long line of Loyola students, and I had just started to snooze when a loud, gravelly male voice shouted, "ATTENNNSHUN, AN OFFICER IS APPROACHING!!!!!" I mumbled, "So what?" and within an instant the sergeant who had shouted at us, was looking me in the face, and chewing me out for my remark, which I still can't believe he heard, and asking me when I had last shaved (two hours earlier) and when I last had a haircut and when I last shined my shoes, and "DON"T YOU GRIN AT ME," and "STAND AT ATTENTION WHEN A SUPERIOR SPEAKS TO YOU!!!!!!!!"

Hey, hey, I was a Loyola University student, and certainly did not consider him my superior. His face and his foul, boozy GI breath were so close to me, I was actually speaking into his nasal passages. Then he shouted even louder, "I'LL DEAL WITH YOU LATER." I have never ever seen that sergeant again. Great start to my military career. I had yet to be sworn in and I already was getting the Hell chewed out of me. Unfortunately, it would not be the last time.

Hundreds of us spent that day being examined, and poked in places I'd never been poked in before, from head to toe. I had no idea what he was talking about when a doctor shouted, "STAND BY FOR SHORT-ARM INSPECTION," and what the heck did he mean when he said, "In the future these tests will be conducted in the middle of the night?" Over the next three years my "short-arm" was indeed displayed "in the middle of the night" for sadistic, perverted medical people who would wake us from deep sleep with the now all-too-familiar SHOUT!! "SHORT-ARM INSPECTION." If one failed it, one would be marched off to the remote small hospital unit at the dreaded "Pecker Hill." Many I saw fail the test, I never saw again.

It must have been horrible, because the film we inductees viewed when we were called to active service at Camp Grant filled the screen with a long thin instrument with extremely sharp twirling blades. The actor, whom we had all seen many times in Hollywood movies, portraying the doctor, explained the instrument would be placed inside the penis and then would open inside the male organ of copulation. The doctor would then draw it "slowly" out of the organ as the spinning blades reamed out the bad stuff. This was before penicillin, mercifully, appeared on the medical scene. I recall Jimmy Flaherty, a student studying for the priesthood at Loyola, fainting, and I, with many others, ran outside the tent and retched.

We were on exhibition for hours in our birthday suits, and then we dressed and took tests. The very first one would measure our "intelligence quotient," and we were told we must answer every question as best we could. Well, when I saw a question like this: "If a bluebird flies from Moscow to Sevastopol in 41 hours and 33 seconds, and Big Ben is chiming in London, what is the temperature in Sioux Falls, South Dakota?" I SKIPPED THAT QUESTION, and moved on to one I could make sense of. I do not claim to be an Albert Einstein, but I can ride a bicycle, something I read he never could learn. I remember a captain who interviewed me the day following the examination, telling me, because I had an "IQ" of 148, when called up, I would be shipping out to

WHOOPIE!!!!! Air Corps basic training, then I would go on to weather forecasting school. He said, "Congratulations, weather forecasting has a very high MOS (military occupational specialty) number, 784." I have wondered over all these years since how they could evaluate me when I skipped a number of the IQ questions. I had hoped they would place me in cryptography school, but the opportunity to study weather fascinated me. When the long day ended at close to 9PM, I felt I had been properly placed. Imagine with my 20/600 vision what might have happened had they placed me in the infantry. I probably would have shot my own men. I was also told, "Don't worry, with your vision, you won't ever be sent overseas." They were right about that. We then returned to the Loyola campus, where we finished another semester on the accelerated program. In April of 1943 the war was not going too well in either major theater of operations, and they needed more cannon-fodder, so we were activated.

Once again the campus emptied, and on April 7, 1943, we reported to Camp Grant at Rockford, Illinois, for more testing and evaluating and we had to view those frightening VD films again. And we had to be assigned to a basic training camp. We also had a lot of spare time, so some obviously sadistic commanding officer wanted us to keep busy.

After we were bugled out of bed at 5AM, we groggily stood outside for roll call, followed by breakfast. Then we reported to a gruff old regular army sergeant who shouted obscenities at us as we dug HUGE, many-blocks long trenches. At 9AM, all sweaty and bone-tired, we would go to classes until noon.

Lunch would follow at the mess hall, aptly named, because it was sort of a cafeteria where they served garbage on plates. 1PM until 3PM, we were back in the classroom, then 3PM until 5PM we would FILL UP the trenches we had dug in the morning. I often wondered if F.D.R. knew this was going on.

At 5PM we would stand "Retreat," and the flag would be lowered as we stood at rigid attention. Then "supper," as they called it in the service, would be served. I had a few dollars with me, and the very first day of my three-year military career I learned the post-exchange had better food than the mess hall. In fact, I have often referred to the PX as the first "fast food" restaurant.

This routine went on for three days, and my back was broken from digging and filling those damn ditches. Then on the fourth day, as I was told I would be, when I enlisted back in December, I was transferred from the infantry to the United States Air Corps, and I would be going to weather forecasters school.

A few days later my parents received a penny postal card: "IN THE SERVICE OF HIS COUNTRY

Headquarters Reception Center

Camp Grant, Illinois

Private Hellyer Arthur Lawrence Jr. United States Army has arrived safely at Camp Grant, Illinois, and has been assigned to the Reception Center for a few days. You will receive notice of his permanent address shortly.

NO VISITORS WILL BE ALLOWED.

B.T. Haines, Captain Infantry"

Mom must have wondered why, when she saw the bold face type informing her, she and my dad could not visit me. My dad had been a World War One hero, and had the French Croix de Guerre personally pinned on his tunic by the Commander in Chief of the Allied Forces, Marshal Ferdinand Foch himself.

So I'm sure dad, who only twice in his life spoke of the horrors he had been through, once to our number two son Michael, and then later in his life to our youngest son Jeffrey, filled her in on how busy I was, preparing for my military career. Right!!!! Digging ditches and seeing VD movies.

That night we who were assigned to the Air Corps were marched to a waiting train, where we boarded turn-of-the-century wooden coaches, to start our journey to a basic-training camp.

This is when the guessing-game started and would continue for the next two-and-a-half days. Where were we going? Only the sergeant-in-charge knew and he could not divulge that information. It might be heard by the enemy, and they might bomb our troop train. This was spring of 1943, and our military was serious, because we didn't know what the enemy might do.

We had heard the Germans had six-engine, very long-range Junkers bombers under construction and maybe they had some ready to fly. Nobody knew...just as no one knew how long the war would last. Some pundits had predicted "up to ten years."

The huge steam engine chugged us off the Camp Grant siding onto the mainline, and we were on our way to basic training. A foul-mouthed sergeant walked through the coaches explaining to we new raw recruits how to pull the "f......ing" back off the seats and make a very, very, very uncomfortable bed that stretched the length of the aisle on each side of the rickety coach. A few hours later that very first night the aisle turned into a cesspool because the one toilet was blocked up, and there was no way for us to ream it out with nothing more than a penknife available. The sergeant promised us that later that night when we stopped for sandwiches, someone at the station would open the "f......ing" thing. When we arrived at the station...Gilman, Illinois, we had our first clue. We were heading south and the only people there were three nice "Gray Ladies," who brought one basket of homemade sandwiches onto each coach. Salami sandwiches. Oh! Boy! Nice and greasy. Just what we needed. And needless to say there was no one with them who could ream out our john. I was starting to sense that I was on the railroad trip to hell. It was a nippy April night, yet we had all the windows wide open trying to eliminate the extreme unpleasantness of our stinky coach. The john never was fixed and we would be trapped in this rolling hell for two-and-a-half days.

St. Louis was our next port of call, and we were allowed to sprint to the station's toilets. It was that first night out I saw one of the most tragic sights I would ever behold. Two grown men, officers of the United States Navy, crying. I was sitting on the magnificent old stations floor when the two officers appeared, staggering down a marble stairwell, one of them cuddling a brown paper bag to his bosom, the other man holding him, so he would not drop whatever was so precious in that bag. Well, with maybe four steps yet to be navigated, tragedy struck. He dropped the bag. The sound of breaking glass echoed in, around and through the marble walls of the gargantuan terminal, and slowly the bottle's contents flowed down the remaining four steps. A tiny, boozy Niagara Falls was being watched in horror by hundreds of eyes. Then the crying started, and one of the officers fell to the floor and started licking the booze off the genuine Italian marble steps. I have never forgotten that heartbreaking scene.

Just like Chicago, St. Louis was a major rail center during World War Two, and I could hear the locomotives of the many troop trains just beyond the doors, huffing and chuffing, and anxiously pawing the tracks, as they waited to take their thousands of GI passengers to cities across the country, and to embarkation points.

This was a good time to guess where we were going. I said; "We're air corps, so we're on our way to Texas." Texas was full of air corps basic training centers. Then someone said "Salt Lake City," another "Alabama." Everyone groaned. "Florida" brought some cheers. We didn't know it, but it would be two more days until, at 2:30AM, we stopped rolling, and the sergeant hollered, "END OF THE F......ING LINE." We pulled our aching, weary bodies off the train into the pleasantly, warm night air of Clearwater Beach, Florida. We didn't have much time to savor it though, because, as we stood under glaring overhead towers of spotlights, another voice shouted, "SHORT-ARM INSPECTION."

Immediately following, we were assigned to our tents on the beach at Clearwater. We were told the great baseball player Jimmy Foxx owned the country club on whose grounds we were encamped.

We who were stationed at Clearwater never had the "country-club feeling" because our accommodations were terrible. The tents were not made of canvas, but rather some sort of ersatz cardboard-paper. The good materials were being used in the jungles of the South Pacific, as well they should have been.

But the government should have given us decent water and food. They did not, and Walter Winchell took on our case on his "Jergens Journal" broadcasts and forced the military to close the training facility and move us into St. Petersburg. One of the young men in my very tent died of dysentery.

My problems with officers continued during my short stay on the Florida sand. One of my tent buddies wasn't feeling well, so I was walking to the mess tent carrying his mess kit and mine, one in each hand, when TWO officers approached me, one on each side. Now I had been brainwashed into believing all officers MUST be saluted, so I threw both mess kits straight up in the air and saluted the officers, one on each side, with my two hands, and, incidentally, I managed to catch one of the mess kits on the way down. WELL I CAUGHT HELL!!!!! I tried to explain I would have thrown one salute had both officers been together on one side of me. But, because one officer was on my right and the other on my left I paid respect to each by saluting with my left and right hands.

They didn't see it that way, and later that day I was ordered by our commanding officer, to serve three nights and days on Kitchen Police (KP). This was my very first time on KP duty, but I assure you it was not the last time I toiled in the refectory.

How in the world could the United States Air Corps move over 300,000 troops into St. Petersburg? Easy…they commandeered the hotels, which is why a week later I found myself assigned to a ninth floor room of The Princess Martha Hotel. My roommate, who announced to me he would occupy the lower bunk, was an extremely powerful man named Harold Heslop, who had muscles on his muscles and was a professional boxer by trade. Within a month Harold Heslop became the heavyweight boxing champ of our basic training command. He certainly was not the ideal roomie for me, if only because I bruise easily, and every time we would pass each other, he would sock me in one of my shoulders, and they have been sore ever since.

Crawling on my belly with a full pack, and a forty pound Enfield rifle on my back, under live machine gunfire at six in the morning, and running two-mile long obstacle courses, and climbing over twelve foot walls, and the rest of what I called physical torture (the army called it PT) beat me up more than enough. I did not need the heavyweight boxing champion of all St. Petersburg pounding lumps on me, too.

This was the first time I'd ever been away from home and I suffered from homesickness. As my bruised by Harold Heslop, and beat-up by the army, body drifted into slumber at the sounding at 10PM each night of Taps, I would be softly crying. God help me if Harold in the lower bunk heard me. More than one night Harold did hear me, but it was not my sobbing he heard. I had a habit of rolling out of that awful upper bunk. Bouncing my head on the concrete floor in the middle of the night might be the reason I've always been as neurotic as Woody Allen. And it didn't help that Harold would always wake up and shout, "STOP THAT, HELLYER!"

My musical career started in St. Pete. On Saturday nights I played with a small big-band-jazz group for dances at the U.S.O., and in the fancy ballrooms of the military-occupied hotels in the St. Pete-Tampa Bay area. We were even written up in the Air Corps Training Command newspaper. I quote from an article of May 23, 1943: "The boys of our group have enough musicians to organize a Philharmonic. Among the prominent performers are Pfc. John Sallee and Pvt. Joseph Imburgia, both accordion virtuosos. Pvt. John Reilly is on trumpet, Pvt. Steve Hathaway is the drummer, and Pvt. Art Hellyer strums his Spanish guitar."

I've never forgotten the lovely warmth of spring in St. Pete, and Sunday mass at the Cathedral, followed by brunch at "The Orange Blossom Café." Sunday afternoons I would stroll by myself along the placid blue waters of the Gulf of Mexico while sipping a huge ten-cent cup of papaya juice. A milk shake today in a McDonald's cup that same size is three-ninety-five or more.

But St. Petersburg had its negative side too: huge cockroaches you could hear running across the floor, called "palmettos" by the natives; clothes dripping wet from the humidity when put on in the morning; unbearable heat; and moss in our GI boots. Plus, and I guess I am the only person alive who has this problem, I hate hot, sandy beaches. And to show you how badly every GI was needed in WWII, the Pentagon went overboard to assure I'd stay in. I have since I was an infant been plagued by allergies. I was allergic to the army woolen uniforms so the UNITED STATES of AMERICA lined my woolen clothing with SATIN. If they did that to assure a lowly private stayed in, imagine what they must have done for allergy-ridden generals and admirals.

Military Service

Basic training ended none too soon for me. I had qualified for more college training in ASTP (Army Specialized Training Program) and soon found myself on the campus of "The West Point of the South," The Citadel at lovely, charming, steeped-in-Southern tradition, Charleston, South Carolina. There on the banks of the Charles River, just a few miles removed from the Atlantic Ocean and Fort Sumter, which was shelled by Confederate gunners in April of 1861 beginning the Civil War, I got my first exposure to a savannah region with its semi-tropical trees and shrubs. I enjoyed doing my homework in the early evening under the spreading branches of the banyan trees.

When I was sixteen years old, I spoke at their monthly meetings to many of the American Legion Posts throughout the West Suburban area of Chicagoland to cobble together "The West Suburban American Legion Baseball League." I received minimal help, and understandably so because we were still mired in the Great Depression. Posts in Glen Ellyn, Hinsdale, Lombard, Arlington Heights, Downers Grove, Wheaton, West Chicago, Aurora, LaGrange and Elmhurst agreed to supply baseball bats and balls, and arrange for their teams to play on local school grounds or city parks. I couldn't ask for more, they were being very generous and helpful. I then went from business to business in each town signing up sponsors for each of the individual ballplayers.

The sponsor would provide a uniform for the player he sponsored and I had an arrangement with a Mrs. Myers, a seamstress in Elmhurst and a friend of my mom's, to sew the letters and numbers on each uniform. My uniform proudly advertised "Pollard Motors." This was a lot of work and running around for me, but it probably kept me in excellent condition, because I also managed "The Elmhurst Elms" team and played in the outfield, and laid out all the team schedules for the entire league, and the fields on which they would play their games in the member communities. I also scheduled the volunteer umpires, which turned out to be a major headache. Morning, noon and night my parents' phone would ring off the hook as the umps would phone in, unable to perform their duties for this reason or that.

And finally, I wrote the articles about as many games as I could for The Press Publications, an Elmhurst firm owned by my dad's good friend Harold Cruger, who owned the *Elmhurst Press* and many other West Suburban newspapers, so I didn't have to run the articles all over the area. I merely submitted them to the sports editor at the Elmhurst Press offices, and he distributed them to their other papers. This was the easiest part of my job.

I still have original copies of some of the articles I wrote during the hot summer of 1940. Here are a few examples, and remember these were not written by Grantland Rice or Jerome Holtzman, but rather by a sixteen-year-old kid who loved baseball.

"THE ELMHURST PRESS
ELMS BEAT LOMBARD BY 11-8 SCORE
The Elms team in the American Legion hardball league led by the fine pitching of Tony Kindl and the hitting of his brother SS Hank Kindl, C Jimmy Greenwood, and 2B Paul Hackert won a hard fought game Monday night at the well-lighted field in Lombard. The Elms team is leading the American Legion League, and Elms First basemen, Big Jim Gruse leads the league in hitting with a .600 average. Center Fielder of the Elms, Art Hellyer is second in batting with a .471 average.

"AMERICAN LEGION HARDBALL RESULTS
The Arlington Heights Redwings defeated the Elmhurst Elms 3 to 1, Wednesday June 26 at their beautiful smaller version of the Chicago Cubs Wrigley Field. First basemen Jim Gruse was the only Elms player to get a hit off the slants of Arlington Heights pitcher, "Fireball" Brunnke.

Military Service

"ELMS HOLD LEAD IN HARDBALL LEAGUE
After finishing the first round of the American legion Hardball League with a record of 7 wins and 2 losses, the Elms team leads the circuit with a .777 average. Three of the Elms players hold high honors in batting stats. First Baseman, Big Jim Gruse leads the league in hitting with a .500 average. Close behind Gruse are two of his teammates with .460 batting averages. These boys are shortstop Hank Kindl, and Captain and center fielder Art Hellyer. In the battle for pitching honors two Elms men are tied with a record of three wins and one loss, Driscoll and Tony Kindl."

My background in baseball, at a very early age had a great deal to do with my being appointed "The Athletic Director for the Military Students stationed at, and studying at the Citadel." I asked the commanding officer what that fancy title meant, and I was told my duties, in addition to my seven hours daily in the classroom as a student, would be to lead the GI's through their Monday through Saturday 6AM PT ("physical torture" as I called it) and to write a weekly column about the sports programs and activities at The Citadel for The Charleston News and Courier. On Page 6 of the paper dated Wednesday morning, September 1, 1943, Sears has their Wednesday values ad "To Save You Money." We were restricted to The Citadel compound, except Saturday night and Sunday until 10PM, but this Sears "value" might have been worth going AWOL for: "An 8-piece 'Fire-King' oven glass wear set, consisting of 4 custard cups, loaf pan, casserole with cover and pie plate. JUST 99 CENTS," and flashlight batteries were 10 cents each "limit 3 to a customer." Of course, there's another way to look at this. My army Private's pay was thirty dollars a month and I had an $18.75 war bond deducted from that every month, so I really couldn't have spent a dollar and nine cents on frivolous things like dishes and batteries.

THE HELLYER SAY

Above this ad on the sports page is a picture of St. Louis Browns pitcher Buck "Bobo" Newsom, who was sold to the Washington Senators for Seventy-Five Hundred dollars on the prior day. Eleven years later I would have an interesting experience with "Bobo" before my WCFL "Downtown Nash White Sox Dugout" radio show at Comiskey Park, home of the Chicago White Sox. Bobo was warming up on the third base dugout side, and he dropped a ball in the dirt. As he picked it up, some fans called to him and asked him to throw the ball to them, and Bobo did just that. A few minutes later another ball got by Bobo so I picked it up and threw it underhanded to a smiling little boy in the stands. Big, huge Bobo came running toward me shouting, "You can't throw baseballs in the stands!" To which I replied, "Why not? You did." Bobo looked at me and very slowly said, "I'm Bobo." I didn't argue the point. Another headline proclaims: "MUSIAL HITS .353 TO LEAD NATIONAL"

The great Chicago Cubs second baseman Billy Herman, who, believe it or not, I would interview for ABC Radio thirty-four years later, on June 25, 1977, was second in hitting with a .334 average. The Cubs' great slugger "Swish" Nicholson, so named because of the sound his bat made when he hit his mighty home runs, was also in the top ten with .312.

The 1943 major league baseball season was moving into its final weeks. Both leagues had eight teams, and the Cubs were in fifth place in the National league race thirty-one games behind the St. Louis Cardinals. Over in the American League, my all-time-favorite White Sox player, shortstop Luke Appling, was on his way to his second batting title on a team also languishing in fifth place, with the hated New York Yankees twenty-one games ahead of them.

The top far right column is headed:
"SOFTBALL TEAMS IN CITADEL ASTP
PLAYING for TITLE, by Trainee Art Hellyer

72

Military Service

"The ASTP softball leagues at the Citadel have concluded their regular season, and the top three teams in each of the two loops are squaring off now in playoffs to determine the section champions."

I then go on to explain about the top three teams in each of the Loops: Section A survivors being Ohio Buckeyes, Fourth Floor (it took a lot of imagination and discussion to come up with that name, I'm sure), T.S., and Section B, Panama Jungleites, Yanks, and White Sox (team I managed). I haven't the slightest recollection of who won the playoffs, but if I were a Pete Rose, I'd place my money on the team managed by two of Loyola's biggest and strongest athletes, Joe Kraft and Art Luxem and their team, with the great name, the Panama Jungleites.

I've skipped five of my Pulitzer prize award winning (HA!) paragraphs, but I find this one interesting:

"In third place is Art Hellyer's White Sox ball club. At the start of the season this was the team picked to win the title, but they were stopped cold. Every man on the team comes from Chicago."

On that very day the Chicago Cubs and the Chicago White Sox were in fifth place in their respective major leagues. All my players were from Chicago, and we were in third place. Not bad.

I had just come out of basic training and I was in great shape. Each morning at 6AM I, yes I, would lead my four hundred some charges through the obstacle course, first running through two long rows of old Jeep tires, then climbing over a twelve-foot wall, after which I would climb a wooden ladder to the top of a ten foot high platform where for twenty minutes each morning I would leap up and down, throw my arms and legs all over that platform and lead them through their calisthenics. Anyone who knows me today I am sure would not believe this tale, but it is true. And by 7AM each morning we all were supposed to be "Fighting Trim." Truth is by 7AM each morning I was in a complete state of mental and physical exhaustion.

In spite of this grueling schedule I fell in love with Charleston and its tremendous history. The city is famous for its many historic homes and the beauty of its fine semi-tropical gardens, and of course, it is the setting for George Gershwin's superb folk-opera, *Porgy and Bess.*

All too soon my stay in Charleston came to an end. There was a war to save the world in progress, and the thousands of men in the Army Specialized Training Program were badly needed elsewhere. The government closed down the entire program and our college days were officially over for the duration, by order of General George Catlett Marshall, Chief of Staff, United States Army.

I was shipped to Greensboro, North Carolina, which to me is one of the three or four most beautiful states in our great country, for assignment. While waiting to find where I would go next, the army couldn't have me snoozing all day, so I was put to work as a payroll clerk in the base finance office. Though this was certainly off the beaten track for me, it earned me my only military letter of commendation. In Finance, yet!! I couldn't balance my checkbook then, and I still cannot.

My stay in Greensboro came to an end, when things had become so bad for us on the war fronts I was shipped to Selfridge Field, Michigan to be assigned for OVERSEAS duty. Someone more blind than I obviously had not seen my 20/600 Camp Grant vision report. I went through all the overseas indoctrination, VD movies again, aircraft identi-fication, etc. Then I was sent to the rifle range where the sudden and continual appearance of "Maggie's Drawers" (the waving red flag that meant, "Man!! Are you a lousy shot!! You MISSED EVERYTHING") every time I was on the firing line, made it eminently clear the United States cause could be in big trouble if my eyes, with me attached, were sent across the great pond. So, I was quietly pulled off overseas orders and shipped to Baer Field at Fort Wayne, Indiana to be just one of four men in an experimental "on-the-line" weather forecasting training program.

It was at Baer Field I fell in love with a pretty WAC from North Carolina, Doris Mosher, and when my folks and her folks learned of our fledgling love affair, our parents all hopped the first trains bound for Fort Wayne. There was a problem that concerned all of them deeply: Doris was Baptist and I was Roman Catholic. We didn't see that as a problem. In fact I love singing those great Baptist hymns. To make a long story short, Doris a short time later shipped out and I never heard from her again.

I cannot think of a worse climate than the Midwest in which to study weather, if only because of the "balloon runs." The information we gathered was minimal and primitive compared to today when everything is done by computers, but in World War Two it was of the utmost importance. Every two hours on the nose during my 8-hour shift I would go to the balloon case and take out one large weather balloon. Then I would climb the steel ladder to the roof, where there was a small room with a helium tank. I would then fill the balloon with the precise measurement of helium. This was critical. The balloon must always be correctly filled or our figures would be incorrect. I would then place a weight at the end of a short line attached to the balloon, again the measurements had to be precise. I would open the little room's door, fight the wind (or rain or snow) across the roof to the theodolite, a telescope with elevation and azimuth angle adjusters. At this point I would put on headphones and a microphone (I've spent my entire working life with microphones) and tell the sergeant downstairs in the weather room I was ready. I would release the balloon, and click another gadget that has been with me forever, a stopwatch.

I would focus the telescope on the balloon and every thirty seconds I would read the elevation and azimuth angles to the sergeant in the weather room. These angles would be plotted on a special chart downstairs, and when I could no longer see the balloon, I would go down to the weather room, and through the readings I had taken, I would chart the direction and speeds of the winds aloft. These we would give to the chief meteorologist who would meet with each pilot before takeoff and give him this information. Every two hours, twenty-four hours per day we would do this. It was most important.

Now, in answer to your questions. On a clear day I could probably see the balloon for ten to twelve minutes which would give us the wind direction and wind speed to approximately six thousand feet. Most planes did not fly much higher in the 1940s. In answer to your second question. How did we see the balloon at night? At the end of the specified length of the special string hanging from the balloon we would hang, believe it or not, a JAPANESE lantern with a candle we would place in it. There were nights in a high wind or rain, or with snow blowing when lighting that candle with a match was almost impossible, but we did it. How? I just don't know. And tracking the damn thing through that Theodolite was no fun either, especially when one's vision is 20/600.

My "on-the-line" weather training days ended and I shipped out of Fort Wayne. I was then stationed, in chronological order, first at Wright-Patterson Field, Vandalia, Ohio, where I had classroom weather school training. I also played center field on the airbase baseball team.

One afternoon in a league game at Bowman Field, Kentucky, I collided with our left fielder, a very large, well-constructed gentleman named Carl Wiggins, as we both chased a long high fly ball. Result? I was hospitalized for a week with a huge bruise that covered my entire chest and abdomen. And because of that missed fly ball we lost the game 2-1, and our chance to play for the national championship.

The next stop on my tour of continental airbases was Selfridge Field, Michigan, on the shores of Lake St. Clair. On a day off, my buddy Sgt. Frank Bronner and I "borrowed" a rowboat, rowed across the lake and thumbed rides into Detroit where we sat through the same movie four times, and saw three live performances by Stan Kenton and his great band at the Michigan Theater. I returned one more time to the Michigan Theater, via a Greyhound Bus, not the water route, to see Hugh Beaumont in the stage play, "The Voice of the Turtle." Some twelve years later the entire nation was watching him on TV as Ward Cleaver, "The Beaver's" father.

My next base, Chanute Field, Illinois, was extremely important in my military career. I attended advanced classes in weather forecasting and received my "ARMY AIR FORCES TRAINING COMMAND" Diploma stating: "Be It Known Cpl. Arthur L. Hellyer, Jr. Serial Number.......Has Satisfactorily Completed the Prescribed Course of Training for METEOROLOGIST—Given at Chanute Field, Illinois from 27 November 1944 to 6 January 1945. In Testimony Whereof and By Virtue of Vested Authority I Do Confer Upon Him This DIPLOMA. Attested —
L. M. Server, Captain, A.C. J.H.Davidson, COL. AC."

My classes each day were from 4PM to midnight with a thirty-minute break for dinner. At midnight we would march to the mess hall for breakfast, and we were often reviewed by our commanding officer Colonel Cooper. As we approached his house, we would quickly know if it was a review night. The Colonel, who was not tall, would be standing atop his garbage can. Trying to keep a straight face and, being sure I didn't look to the right to see this unusual spectacle was tough enough. But the sight of one of my classmates marching upside down on his hands was too much. Colonel Cooper would shout, "TROOPS HALT!!!! ONE-TWO." Then he would order our sergeant to approach the "Reviewing Stand," and he would always ask the same question, "Sergeant is that soldier marching upside down?" At this point all of us would be trying to stifle our laughter. The sight of the colonel on the garbage can, and now private (he'd been busted a couple of times from corporal for this same antic) Leonard Fleisher marching upside down was more than we could take. Many nights I returned to the barracks with wet drawers from trying so hard to control myself.

But there was always more. When we climbed into our bunks each night after 1AM, Leonard Fleisher would be seated NUDE atop his bed, crunching corn flakes from a small Kellogg's box he had brought with him from the mess hall. My stay ended at Chanute Field all too soon, because I enjoyed getting home to see my folks in Elmhurst two Sundays each month.

So it was onto Hensley Field, Dallas, Texas, Midland Texas Army Air Base, and Sheppard Field at Wichita Falls, Texas, where I paid out of pocket for flight lessons on the civilian side of the field.

I actually soloed without crashing the little Taylorcraft or killing myself or any other people. I found it most difficult landing the little plane, because to do so, I was required to glide down right over the base hospital and dozens of "meat wagons" with Red Crosses on top. Not exactly the best view for a student pilot.

Kirtland Field at Albuquerque was next on my all-expenses-paid tour of Air Corps bases, and it was here I would have some experiences I would remember as long as I live. I traveled from Wichita Falls to Albuquerque, New Mexico, through some of our most gorgeous country in a single gas-electric Santa Fe Railroad combo locomotive and mail-car-passenger car. I have never enjoyed any trip as much as I did that jaunt through a small area of America's stunning great Southwest.

Kirtland Field, a B29 base, was on a plateau high above the city, and unfortunately I watched many planes crash on takeoff, almost every one due to mechanical failure, into the valley south of the airbase.

One Friday night a happy, laughing wedding party accompanied the bride and her Air Corps sergeant-groom to the doors of our weather station. I briefed the flight-crew, including the sergeant-groom on the weather, which was excellent, and the bride kissed her brand new husband for the last time. The B29 crashed and burned in the valley on takeoff. No one survived.

Another crash involved Angie and me. Angie, a WAC from Detroit, whose folks kept her well supplied with homemade "Dago-Red" wine was a fine meteorologist and I enjoyed working with her. I was drawing the latest weather map, adding to my vision problems. I have no idea how Tom Skilling does it today, but in 1945, every four hours each weather station in the country would transmit their latest figures on the teletype: temperature, humidity, dew point, barometric pressure, rain, snow, sleet, fog, cloud cover, etc. I would then place this information for each reporting city on the new weather map, in a space a dime could cover. More than once Angie would say to me, "Art, I can't read your chicken-scratching for Denver." Or, "Art, I can't tell what the cloud altitude is for Los Angeles. What does this say?" I would take a close look at my own printing and say, "I'm sorry Ang, I can't read it either." MY OWN PRINTING!! I've suffered with this affliction all my life.

Suddenly, Angie screamed, "ART!! MY GOD!! IT'S

COMING RIGHT AT US!!!!!!" I looked up just in time to see a B-29's wing lights bouncing up and down as America's largest bomber bore down on us. Angie and I hugged each other, as she grabbed her bottle of "Dago-Red" and we ran down the single flight of stairs into the hangar below, AS THE PLANE ROARED THROUGH THE BUILDING WITHIN INCHES OF US!!!! We were so close we actually saw the crew in the greenhouse, and could see one of the men slumped forward.

One of our weathermen, Larry Edwards, had stopped in the downstairs men's room on his way to work at that moment, and he staggered out to the tarmac with us, not aware he had no pants on. How everyone in that hangar got out alive, including the plane's crew, none of us will never know. We were all treated for shock, by hospital people who were among the hundreds of GI's who came running from all over the base. And each of us spent the night in the base hospital. That night I had my first ever session with a psychiatrist. My high regard for them continues to this day.

The air-cooled B29 engines were often to blame for the crashes, but this one was caused by "tire failure" the report said. The plane had a blowout when it touched the runway, then swerved, out of control toward our hangar. That was about the moment Angie saw it heading our way. Before it hit the hangar, it wiped out twelve or thirteen smaller planes parked just across from us. Everyone involved in that episode was very fortunate.

July 16, 1945, I heard a muffled explosion, and I saw and watched a non-weather type cloud forming in the sky. A number of us saw it and wondered what the heck it was. There were no television stations then, and the radio newscasts we heard said nothing about it.

Later that day when my weather shift ended I hopped a bus and went downtown, passing on the way Ernie Pyle's home, and the University of New Mexico's beautiful Spanish architectural buildings.

No newsboys were shouting "Extra Extra…Read all About it" as they did on December 7, 1941. I bought a paper at a corner newsstand. There was nothing about what I had seen that morning anywhere in the paper on my first perusal. Then as I searched more carefully, I found a small item, maybe on page 14 or page 15. It was a tiny story under a small heading, "Ammunition Dump Explodes At Alamogordo." In the account it was stated, "no one was injured," but one line made me wonder, "A blind girl at the University of New Mexico in Albuquerque saw the flash."

On August 6, 1945 I was at my parents' home, on a three-day pass for my birthday, and we heard on the radio the bulletin about the USA dropping the first atomic bomb on Japan. That day I knew, I had seen the first ATOMIC BOMB EXPLOSION.

Kirtland GIs would stand in line every night at "The Copper Kettle," a tiny eatery in downtown Albuquerque with only a counter that seated ten to twelve steak-hungry souls. What was the attraction? For 99 Cents we would be served a delicious FIVE-COURSE STEAK DINNER!! No one seemed to care where those wonderful steaks came from or how in the world the proprietor could get them.

One evening I was standing alone at the bus stop after the steak dinner when I saw a man beating the daylights out of a small woman across the street in the v-shaped entry way to a store with a "closed" sign hanging on the door. Just a few feet from me was a police callbox. I pulled the switch down, and almost immediately a squad car pulled in front of the store, and two of Albuquerque's finest jumped out and started pulling the assailant off the woman. It was at that moment I learned a lesson in life. The woman being attacked screamed at the cops, "DON'T HURT HIM…HE'S MY HUSBAND."

It was at Kirtland Field I played, until I was shipped late that summer to "The West Point of the Air," Randolph Field, as an outfielder on the team that would later that year win the Air Force national championship. Our pitcher was the star, a fellow named Jess Dobernik, who played for the Chicago White Sox before the war, and then for the Chicago Cubs after the war.

I fell in love with my last two Air Corps cities, Albuquerque and San Antonio, and its fabulous River Walk. I even applied at radio stations in both cities in 1946 when I was studying at Radio Institute of Chicago, and the program director at KOB in Albuquerque was nice enough to answer me and advise me to get started in a small city and get some experience. Good advice I would follow to the letter.

Winter 1945 was so pleasant at San Antonio, Texas. The war was over and some fifteen million of us all over the world were awaiting discharge from the service. I would be a civilian once again the following February. I had no duties at all now, so I read many books, strolled the Riverwalk, visited The Alamo, which looked then, at least to me, just as bad as it must have looked to Davy Crockett, Jim Bowie and 180 other Americans who were slaughtered in 1836 by Santa Anna and his 4000 cohorts in the battle that rallied Texans in the Texas War for Independence from Mexico.

It was also while stationed there I took my meager monies to Neiman-Marcus and purchased a very colorful SILK tie. Right there in the store I took off my drab GI tie and placed the new one on me. I thought it brightened up my uniform considerably and later that night as I flashed my pass at the MP at the gate, he gave me a ticket for "being out of uniform." Frankly, my dear, I couldn't care less.

One mid-morning as I was reading at the base library I heard "it" for the very first time. "It" was a jet streaking overhead…low and LANDING.….WOW!!!! Every GI at

Randolph Field must have joined me as we ran hell-bent for the landing strips, which already were being guarded by more MP's than I had seen collectively the past three years. The tiny jet-fighter landed, but I could get nowhere near it. It was a thrill I will never forget.

February 16, 1946, I left behind me the lovely weather of San Antonio, Texas and stepped aboard a KATY Railroad day coach to St. Louis, then Chicago. And on February 18, 1946 as I walked out of the west gate at frigid Fort Sheridan, Illinois on the frozen shores of Lake Michigan, I took off my GI tie, put on my Nieman-Marcus tie, walked across Sheridan Road and boarded a southbound Chicago and North Shore "Electroliner," and returned to whatever it was CIVILIAN life had in store for me.

RADIO INSTITUTE OF CHICAGO, AND WHAT FOLLOWED...

* Essay 4 *

When I was mustered out of the Air Force in February of 1946 I had served three years two months and seven days toward my twenty years retirement. I enlisted when I was nineteen years old, which meant I could have retired at age 39, and received a nice check the first day of each month the rest of my life, but no, I had to go into radio where at any given time the average broadcaster earns minimum wage.

And why did I go into radio? It was one of three things I always wanted to do: play major league baseball, be a broadcaster, teach American history at a small college. Well, I got out of the service too old to start playing minor league baseball, I had a smattering of broadcasting in the service, and I had no credentials for teaching American history, so when my mom saw a broadcasting school ad in the paper, I was interested.

"A glamorous well paying job can be yours. You can become a STAR and work with THE stars. If you are a veteran you are eligible to enroll under the GI Bill. Radio Institute of Chicago, 165 N. Michigan Avenue, Chicago, Illinois."

I lived in Elmhurst, Illinois, sixteen miles west of the loop, and train service on the Chicago Aurora and Elgin electric line ran every half hour 24 hours a day, so getting to and from the loop was a breeze. Not a breeze was the 20 block walk each way to and from the Elmhurst station from my parents home, and the very long walk from the Chicago Aurora and Elgin terminal at Quincy and Wells to 165 N. Michigan Avenue. But what the heck? I was young. I was only twenty-two years old and I was going to end up in a glamorous place and be well paid and be a star. So I enrolled under the all-expenses paid GI Bill and I was on my way to stardom, fame and fortune. Yeah, right!

I did have fine instructors. Chicago's best commercial announcer, "The Man of a Thousand Voices" Paul Barnes, had impressive credentials, as did Ted Liss and Sidney Breese (both were on many of the daily soap operas out of Chicago) and NBC Director Larry Kurtz, and CBS Chief Announcer Bob Cunningham, just to name a few. And I was teamed for our work projects with an apple-cheeked, 19-year-old student named Tom Bosley, who in years ahead would enjoy many years of "Happy Days" as Richie Cunningham's father.

Radio Institute of Chicago was founded, and operated by a former "Opera Star" and small radio station owner in Northern Indiana named Doris Keane. I never heard a woman give people a snowjob the way she did. She could make a person believe anything. The man who unwittingly fronted the school, which would turn out to be a fraudulent operation, Dr. George Currier, was a fine Presbyterian minister with an equally fine church in upscale Woodlawn. Dr. Currier, thank God didn't end up in the federal penitentiary, but Doris Keane did. Unbeknownst to the world in 1946, Mrs. Keane was not playing straight with the United States Government, which, under the GI Bill of Rights, subsidized our schooling. All this would become public knowledge some years later.

Fortunately for me, Bob Cunningham took me aside one day in late fall 1946 and told me there was no reason I should stay there for the two- or four-year degree courses. He said I was ready to get into the field, and he had recommended me to his fellow University of Michigan graduate and friend, Mr. Jack Gelder, General manager of WKNA, Charleston, West Virginia which would be signing on the air for the first time on New Years Day, 1947.

New Year's Eve 1946 found me the only passenger in the club car on a Chesapeake & Ohio Railroad "Budd-built" streamliner, bound for Charleston, West Virginia. I had never had a drink, so though drinks were free that night, I saved the railroad money. I arrived in Charleston shortly after midnight, phoned the program director, Frank Shaffer, who told me I had a room reserved at The Kanawha (pronounced "KUHNAW," I quickly was informed) Hotel, the building this brand new radio station WKNA was located in. He told me to get some sleep, then sign the station on at 5AM. Well come on now. This was to be my maiden broadcasting venture and I was a basket case. Needless to say I didn't sleep a wink, and at 4:30AM, I showered in COLD water, dressed and took the elevator to work. It would be the only time in my 55-year career I would take the elevator from home to work.

At 5AM, January 1, 1947, I was the first announcer to ever, officially, sign on WKNA. The prior night, New Year's Eve, Manager Jack Gelder, Program Director Shaffer and News Director, Bob Provence, and the owners, hosted a huge party for the fledgling station. I was on the train on my way to Charleston, so I didn't get to meet the mayor and all the honored guests, but I could certainly smell the party as I entered the station for the first time. The smell of stale cigarettes, perfume and booze permeated the air, polluting the freshly painted walls, the new furniture, the newsroom and the two studios and their control rooms.

The engineer welcomed me to "The Kanawha Valley, Charleston and WKNA," and I went into the newsroom to prepare my first-ever on-the-air broadcast. This was no longer the dummy studio at Radio Institute of Chicago. This was THE REAL THING!!!! Was I nervous? Is the Pope Catholic? I was trembling all over, but I was ready. Then I FROZE in my tracks!! THE AP AND UPI NEWS MACHINES WERE NOT RUNNING!!!

There is an unwritten law in radio—news machines must run twenty-four hours a day, three hundred sixty-five days a year. Both switches were in the OFF position. I noted each had a fresh roll of paper. Each machine was eagerly waiting to print the news from Charleston and the world so I could deliver my first ever on the air newscast to thousands, hundreds, well...it was New Year's Day and a few people surely were waiting with bleary eyes and anxious ears to hear if the world survived the transition to 1947.

What in the name of heaven was I to do? Well I did the only thing I could do. I ran downstairs to the 24/7 coffee shop, bought the daily paper, and delivered the news from pages of the paper. About ten minutes into this historic, for me, newscast, the studio door in back of me opened with a bang. A bass drum hit the doorjamb, and five huge men smelling like a distillery staggered in around me.

At 5:13:50 I concluded the news with a rapid reading of the local weather from the front page of the paper, closed my microphone pot, opened the turntable pot and put on the air a scheduled sixty second commercial I had cued up just prior to the news. During these sixty seconds the five musicians introduced themselves, and as the commercial ended I closed Turntable number one pot and opened the Microphone on number two pot. I then pointed my Radio Institute of Chicago trained cueing finger at the swaying bandleader, and ridge runner twanging, howling and screeching started.

WKNA's first musical show ever was on the air. I opened microphone number one, and said, "Happy New Year, Charleston. I'm Art Hellyer....the red-headed announcer...

one of the new guys in town...and you are listening to music by Slim Drye and The Carolina Hillbillies." I remember nothing else about that show but caterwauling and the smell of booze and sweat. Slim was anything but DRY(E). My first hour ever on the air had been most eventful. Later that New Year's Day Manager Jack Gelder phoned me to welcome me to the station, and he asked me how things were going. I told him the day had started with the news machines turned off. He said he certainly would check on that.

The following day he told me in person what had happened. It seems Waverly Graverly, the maintenance man, was cleaning up the station after the big New Year's Eve bash. He told the station manager, "I turned off those machines Mr. Gelder because you all went home last night and left them running." As I look back on my career I guess that was the way it should have started, complete chaos and drunken hillbillies.

In March of 1947, Jack Gelder gave me three days off so I could go to my folks home to marry Elaine Miller. One day was consumed by traveling back on the train. The next evening at 7:30, Elaine and I were married in the Catholic church rectory because Elaine was a heathen (Lutheran) in the bigoted eyes of the Roman church in those days. In fact my dad and Elaine's father were barely civil to each other or toward us because we each, according to the other father, were heathens.

My mom, who at one time was a Catholic novitiate, studying to be a nun, and Elaine's Lutheran-all-her-life mom, were on our side. Their support meant so much to both of us. Elaine was gloriously beautiful in her long white wedding gown, and I've always felt terrible that she was not permitted to be married in a church. It is just one of many reasons that years ago drove me from ever again going into a Roman Catholic church. When my brother Dick also married a

Protestant, Edith Jorgensen, now his bride of 50 years, the Catholic church just ten years after Elaine and I were married, had seen the error of its ways. Or was it the pressure of watching millions of young people leaving the Catholic church because of that dumb man-made rule?

I must be fair and say that my father-in-law and I, over the years that followed, became the best of friends. And he did give us a beautiful wedding reception at a fancy suburban country club. Then my brother drove us to Grand Central Station in Chicago. We boarded The Twentieth Century Limited, which dropped our Pullman car at Toledo, where it was attached to another NYC train bound for the southeast. My new bride and I arrived in Charleston, West Virginia, just in time for me to go to work, and for Elaine to take the elevator to my hotel room. I was away from my job less than three days, the three most important days of my entire life, because this lovely lady would light up my life, bear our five wonderful children, Larry, Mike, Debbie, Vickie and Jeff, and she would show me the way, for the next fifty-one years.

A year and a half after the war officially ended found me a newlywed, with six months of radio schooling under the GI Bill, and a new job. Now for the tough part, finding an apartment in postwar America.

I keep everything, so why wouldn't I have this ad I placed in the Charleston newspaper sixty years ago: "RADIO ANNOUNCER—EX GI and WIFE of FIVE days in need of furnished apartment. We like Charleston, hate to go back to Chicago—it's up to you. Art Hellyer...Radio Station WKNA." The day the ad ran I had five phone calls at the station, and by nightfall we had settled into a second-floor bedroom in a private family home. We bought a hot-plate for a dollar at a big local drugstore, and Elaine prepared and cooked a delicious pork chop dinner for us, and we dined in front of the fireplace. In 1947 every home in the south had a gas-fired fireplace in every room of the house. A luxury? No way! There was no central heating in Southern homes. The gas-fired fireplaces heated the homes. And where did we wash our dinner dishes? In the sink of the bathroom we shared with our landlord and his family. It was a start.

Look out world!!!!! Here come Elaine and Art Hellyer!!!!!

MILWAUKEE

* Essay 5 *

**"The TOWN CRIER
Chicagoan Art Hellyer, now Milwaukee's favorite disk jockey,
has opened at the Riverside Theater there with Dave Garroway,
Lynn Burton, Eddie Hubbard, Mel Torme, The Harmonicats,
and Two-Ton Baker and Bonnie Baker."**
Chicago Daily News, Jan. 20, 1948

Woody Dreyfus was the program director at WMAW, Milwaukee, a radio station, like so many others after World War Two that was getting ready to sign on for the first time. I was looking for work, and I had to provide for my beautiful bride of one year, the former Elaine Miller of the Elmhurst, Illinois, Millers. Elaine was well along carrying our first to be born, Arthur L. Hellyer III, Larry, so I answered an ad in *Broadcasting Magazine* hoping it would land me a job in Milwaukee radio.

My eventual goal was Chicago radio, and Milwaukee, Wisconsin, was closer to Chicago than Charleston, West Virginia, and Fort Wayne, Indiana, and paid better than Aurora, Illinois, the three cities I had worked in to this point. Elaine and I were living under less than ideal conditions with my in-laws in their modest home in Elmhurst, Illinois, so when Mr. Dreyfus sent me a letter asking me to come see him in October of 1947, I jumped at the opportunity, and we took off for Beertown, USA, in a flash.

We were aboard an "Electroliner" on the Chicago, North Shore and Milwaukee Railroad, one of the first streamlined electric commuter trains in America. We loved the comfortable seats in the little four-car rocket, and the miniature dining car was equally enjoyable. As I look back over the years I realize the simple moments in my life were the nicest moments.

We rode the Chicago Aurora and Elgin electric railroad from Elmhurst to the CA&E station at Quincy and Wells where we boarded the little pride of the North Shore Line on the elevated loop lines. The train swung around the perimeter of Chicago's loop, then made a quick right turn at The Merchandise Mart. This was the flagship of the fleet so we stopped at only a few stations as we roared northward. Soon after we left the Howard Street station on the far north side of the City of Chicago we descended and took the trackage which included a trip right down Main Street in Wilmette.

We practically flew the rest of the way into the heart of downtown Milwaukee where we came to rest at the end of the line. This final station on the North Shore Lines was at 7th and Wisconsin, adjacent to the Schroeder Hotel, where I would not too many months hence be doing NBC radio network half-hour late-night dance band broadcasts (remotes) with Shep Fields and his "Rippling Rhythm." Mr. Fields would get his Rippling Rhythm effect by blowing bubbles with a straw into a large, water-filled Mason jar while his orchestra was playing their theme song.

WMAW was on the second floor of The Town Hotel, above the Town Theatre, and it was under big time construction. The construction firm had a fast-approaching FCC deadline to meet. They couldn't care less about the FCC, but they wanted "Construction completed on time" money

Milwaukee

from WMAW.

Elaine and I picked our way through piles of two by fours, bx cable, electric junction boxes, control panels, consoles, four RCA Victor turntables still in their factory cartons, RCA 44 microphones and other broadcast equipment. This mess looked like it might take five years to organize it into a sleek, modern post World War Two radio station.

A few minutes later as we sat with Woody Dreyfus he told us the work had to be completed for a Christmas Day sign on. Why not? I signed on the first station I ever worked for, WKNA, Charleston, West Virginia, on New Year's Day 1947. I just could become famous as the announcer who signed on the most postwar new radio stations on major holidays. Elaine and I left Woody Dreyfus feeling I had an excellent chance for the one remaining announcer's opening. Mr. Dreyfus said he would send me a letter either way, and we believed him.

We had a few hours before the next "Electroliner" left for Chicago so we slipped into a theater on Wisconsin Avenue, and saw "The Foxes of Harrow" starring Sexy Rexy and gorgeous Maureen O'Hara.

Within a week I had a very complimentary letter from Woody Dreyfus, and I would start the Milwaukee portion of my already unusual radio career within two weeks. Good news indeed, because we were flat broke. But that would be the story of the majority of my years as a broadcaster. So what else was new?

I moved to Milwaukee, started work at WMAW, shared a room in the Town Hotel with fellow-announcer Cy Nelson, and started the hunt for an apartment in post-World War II Milwaukee. I had no car so Woody Dreyfus let me use his Cadillac. I would answer "apartment for rent" ads in The Milwaukee Journal newspaper. My weekly pay before deductions was $17.95, and the few apartments available were priced WAY out of my range. It was most discouraging to say the least. Then aid came from an unexpected source.

WMAW finally signed on, well after Christmas Day and the Uehlein family, owners of Schlitz Beer, "The Beer That Made Milwaukee Famous" had an open-house honoring all of us at Milwaukee's newest radio station. Mrs. Uehlein was a charming woman who welcomed us each individually and told us if there was anything she could do for us, all we had to do was ask.

I was, as I have always been, at the few parties I've been brave enough to attend, hiding in a corner behind a huge potted palm, afraid to speak to anyone, when Mrs. Uehlein, suddenly like a huge ocean-liner, floated into my presence, brandishing a martini. She saw I wasn't holding a glass, so she thrust the martini into my right hand, and asked if she could do anything for me. I stammered something about a wife and a baby and I said we badly needed an apartment. She wrote my name in a small solid gold pocket notebook and said, as she glided away, "You'll be hearing from me. Now enjoy your martini, and do have more."

Well, I took my first-ever taste of booze and it was AWFUL!!!!! It tasted like what varnish must taste like, so when nobody was looking in my direction I did for the first time something I would do hundreds more times over the years ahead...I poured the varnish into the potted palm.

Within forty-eight hours Mrs. Uehlein was true to her word. She called me at WMAW and said the 770 Marshall Apartment Hotel had a rare studio apartment vacancy. This was right after World War Two and finding a place to live was extremely difficult. I didn't have a penny to my name, so the fact that 770 Marshall Street was within walking distance of WMAW in downtown Milwaukee was a bonus. My daily nine-hour shift at WMAW ended at 5PM, with a return to the Town Hotel each night from 11:30 until midnight to host the ABC radio network show with the Hal Otis Trio. I would walk the eight blocks each way, and save the ten cents a bus ride would cost. With that one thin dime I saved, I could buy a quart of milk or a pound of cheese. Things were really looking rosy for the A. L. Hellyer, Jr., family.

I moved all my worldly belongings (an army duffel bag with my clothing and shaving gear) into the "Studio Apartment" at 770 Marshall, and awaited Elaine's arrival with infant Larry, at the Chicago and Northwestern Railroad station six blocks away. I remember we splurged and hailed a Yellow Cab to take our little family to our fancy new digs. Well, it really wasn't much of a place, but it had a roof and we were together. This was a tiny apartment, but it was our first real home.

Elaine and I slept in the Murphy bed, which would have been fine, but the first time we opened it, Murphy was in it. Old joke. Sorry about that. Larry slept in his buggy which had been a gift from Elaine's family, and Elaine prepared meals in the only other room, a very small "Pullman Kitchen," with a combination ice box, sink, one-burner range. There was no room in the kitchen, so Elaine and I sat side by side on the bed to eat our meals.

This was not a very large place. Thank goodness I only weighed one hundred sixty pounds. If I were ten pounds heavier I would not have been able to turn around in the room. If you've ever traveled cross-country in a roomette on a train you know how much space we had.

The monthly rent was much more than I earned at WMAW, so I worked four hours each night in the kitchen of the Pfister Hotel, midway between WMAW and our apartment. Saturday was my day off at WMAW so I got a full eight-hour job pumping gas at great University of Wisconsin and Chicago Cardinals football star Pat Harder's Pate AirGlide Gas Station. Somehow we managed to keep body and soul together.

One day I interviewed the Lieutenant Governor of Wisconsin, Jim Callan, on WMAW and mentioned, as I did to everyone I met, I was looking for a real apartment. Well, Mr. Callan had just built a brand-new apartment building at Fifty-One Hundred North Teutonia Avenue, and he had a one bedroom apartment available for seventy dollars a month, half of our monthly rent at 770 Marshall, and Elaine could choose the paint colors for the rooms. WOW!!!!! I jumped at it. BUT, where would I get the first and last months rent money to seal the deal?

Household Finance sponsored my noon newscast on WMAW, so I went to their office on Wisconsin Avenue, and because the people in the office listened to me on "their show," and thought I was a big radio star, I secured a "signature-only loan" just as I said on their commercial each day, and within two weeks we were settled in a REAL apartment.

We lived there for close to two years, during which time I really got the feel of family life and real radio. When Gene Autry brought his "Melody Ranch" broadcast for Wrigley's Chewing Gum to Milwaukee I won the announcer's audition for the show from the stage of The Riverside Theater. This was my first coast to coast broadcast and it was a major thrill. The check for fifty dollars was a tremendous thrill, too. Fifty dollars for one half-hour show. We couldn't believe it!!! My shift stayed the same, Monday through Friday from 8AM until 5PM, and the 11:30PM to Midnight broadcast on the ABC Radio Network, with its talent fee of five dollars per show was wonderful.

I also worked Sundays from 6AM to 2PM, and did the German Hour from 11AM to noon with a gentleman who would repeat in German everything I said in English, and also gave special announcements of upcoming events, and for all I knew of Bund meetings. My talent fee for that show was a case of Michelob Beer each month. We didn't drink, so we would put the case in our apartment locker, and save it for Elaine's dad. In 1948 Michelob was a German-import beer. Today it is an import from St. Louis…a product of Anheuser-Busch.

Were I not a packrat, keeping every scrap of paper through my entire lifetime, I would not know the very afternoon I introduced voice tracks and sound effects and other programming bits that turned front office suits into blithering basket cases. This Interoffice-Memorandum from WMAW answers the questions. It is dated April 12, 1948, and it reads thusly:

"To: Art Hellyer
From: Hal Walker, program manager
SUBJECT: MAW'S MATINEE.......A darned good show...

It has been suggested by both the front office and the sales department that your show continue along the same format as originally established, i.e., informal and entertaining. However, there has been some thinking about the use of sound effects, slowing down and speeding up turntables while the artists are singing, voices coming in out of nowhere, etc., etc. The general opinion is that the time of your show is too early in the afternoon to make the use of such material desirable. So let's leave the special effects off for a while, OK? Not by a darned sight do I mean that you should leave your personality out of the show, but I believe a little more of the 'brassiere salesman' approach (Martin Block, for instance) would sell the good Housefraus on the Matinee."

Well the first thing I did, of course, as I always did with stations' "Inter-office Memos," I read it on the air, interjecting my personal comments. An example would be the "darned good show" statement which was to butter me up for the assault that would follow. And how about the line, "So, let's leave the special effects off for awhile, OK?" Well, I could discuss that line until doomsday and they would never let me do it, so of course, it was NOT "OK"...And Mr. Walker sure liked to use "darned sight" in his conversation. I can hear his long-suffering wife shouting, "WILL YOU PLEASE KNOCK OFF THAT 'DARNED SIGHT' CRAP?" It would be three more years before I could make all those "special effects" a regular part of my show, and it wasn't over WMAW's 5000-watt airwaves in Milwaukee, but on a Chicago 50,000-watt powerhouse, WCFL.

A young lady from Claremont, Oklahoma, the former Clara Ann Fowler, came to the Town Room of the Town Hotel in Milwaukee in 1948 and I had the pleasure of being her first network announcer.

Mr. Jack Rael of Mercury Records drove into Tulsa one night, and heard Clara Ann warbling country songs on the radio. When he would leave Tulsa a few days later, his life and Clara Ann's life had changed forever. Jack Rael became her manager, gave her a new name, Patti Page, and the rest is history. She thought she would sing a few years on Tulsa radio, get married, have children and that would be that. Instead she became "The Singing Rage...Miss Patti Page," and sold millions of records.

Patti was twenty years old and I was twenty-three when we worked together in Milwaukee. I remember one night when WGN's Eddie Hubbard was in Milwaukee for an emcee gig, he stopped in for our radio show. After the show, Eddie went out to his car, got his famous ukulele, and Patti, Eddie and I sang songs until the break of dawn. Many, many years later I recommended Eddie to Ralph Sherman for a Satellite Music Network announcing job. In 2007 Eddie was still doing it.

It was during this period I acquired my first car. The station had a trade-out with a local English Austin dealer. A trade-out is perfectly FCC legal, and is common practice. The station accepts a product, and in return gives the client equal value in radio commercials.

The Austin was brand new, had a dyed-blue kangaroo leather interior, a heater and a radio and was valued at twelve hundred dollars. The station had no real use for the car. I needed a car badly, especially its 45 miles per gallon of gas, so the station manager, a fine gentleman named Jerry Sill, sold me the car for six hundred dollars. I secured a bank loan for the full amount, and over the next thirty months I paid it off. Everyone was happy, everyone was a winner.

Once a month during my Milwaukee apprenticeship I would go to the MASSIVE Wood Veterans Hospital and provide those poor souls some entertainment. Many of them were terribly wounded World War One veterans who had known no other home. And, of course, World War Two veterans were also there by the thousands.

I asked Patti if she'd accompany me and she agreed. I picked her up at the hotel in my new English Austin and we drove to the hospital. Patti's career, like mine, was in its infancy, but when she walked on stage with me the applause was deafening. There were men in wheelchairs, and on gurneys, some were leaning on wooden crutches, and many were standing against the walls. These mostly were men who were spending or would spend their entire lives in military hospital beds.

Patti Page brought down the house. A hospital patient-pianist accompanied her and she sang the great songs of two wars, from "There's a Long, Long Trail A-Winding, Into the Land of My Dreams" to "Kiss Me Once, and Kiss Me Twice, and Kiss Me Once Again, It's Been a Long, Long Time." She stood there, alone at the front of the stage for almost three hours, and then she spoke quietly into the microphone thanking the veterans for giving her a free country in which to live.

When she concluded the program with Irving Berlin's "God

Bless America" there wasn't a dry eye in the house. Then she came down from the stage and walked up to each and every gurney and wheelchair, and talked to each and every veteran individually, and those who could stand did so, and there was thunderous applause for many minutes. Although "Tennessee Waltz" was written in 1948 by Pee-Wee King and Red Stewart, it would not become a smash hit until 1951 when Patti Page recorded it and sold over a million copies, and over the next twenty years it sold over SIX million copies. These veterans were in on the ground floor of Patti's career which over the years ahead would find her forever in the top three all-time female singers. Patti Page has a very special place in my heart.

After the program Patti went to as many rooms as she could in those vast buildings where loneliness and despair pervaded every nook and cranny. She shook hands with the veterans and she kissed many of them on the cheek, and for a wonderful moment eyes lighted up for the first time in years.

No one who saw Patti Page that magical afternoon ever forgot her visit. I often spoke of it on my shows. I have loved that lady for over fifty years, yet except for TV I have never seen her again. Son Michael wanted to buy tickets for me to a Chicagoland Patti Page concert recently, but I chose not to go. I'd rather remember 1948 when we were young, and our lives were ahead of us.

I had, at this very early point in my career, interviewed quite a few people, and I always had a fear that would give me panic attacks prior to and during the interview. What would I do if the person across the microphone from me were to say forbidden words on the air? Words like "hell" or "damn" or "pregnant." I, of course, would be fired INSTANTLY and the station would be fined a substantial amount of money by the FCC, and put on probation. Should it happen at the same station a second time, the FCC would pull the station's license, putting a lot of innocent people out of work. It really frightened me, though I had no control over what came out of people's speaking tubes. Yet, I as the announcer and person closest to the culprit, would be held responsible. Management somehow believed, as the announcer, I should have been aware of the possibility the interviewee might foul the hygienic airwaves with a Hell or Damn, or, God forbid, something worse. Before each interview I would be vomiting in the men's room, and then having violent stomach spasms during the interview.

My first major interview, conducted in 1948, was with the Honorable Basil O'Connor, the man whom President Franklin Delano Roosevelt had appointed head of "The March of Dimes." The organization was in the front lines in the fight against the health scourge of the forties and fifties, POLIO. Can you imagine, I so shook during my conversation with Mr. O'Connor, he asked me if I was all right? Right on the air! I was even frightened to death a man of his stature might slip and say one of the forbidden words that would surely put to an end my career, which was just getting started.

Polio was so epidemic, parents would not allow their children to go to the local swimming pool or play in the hot sun. Polio was everywhere! President Roosevelt, once a fine athlete as a young man, was crippled for life by this most dreaded of all diseases. I had it in 1938, but it was not diagnosed as such until I was in the army, and a sharp doctor at Randolph Field, Texas, discovered it through x-rays he had taken following a baseball injury I'd suffered. Thankfully, in 1954 Dr. Jonas Salk, a microbiologist at the University of California at San Diego, developed a vaccine that all but eradicated this killer.

1948 was an exciting year for me, and a transitional one in my formative broadcast years. World War Two was now three years behind us, and our uniforms were in the ragbag. Fellow announcer Tom Mercein and I, dressed in blue suits, white shirts and ties, were in the music library at radio station WMAW in Milwaukee. The station was on the second floor of The Town Hotel and I was about to start my Noon to 4PM "Maw's Matinee" show when this fellow with lots of hair piled up on his head strode in with a 78rpm record in each of his hands.

He introduced himself as "Liberace," then with sort of a shy look he said, "My full name is Walter Valentino Liberace and I was born right here in town." He then gave us each one of the records to play, "if you can," on our shows. He wrote our names on a slip of paper, put it in his jacket pocket, and he was off to the next station. He was planning on getting a lot of plays in his hometown.

Well, Tom and I put the "A" side on a record player, and we were fascinated by all the songs he had worked into "Tico Tico." If you grew up with 78s as I did, you are well aware only one song could be recorded on each side and most songs ran approximately two-and-a-half minutes. It astonished us to note he played melodies from twenty-one songs in that short period of time. Needless to say, we looked at each other and said "Wow!! I'm playing this one today."

Well, I was on until 4PM, and Tom was on 4 to 8PM, which is why I have an autographed picture of Liberace wearing one of his jackets you must see to believe. With his diamond-encrusted fingers and pen, he has written: "To Art Hellyer, the first DJ to play my records, Gratefully, Liberace."

His rise to superstardom, and to now be spoken of by millions of people as, arguably, "The entertainer of the Twentieth Century" is astounding when one recalls when Tom and I met him in 1948, he was earning fifty dollars per week.

Yet three years later, in 1951, he was working the top clubs in the country, and was rapidly becoming the most popular entertainer in the world. In 1952 he landed a weekly TV show, and was a television regular through 1969. Liberace made an enormous amount of money on TV and it was he who coined the phrase, "I laugh all the way to the bank."

RADIO 1950–1955

* Essay 6 *

**"As one who grew up in Chicago during the 1940s and 1950s,
I well remember Art Hellyer on radio, just as I remember
Mal Bellairs, Dave Garroway, Eddie Hubbard, Howard Miller,
Mike Rapchak, Ernie Simon, and Ken Nordine.
Art, because of his terrific sense of humor, has always stood
above the rest. And, as you may know, Art has remained in
broadcasting far longer than the rest—for good reason."
— George Spink,
TUXEDO JUNCTION NEWSLETTER," July 2003**

My Chicago radio career started because of penny postal
cards. I was employed in 1948-50 by WMIL ("Means
Milwaukee"), and I would listen to the great pros on Chicago
radio whenever I was not on the air myself....people like Dave
Garroway, Myron (Mike) Wallace, Hugh Downs, George
Stone, Dick Noble, Wed Howard, Les Tremayne, Barbara
Luddy, Olan Soule, Parley Baer, William Conrad, Jim
Ameche, Pierre Andre, Mal Bellairs, Paul Gibson, Franklin
McCormack, Virginia Payne, Norman Ross, Sr., Howard
Miller, Bill Evans, Alex Dreier, Paul Harvey, Fahey Flynn,
Jane and Goodman Ace, John Harrington, Mercedes
McCambridge, Clifton Utley, Studs Terkel, Cliff Norton,

Eloise Kummer, Eleanor Engle, SaraJane Wells, Sid Breese, Arthur Peterson, Betty Lou Gerson, Hugh Studebaker, Willard Waterman, Jack Haskell, Connie Russell, Jill Corey, Bette Chapel, Carolyn Gilbert, Bob Elson, Halloween Martin, Don Gordon, Bill O'Connor, Bill Hamilton, Jack Quinlan—with most of whom, believe it or not, I would soon be working, but I hadn't the vaguest idea it would happen. It never entered my mind.

It all suddenly happened because of penny postal cards I would send daily to the program directors at the Chicago radio stations. On each card I would print (my handwriting has always looked like a chicken stepped in an ink spill, and then walked across a sheet of paper) "HELP!!! SAVE ME!!!!!!! GET ME OUT OF MILWAUKEE RADIO!!!!!!!!! ART HELLYER."

In early 1950, Mal Bellairs informed WCFL program director Bob Platt he would be leaving the WCFL staff to go freelance. Well, Mr. Platt looked in his file of announcers looking for work...cards, letters and piles of audition electrical transcriptions and a few tape reels (this was early for tape and too expensive for the average starving announcer to afford...I couldn't afford anything but penny postal cards and even they were a strain on my budget) and he called in over two hundred people to audition for the soon to be vacated Bellairs position. I did not attend because I was too broke to ask for a day off at WMIL and even if I did get the day off I did not have money for a ticket on the North Shore Railroad to Chicago and back to Beertown, USA. So the audition was held over a period of days and a very young and highly talented broadcaster named Jack Taylor won.

Then Bob Platt did what was common practice. He threw out all the cards, letters, ETs (sixteen-inch shellac electrical transcription discs that would spin on the turntable at thirty-three-and-a-third revolutions, becoming the forerunner of the LP), and the recently introduced reel-to-reel tapes. Some weeks later he realized he must soon hold auditions for the 16-week summer-vacation relief announcer position and he had only a daily postal card from some kid announcer in Milwaukee on his desk. So he called the kid...a kid named Art Hellyer at WMIL. Lucky for both, the kid was on the air, so Bob Platt said he'd like Hellyer to send him an ET. Hellyer couldn't afford an ET, so Hellyer opened the microphone to all of his listeners and said, "I'll audition for you right now Mr. Platt....Let's see....I'll give Parkway Tavern an extra FREE spot right now." And I read the Parkway Tavern commercial for Bob Platt. Bob Platt said, "Thank you Art. You are hired...you start May 27 (1950)...BUT IF YOU EVER GIVE ANYONE A FREE COMMERCIAL ON WCFL I WILL FIRE YOU!!!!!"

Late in my 1950 WCFL summer-vacation relief job I had a call from Walter Schwimmer....THEEEEEE MOGUL at Schwimmer and Scott Advertising. Mrs. Charles R. Walgreen had been listening to me and would like me to do a new Walgreens show starting in September on WCFL. WOW!!! GREAT NEWS!!!! The show was at the moment nameless, but I was to sit in at Schwimmer & Scott Advertising and help the agency and Walgreens people select a name for the show. You would assume that I should have felt honored, but this is just part of the lunacy of the business. The meeting would start as soon as I could get from the station at the end of my show to the agency a few miles away on Michigan Avenue.

When I arrived, the meeting started with agency man Bob Knapp saying, "we can make this a short meeting because I have come up with the ideal name for OUR PROGRAM....we'll call it "The Morning Show"!!! HOW BRILLIANT!!!!!! This from a man with a degree in advertising from the University of Michigan. In fact he had graduated in the same class with Bob Platt, who hired me at WCFL, and Mike Wallace, in the forties and early fifties a staff announcer at WMAQ NBC and the nightly newscaster on "The Bond Store News" at 11PM on WMAQ. And yes, the same man who would go on to even greater fame as one of the forever excellent hosts of "60 Minutes" on CBS-TV.

Many, many hours later, after lunch had been catered by Fritzel's and dinner hour was fast approaching, it was agreed we still didn't have a name for this, at the moment....stuck on the drawing board....radio masterpiece, so we would convene for the day. "Give it a great deal of thought in your homes tonight, open it to family discussion, etc., etc." said the mighty minds from Walgreens and the agency. Then we'd meet at Schwimmer & Scott Advertising, same time tomorrow.

This was my first experience....I was 26 years old....with the giants of advertising and broadcasting, meeting to discuss something they considered to be a major decision.....the naming of a stupid twenty-nine minutes and thirty-seconds radio program on just one of the over four thousand radio stations then on the air in America.

This was the meeting that early in my career decided me to stay away from meetings. They were meaningless, and deadly boring. These were a bunch of pompous, top-level executives trying to justify their jobs, and I wanted no more of it. I did not go home and ask Elaine or baby Larry to seriously help me come up with a name for the show. In fact, I bowed out of the stupid meeting the next day, and was informed by telephone by Bob Knapp much later that day that the mighty minds in their infinite wisdom had decided to call the show, "Walgreens' Headlines and Music." That only took approximately sixteen hours and two catered meals to come up with.

Jump forward now to September 25, 1950. We were living at my in-laws' home in Elmhurst, Illinois, while we tried, in post WWII America to find a rental somewhere, anywhere in Chicagoland. Housing was most difficult to find, and though my salary had risen from $32.50 a week in Milwaukee to $52.50 for a 48 hour week at WCFL, we could not afford the few rentals we did find. So we were temporarily the guests of my father-in-law who early on hated me because I was "a radio tramp who will never make any money" and who stole his lovely eldest daughter from him and was worst of all "a follower of the Pope." Truth is although I was baptized Roman Catholic I have always said on and off the air, "The Pope puts his pants on one leg at a time just as I do," and not only that he is a mortal man like most of the men I'd ever known.

9-25-50 I drove my little 45 miles to the gallon of gas, English Austin from my in-laws' home in Elmhurst to the loop for my first freelance show. Freelancing was when you had no regular job, but went to hundreds of auditions, and hoped and prayed you'd win one once in awhile. I won one out of seven over the following years, which Super-Agent Shirley Hamilton told me, was a very high percentage.

Let us pause now for station identification (If I said that once over the years I probably said it fifty thousand times). Let us pause now as I am driving to the city for my first "Walgreens' Headlines and Music" program, and discuss auditions. Webster's 50 pounds of words describes it as…"Audition…noun….the act or sense of hearing, a hearing to test the fitness of an actor, musician, etc., as for a particular job." I would call it, in over 90 percent of the cases, a bloodbath to justify an advertising person's job, because in many cases the ad agency has already decided who they want—as in my own case when I won the auditions for Kellogg's, where I introduced to an already overly cerealed-and-sugared world, their cavity-causing, dentists' favorites. The agency people heard me delivering commercials on my various radio shows, and decided I would be their choice.

The audition process is one that has brought on many heart attacks. At least twice weekly in the early fifties, I would run up and down Le Boul Mich carrying a back-breaking, and I might add, pocketbook-breaking load of 12-inch to 16-inch electrical transcriptions. Recording them was expensive, and unlike tape, if you made a mistake there was no way to correct it. I used Don Lavery's Globe Transcription Service studios to record all my shows because for broadcasters like Bill O'Connor and me, Don knew most of us were on the brink of disaster and bankruptcy. Don Lavery did a lot of major client recording work, but he had a special much lower rate than the huge studios. World-famous runner Jesse Owens, who showed Adolph Hitler and the world at the 1936 Berlin Olympics that a black man from the United States of America was the best in the world, recorded his audition transcriptions at Globe Recording Studios. Even he was on a broadcaster's budget.

As I sat in the right lane at the corner of Clinton and Randolph Streets preparing to make a right turn, on my merry way to the premiere of my first freelance show, a huge green and white Chicago Motor Coach Company bus made a right turn from the wrong lane and in one swift crunching moment took off the front end of my car. I, of course, had not a penny on me, as was almost always the case, so after police reports were filled out I walked the over two miles across the city to the Furniture Mart at 666 N. Lake Shore Drive. I took the elevator to the WCFL studios on the 19th floor and entered the studio as Howie Roberts greeted me with "Good morning, Art. What the heck happened to you?" I told him of the accident as I sat in a chair, shaking from head to feet trying to compose myself for THE BIG SHOW!!!!! That calamity should have convinced me to get out of this absurd business, but somehow I did the show in a blur. I know the agency assigned a producer and a director to the show. They threw signals at me, waved their arms around a lot, made circles with their fingers and drew their index fingers across their throats and tapped their noses many times. They waved their fists at me, and made all the other signs by which we live in radio. I guess the show went OK because those two people never showed up again and I did the show for over three years until the morning I decided to have the "LATE" Charles R. Walgreen as a guest, and I said, "For Mr. Walgreen's appearance on today's show we now leave our studios" and Dr. K brought on a harp solo, and Walgreens fired me.

I was summoned to appear in the august presence of Mrs. Walgreen in her lavish mansion on the lakefront. She apparently wanted to ask me but one question, "Young man why do you say the things you do on radio?" My reply was brief, "Ma'am...I believe I was put on earth to puncture pomposity." The stuffy butler ushered me out the door without another word being spoken by any one. It was while I was doing the Walgreens show Marty Hogan and others in the front office at WCFL decided to ask me to take over the station's morning drive time, and the rest is history, or to make the feminists happy, herstory.

One day in 1950 I received a phone call at WCFL, where I was the summer vacation-relief announcer, from producer Larry Kurtz. He had been my production class instructor at Radio Institute of Chicago back in 1946, and he was going to produce a new television game show...on NBC Central Division Network. If I recall correctly we were not yet connected to the nets west of Chicago and St. Louis, and this show would come out of WNBQ, the Chicago NBC-TV affiliate, and would be seen in about ten cities in the Midwest.

The show would run live (no videotape yet, and filming was far too expensive) at 4:30PM Sunday afternoons, and would be called "Rate Your Mate." Jack Holden, the announcer, and Paul Barnes, the host, had to be very careful as they pronounced the show's title, because the show was sponsored by the Sealy Mattress Company. And though both announcers were professional masters of voice and diction, NBC still received many letters each week objecting to the show's title.

Carmelita Pope had been hired as the young actress for the show and Larry Kurtz asked me to be the young actor. We would assemble at 9AM on Sunday morning for the "non-rehearsal" rehearsal. I call it that because Carmy and I would perform ad-lib skits suggested by the listeners' postal cards drawn from a spinning container. We would not see the actual cards, but Larry Kurtz would have us perform our skits using the hundreds of leftover cards from the previous week so we'd, over the hours ahead, become used to the idea of what we would be doing on that day's show.

It was interesting as the weeks flew by to note many viewers would send in their same suggestions each week, so some of them we actually would have rehearsed. The stagehands unions had not yet signed contracts with the TV stations, so Carmelita and I would set the stage, dragging out park benches, street lights, fake shrubbery, shaking snowflakes over each other, etc. One scene called for a bathtub, which Carmy was supposedly bathing in, while I, her husband (no "significant others" in those days) stood at the prop sink shaving as we played whatever the heck the scene was. We would rehearse by woodshedding some of the prior week's suggestions from 9AM until noon...break for lunch...most of us were so poor we brought a sandwich from home, then talk about the show most of the afternoon until 4:30-5PM when we would do the show live on the Midwestern leg of NBC. After the show we'd all talk about it for a short while, then Larry Kurtz would pay us for our day's work. We would each get a crisp five dollar bill, and walk to public transportation to get back to our living quarters.

Early in 1952 I had a phone call from a small advertising

agency owner, Charlie Temkin. He was small in stature, and his agency was small, but HIM? He worked, as we called it, "out of his hat." Over the next ten years I would do hundreds of television commercials for him. He would buy the cheapest old films, not the ones that ran after the 10PM news, but the ones that played after the films that followed the 10 o'clock news. And the commercials would not run 30 seconds or 60 seconds to the thousandth of a second, but rather for 10 to 20 MINUTES.......and I would shout at the viewers, and wave my arms and point my right index finger at the camera and many times during the message I would COMMAND....."GO TO YOUR PHONE RIGHT NOW!!!!! RIGHT NOW GO TO YOUR PHONE AND CALL 555-1234. THAT'S 555-1234 555-1234....DO IT NOW!!!!!!!! CALL 555-1234.... 555-1234....555-1234."

Thanks to Charlie, and other admen for whom I did these TV pitches as we called them, Jack Scott, Walter Schwimmer, Ray Freedman, Sandor Rodkin, Mike Barkas, etc., I led the strange life that only my fellow freelancers Bill O'Connor, Marty Faye, Al Parker, Mal Bellairs, Howard Miller and a few others knew. At one time I had over 200 quarter hours a week, on seven radio stations for Downtown Nash (not exactly "Downtown," but close at 1200 W. Madison.....in the heart of "Skid Row"). In fact, to further entice listeners to come to Downtown Nash I would often say on my shows, "Folks come out right now to Downtown Nash. Twelve Hundred West Madison Street and meet Jack Metnick, THE KING OF THE BUMS."

I often did the shows live from the front windows at 1200 W. Madison Street, and strange things would occur that wouldn't happen if I were sitting in a studio in the loop. Strange things indeed, like the woman who would back up to the showroom window behind which I was broadcasting, bend over, pull up her skirt and present to me for my edification her extremely large bare-naked, pressed-against-the-window, posterior, or the highly inebriated male who would throw empty beer bottles at the window, or the couple who would fornicate on the sidewalk possibly expecting I would broadcast the activity as one would a wrestling match. They were arrested a few times and charged with "open lewdness."

Sometimes the activity would be inside the showroom when a salesman would lose a sale and a shouting match would be heard as I was talking about the friendly salespeople at Downtown Nash.

Where were the police? One block away at the West Madison Street Police Station. I think they looked on these activities as part of the show I was doing. In fact, some of them became part of the show as they would slap with their open hands, the bare posterior the lady was displaying to me. Believe me, it was most difficult to keep a straight face when these activities were going on, and most difficult for me to talk of all the advantages of shopping for your car at Downtown Nash, especially when those two fat cheeks were pressed flat against the window directly in front of me. Most of the car dealer employees thought it was a scream....I didn't....I was forced to sell cars verbally under most difficult circumstances.

My weekend schedule for Downtown Nash was different every week, because all the Chicagoland radio stations would start phoning the Metnick brothers around one o'clock on Friday afternoon....the station salespeople would tell the brothers what time slots were still available (not sold) for the weekend, and the Metnicks would buy those availabilities for well-below rate card. I would get there about 2:30PM Friday afternoon, pick up the unbelievable weekend schedule, then head for Globe Transcription at 230 N. Michigan where I would record for the next 5 to 6 hours and Don Lavery would make the number of copies that were needed for the stations I was on that weekend. By 9-10PM I would hit the streets

RUNNING with a huge pile of 12-inch electrical transcriptions. (I was so glad when cassette tape came along a few
years later.)

I would go from one station to the next, and drop the
recordings and a list of the times they would play at WGN,
WMAQ, WIND, WLS, WAAF, WCFL and WJJD. I also
printed on individual file cards the call letters and frequency
of each station, then when I sat down at the microphone for
the live shows I would put the proper card at the base of the
mic so I would always properly identify the station I was on.
Only once do I recall slipping up and it was a Freudian slip,
because at WIND I once said, "For Downtown Nash I'm Art
Hellyer and this is WBBM...Chicago." Why? I don't
know...I wasn't yet on WBBM in the early to mid-fifties.
Strange how the mind works, isn't it?

It was also at WIND in the early fifties I met a staff
announcer named Milo Hamilton. I was born in 1923 and Milo
was born in 1927, so we were just a couple of youngsters early
in our broadcasting careers. At that time Milo was famous for
only one thing. One Saturday morning, in a fit of pique, he
pounded his fist through a plaster wall in the outer lobby, and
for years employees would hang the current calendar over the
gaping hole. More fame came Milo's way on October 1,
1961, when on the closing day of the baseball season Milo
would announce Roger Maris' season record-breaking 61st
home run.

But wait baseball fans....there's more! On April 8, 1974,
Hank Aaron broke another Babe Ruth record of 714 lifetime
homers and guess who was at the WSB Atlanta Microphone to
call it.....our favorite wall-smasher MILO HAMILTON. And
Milo is now in a bunch of Halls of Fame. And I still hear
Buck Martinez and Mark Patrick on their number one baseball
talk show on XM Satellite saying "Here's Milo calling yet
another home run!" Yes at age 81 his voice is just as vibrant

as it was back in the early fifties when he was delivering WIND station breaks. Good for you Milo. Way to go.

By 1AM Saturday I would be in bed and at 6AM Saturday morning I would be on my first live show, usually WIND in the Wrigley Building, then off at 630, then on WMAQ in the Merchandise Mart also at 630. How would I do this? I would close the WIND show at 627, the record turner would play my instrumental theme "Hi Ho Hi Ho it's off to work we go" until 6:30. I would run out the door...hopefully catch the elevator quickly, then run from the Wrigley Building to the Merchandise Mart, jump in the elevator....get off at the 19th floor and run to the assigned studio where the record turner had started my theme playing at 6:30 straight up. I would sit down and at 6:33 fade the music to background and I would start talking. I would generally do that in the six-minute interval.

Meanwhile, the shows I had recorded the past evening were playing on the other stations at the same times. The rest of Saturday until 6PM would be exactly the same as I ran from one station to another...WGN in Tribune Tower, WIND in the Wrigley Building, WMAQ in the Merchandise Mart, WLS at 900 W. Washington, WCFL in the Furniture Mart at 666 N. Lake Shore Drive and WJJD in the Carbide and Carbon Building at 220 N. Michigan.

Why live shows, too, all day? The Metnicks wanted it that way. They almost killed me. I met myself coming and going, back and forth across the entire downtown Chicago area, and during one period they added WAIT, which was broadcasting those days from their transmitter next to the Elmhurst Airport, and yes I would hop in my Nash Rambler, and drive myself out to WAIT, too.

Did I crack up? You betcha I did. There were times when I was so exhausted I would just sit in the car and shake all over and cry, cry, cry!! It was a tough life and, in those early days, radio did not pay big money as it would today.

Often I had a TV show to do on Saturday and Sunday night. I used to stagger home, sleep a few hours, then do it all over again on Sunday. Yet between shows on the less hectic weekdays (my morning show at WCFL was on 6:30-10AM) and a few shows scattered through the day and a TV show for an hour-and-a-half two or three nights a week, I spent a great deal of time with our growing family. I would drive the 13 miles from the loop in off hours and then rush home to play with Larry, Mike, Debbie, Vickie and Jeff, then shoot back into the loop for a show or two, then back to the house. Hectic? And how, but I had youth and excellent health in my favor.

The hours I worked were taxing enough, but I also had to put up with guff from top management. This is a copy of a memo that the VP/GM of WJJD sent out on October 19, 1954:

"ANNOUNCERS, RECORD TURNERS, ENGINEERS!
Effective immediately...this is to advise that we are standing by our policy on our commercials 100%. In a 25 minute program where we allow one minute after every record, it is to be one minute, and at the close of the program there is to be NO fading of records to put in a close. If there is no time to complete the entire record, sign the program off by saying, 'This program has been brought to you by...(sponsor ID)'...AND THAT'S ALL!

"In the event the program is done live and the disc jockey signals to cut the music to bring in a long close...DON'T DO IT! Run the record as long as you can, and then the program is to be closed off by 'sponsor ID.'

"In the case of DOWNTOWN NASH with Art Hellyer on Sunday mornings, he is allowed from one up to two minutes after every SECOND record with a 15-second open and close...NO MORE! If he runs any more, CUT HIM! Any question concerning this...see me! I am holding each man responsible, and any violations of this rule will be taken up in the front office!

        — Fred Harm   VP/GM WJJD"

I might add this is the same music-happy manager who phoned me on Armistice Day to tell me to "observe 60 seconds of silence at 11AM, but play music in the background so we don't lose the listeners."

I look back on it all now and I can't believe I did it. I went one period of time 4 1/2 years with not a day off, 7 days and nights a week. Did Downtown Nash sell cars off this complete Chicago weekend saturation??????? They SOLD TONS OF THEM!!!! Downtown Nash was the number-one Nash dealer in America during those years.

The following page shows my schedule every Saturday and Sunday for almost seven years. I did all the above shows live, while shows I had recorded at Don Lavery's Globe Transcription Studio on Friday afternoon and evening were playing on up to six other stations opposite me at the same time:

THE HELLYER SAY

REGULAR WEEKLY SHOWS I DID.......1950-1956

Time	Station	Where	Program
6:30-7AM Sat.-Sun. Live	WGN RADIO	Tribune Tower	AH for Downtown Nash
7:00-8:00AM Mon-Sat. Live	WCFL	Furniture Mart	AH for Walgreens and Zenith Radio
8:05-9AM Sat.-Sun. Live	WIND	Wrigley Building	AH for DT Nash
9:05-10AM Sat.-Sun. Pre-recorded	WAIT	Elmhurst Airport	AH for DT NASH
10:05-11AM Sat.-Sun. First station Live...All others prerecorded	WMAQ WGN RADIO WIND WAAF WCFL WJJD	Merchandise Mart	AH for DT Nash
1:05-2PM Sat.-Sun. Live	WJJD	Carbide & Carbon Building	AH for DT Nash
2:00-4PM Sat. Live	WBBM RADIO	Wrigley Building	"The Art Hellyer Show"
5:05-6PM Sat.-Sun. First station Live... All others pre- recorded	WLS WMAQ WGN RADIO WAAF WIND WCFL WJJD	Stone Container Building	AH for DT Nash
10:30PM -12:30AM Live	WGN-TV	Tribune Tower	"Movie Playhouse" Art Hellyer Emcee
Drive	HOME	To Skokie to SLEEP	UNTIL 5AM

Weekends were terribly rough, but I was in my late twenties and early thirties. Ten years later I could not have carried a schedule like this, which is why I was thrilled in

April of 1959 when Channel 7, WBKB, now WLS-TV, for whom I'd been doing TV shows since 1950, offered me a full time forty hour week, and the right to continue freelancing.

Most stations did not allow their broadcasters to do both. I stayed with Channel 7 and the ABC-TV Network over 30 years, doing local announcing, and network announcing on shows like "Wide World of Sports," "Monday Night Baseball," "Monday Night Football," "Bewitched," "The Lawrence Welk Show," "The Real McCoys," "Naked City," "77 Sunset Strip," ABC-TV news, and Channel 7 news, plus many other shows on ABC-TV. Sounds almost as hectic, but it really wasn't. AND it lasted until automation reared its ugly head, and they had no need for live broadcasters except on the nightly newscasts. I had a long run in the broadcasting business and could not complain.

In 1952, after almost two full years of my freelancing on WCFL, Marty Hogan called me one day, and said he'd like very much for me to take over the morning show at WCFL. He said it had "nothing but goose eggs" in the ratings books, meaning no one was listening, and that I could do and say anything I wanted. I could have "carte blanche....just bring us listeners, Art...I know you can do it."

I asked if I'd be able to continue freelancing, and Marty told me I could. That started a relationship that would see WCFL in the morning go from last in the ratings to first in the ratings. The next day I met with GM Marty Hogan in his offices on the 19th floor of the Furniture Mart where just two years earlier I had won the summer vacation relief announcer's job with my daily postal cards to program director Bob Platt. And now I was taking over the morning show...the best spot in radio in those days, but on a station with "no listeners" in the morning.

I asked Marty who the best record turner was in town...not just at WCFL, but in all of Chicago. He said he had heard

Lenny Kaye at WBBM was said to be tops. I said, "Please get him for my show?"

Marty then explained all record turners in Chicago were members of the American Federation of Musicians, and each could have only one job. It was union chief James Caesar Petrillo's way of seeing to it that all musicians were working for a living wage. Not a bad idea, of course, but I wanted this Lenny-what's-his-name, who worked at WBBM.

Well, WCFL had an ace in the hole...James Petrillo's son Lee Petrillo was the WCFL music librarian, and he and his wife Mary would join Bill and Dorothy O'Connor and Elaine and me for weekly poker games. Let's see if he could work on the old man and allow Lenny Kaye to work two jobs, and do it without it causing the other AFM members to get out the signs, and march on us. It would not be easy, but at the time Marty Hogan was also County Clerk Richard J. Daley's campaign manager and I did the daily "Marriage License Show" from the county clerk's office. Maybe, just maybe, all the things would gel, and a compromise could be struck that would allow Lenny Kaye to work my show.

Well, lots of strings were pulled, many behind the scenes deals were worked out and Lenny Kaye could work my show just so long as he was at his post at WBBM at 9AM daily. Good enough...I would have his services 6:30 to 9AM, and I could go it alone just fine each day to my show's conclusion at 10AM. GOOD DEAL....LET'S GO...LET'S GET THE PEOPLE LISTENING TO WCFL IN THE MORNING ONCE AGAIN!!!!!!

And we did just that..........

THE ART HELLYER SHOW...
May 27, 1950, to July 12, 1957

* Essay 7 *

"Good Sunday morning radio listening:
Art Hellyer's program on WMAQ-NBC from
11 to 12. Hellyer sells used cars with the most
painless commercials on the air. They Are Funny!"
— *Jack Mabley, Chicago Daily News, 5-21-51*

"Marty Hogan GM/WCFL demanded that
Hellyer tape an immediate apology to the bank."
— *Variety Magazine*

" I feel that Art Hellyer is the outstanding
morning radio personality in the country today."
— *Marty Hogan, VP/GM, WCFL*

"New York Advertising Club's winners for 1958,
Television: Arthur Godfrey / Bufferin
Radio: Art Hellyer / Simmons Mattress"
— *Advertising Age Magazine, 8-11-58*

I would like to say a heartfelt thank you to Jim Lounsbury before I start this essay of "The Hellyer Say." Five years before Dick Clark, Jim started the television teen dance shows, and twenty-five years later he became a respected Washington, D.C., television journalist. But most important of all he saved our first child's life. In 1950, at age 26 I was in my first year realizing my childhood dream of working on radio in the only city I ever wanted to work in, the city I was born in, Chicago.

TV Guide magazine was having its first annual golfing, swimming, dinner outing for all of Chicago's radio and television people, and I, the newest kid on the block, was invited. My young bride, the Lovely Elaine, and our two-and-a-half-year-old progeny, Larry, were invited to attend with me.

I had tried to learn to play golf under the tutelage of my father in law, Erv Miller, who shot in the high sixties and low seventies, and at age fifty already had three PGA sanctioned "Holes-in-One." Attempting to learn in his presence proved to both of us I had no future in golf, so my day at the TV Guide Outing at the North Shore Country Club would be spent swimming, which I've always loved to do, and eating, for which I had the same proclivity.

So I dived into the greenish, chemically treated pool waters and with my 20/600 vision, blindly groped my way around. After maybe two minutes I surfaced to hear everyone present screaming and pointing. Well, I being blind as a bat assumed they were pointing at me, and thought, "Ye Gods! I must have lost my trunks," so I felt below my waist and found my Jantzens were secure.

It was then I heard Elaine and others screaming "Larry, Larry," and pointing into the pool. I still had no idea what was going on when a male body dived into the water and sank to the bottom. A moment later, the diver surfaced carrying our young son Larry in his arms.

He quickly stretched Larry out and applied artificial respiration and in a moment Larry was spurting green chemical water like a whale. Jim Lounsbury had saved our beloved son's life. Elaine and I were both crying, everyone around was crying, and now that Larry was definitely alive and well, thanks eternally to Jim, someone asked him why he dived into fifteen feet of water. His answer was that his daddy did it, so he did it too.

For years after that harrowing episode, every time I would meet Jim Lounsbury in the halls as we were running between radio and TV stations where we were doing our shows, I with tears in my eyes would gratefully thank him for giving our first-born back to us. I just can't imagine what life would have been like for Elaine and me if we had lost Larry.

And now especially as I write this in 2007, with the Lovely Elaine already gone for over nine years, I can't imagine what life would have been like without Larry and Mike, Debbie, Vickie and Jeff.

As I was completing my summer of 1950 vacation-relief stint at WCFL, Walgreens and Downtown Nash (as described elsewhere) came into my life. Those were exciting of course, but the best was yet to come. Late in 1951, Marty Hogan, general manager of WCFL, and Bob Platt, his fine program director who had hired me, offered me the morning drive-time show. There was nothing bigger in radio in those days and that spot was cherished by every broadcaster. However, there was a good possibility this would not be a good choice because WCFL drive time showed zilch in the ratings books.

And then again I had nothing to lose…this could be my big break….it would indeed be a challenge, and, if I could build the ratings, the sky could be the limit. I've told elsewhere how we secured the services of WBBM's music chief Lenny Kratoska, and how he would work with me from the start of my show at 6:30AM, then go across the street from WCFL's studios in the Furniture Mart at 666 N. Lake Shore Drive to his office at WBBM-CBS at 9 AM, and put in his eight hours there.

From the day we started "The Art Hellyer Show" until I was

fired five-and-a-half years later, on July 12, 1957, we must have done extraordinary things, because we moved the station from zero rating points to number one in Chicago morning drive time. I say it this way because I don't really recall what we did. I would be parking my car listening to Lenny, whom I had dubbed "Dr. K....TT (Turntable Technician)," playing my recorded opening, then I'd take the elevator to the nineteenth floor studios, sit down, and put on my headphones. Dr. K would "fade to background" my theme music, my wonderful engineer Ernie Nottger, who had only one arm and always astounded me with his dexterity, would open my microphone and things would start to happen. What things? I don't recall. Nothing we did was planned...the entire show all those wonderfully hectic years was ad-lib. Never did Lenny and I sit down after the show and talk about what we had just done or what we would do the next day. Even if we wanted to we couldn't, because the good doctor bolted out of the WCFL studio at 8:58AM as instrumental music played to the break, and I delivered the voice-over-music station break, "I'm Art Hellyer, and this is WCFL, The Voice of Labor, Chicago.... One thousand on your radio dial....I'll be back for one more hour after WCFL News Director Vic Barnes updates us on the latest disasters. Good morning, Vic."

Mr. Barnes would tell us all the latest terrible things that were happening locally, in Washington, and overseas. After all, that is the meaning of "NEWS"—North, East, West, South, all the directions and the only directions from whence all the latest tragedies could come, right? When I came back on at 9:05AM, Lenny (Dr. K) had already been seated at his desk across the street for five minutes, and I would do the final hour alone.

Doing an unplanned, ad-lib show had been my way as I worked my way up the radio ladder through Charleston, West Virginia; Fort Wayne, Indiana; Aurora, Illinois; and Milwaukee, Wisconsin. Doing it "my way" also got me fired at five of the stations in those four cities, but in Marty Hogan I had a manager who gave me "carte blanche," his very words the day he hired me, as I sat in his office, dressed in my army fatigues with a White Sox baseball cap setting off my haute couture attire.

A number of "Art Hellyer Shows" are enshrined in the Radio Archive of the Museum of Broadcast Communication in Chicago, thanks to America's foremost radio authority, Chuck Schaden. So I have been able to hear some of the things we did, because it all happened so quickly as we moved from one thing to another, I never remembered anything.

Just recently I discovered on the internet one of my WCFL morning shows is in a Hollywood radio station's Hall of Fame. How or why it is I have no idea. But it's nice. Thank you.

I've always believed "The Art Hellyer Show" on WCFL started as a two-hour live audition, and grew to three, then four hours because the only thing that matters in the broadcast industry happened. Sponsors bought the show...and DID THEY. Most of the time it was SOLD OUT, and we had a waiting list. In fact Dr. K and I had so many commercials, many mornings we never played a piece of music. The show became so clogged with commercials, one morning when Ernie opened my microphone, I shouted..."Help....Save us! We're drowning in a sea of commercials!!!!!" That very morning we invented, or concocted......whatever? We started our first "COMMERCIAL FESTIVAL."

Dr. K had three RCA turntables lined up in front of him, each with three speeds, 33 1/3, 45, and 78. All three were needed in the mid-nineteen-fifties because half the records we played on our show were still at 78 revolutions per minute, and the "Long-Playing (LP)" 33 1/3 RPM records, and 45s were just starting to make major inroads.

The great majority of commercials since back in the nineteen-thirties were recorded on twelve-inch to sixteen-inch discs with a sheet of aluminum sandwiched between two layers of a thin shellac coating. They were recorded at 33 1/3 RPM, and were the forerunner of the LP (Long-Playing) record, which came along in the late forties.

Dr. K slapped three of these discs with scheduled commercials recorded on them, and on my cue he started them all running. At the same time I read a scheduled commercial into the microphone. An absolute first in the broadcasting industry...Four....count them....FOUR commercials being heard by the listeners, and all at the same time.

Well to say that the phones started to light up is putting it mildly. Lou Ronder, who now was our program director, since Bob Platt had left to open his own advertising agency, was the first to call and shout, "ART WHAT THE HELL ARE YOU DOING?" I told him he could hear what the hell I was doing. He told me to stop it instantly, which, of course, inspired me to continue doing it.

In fact, in spite of WCFL management blowing its stack, and the ad agencies and sponsors screaming bloody murder at me, from that moment on, Dr. K and I had "Commercial Festivals" whenever we were terribly clogged with sponsors' messages. I would just holler, "Dr. K, it's commercial festival time," and away we'd go. I didn't care what the front office or the sponsors thought. After our very first one, I found the listener, the most important person, loved our festivals.

And guess what...the clients and agencies eventually liked them, too. If they were not selling the clients products they would have continued objecting to them, BUT THEY SOLD! And that was ALL the clients cared about. Radio and TV is NOT about entertaining you or your Aunt Minnie. It is about only ONE thing.....THE BOTTOM LINE!!!! And at any given time, it is run mostly by idiots.

Nathan Godfried, in his fine history book "WCFL, Chicago's Voice of Labor, 1926-78," published by The University of Illinois Press writes, "Art Hellyer became a popular disk jockey during the fifties. Combining wit, charm, and an amazing sense of humor, Hellyer created an alive, bubbling program of daily entertainment."

And in a passage from Arnold Passman's book "The DeeJays...How the Tribal Chieftains of Radio Got to Where They Are," published in 1971 by The MacMillan Company, Mr. Passman writes, "Less concerned with music, the powerful morning man was in the advance guard in adding what was called 'The Third Man Theme' to radio. The production of sound effects and voice-tracks contributed to a bewildering pattern.

"Art Hellyer was a Chicago joculator who gave Howard Miller a good run over WCFL from 1952 to 1957. Hellyer was given free reign by general manager Marty Hogan, who had begun as an announcer with WCFL, and compared to the run-of-the-mill station head, had to be called courageous.

"Hellyer acknowledges the incalculable assistance of a nimble partner. This was his record turner, an American Federation of Musicians member named Lenny Kaye, whom Hellyer dubbed Dr. K, T.T. (Turntable Technician). 'He was the greatest talent I have ever known', said Hellyer. 'I paid him out of my own pocket, above what the station paid him, because he made me. It was a combination on his part of total involvement, photographic memory, and an anticipation of what I would do. We saw each other for just three hours a day, and it was just remarkable. We had no idea of what was going to happen until I sat down at the microphone.'

"At one point in their spree, which was truly cacophonous, it was decided to send Hellyer and Kaye to New York for a month in a talent swap with WINS's Bob and Ray. But it was called off because Hogan would have the expense of putting up Bob and Ray and eleven other people, whereas only Art and Dr. K would be going to New York.

"The pair's greatest moment probably came when they 'covered' the 1956 Democratic Convention from a broadcasting booth that was obviously the men's room. Hellyer pleaded daily for access to the convention and was finally granted the inside privilege. It included some tongue-in-cheek plusses as a one-way mirror, voting booths where everyone voted with the toes of their shoes pointing out under the door, etc., with inserted tracks of toilets flushing. Like everything else we did, this was a spur-of-the-moment, off-the-top-of-the-head ad-lib bit.

"'When I listen to those shows from back in the fifties, I am astounded. How in the world did Lenny and I do all that? There is no way it could have been scripted. Dr. K fired hundreds of voice tracks at me each and every show, and I with my wild imagination would conjure up something, blurt it out, and Dr. K would have THE appropriate voice tracks ready.'

"'It was an amazing association that has never been duplicated. Bob and Ray, Ernie Kovacs, Jonathan Winters, Soupy Sales, Tim Conway and others all were magnificent humorists, but it was Lenny Kaye's genius, his ability to always come up with just the right voice, just the right statement on the spur of the moment that made our shows uniquely different.'

"'Many mornings after the show I had commercial recording sessions or agencies to call on, and I would be walking with the hordes of people on Michigan Avenue or State Street, and I'd often hear a stroller say, "Did you hear what Art Hellyer did today?" Then I would hear what I had done. Had you asked me to recall it myself I could not have done so. It all was off the tops of our heads, and we did so many bits daily they were forgotten by us when the show was over.' "

From The Chicago Federation of Labor News   June 1952
By Irwin Klass

"Everyone in town is talking about WCFL's morning madcap, Art Hellyer. His zany antics during the 6:30 to 8:30 AM spot on our station have made him a Chicago household word. Art has built a fantastic audience by daring to be different on the air. His original ideas are unique, as he kids recording artists, and throws in sound effects unheard of on disk jockey programs.

"Now his face, too, is becoming just as familiar as his voice. WCFL has contracted with Illinois Outdoor Advertising for the posting of 40 billboards in the Chicago and suburban area. They are located at busy intersections and are seen by over 2,000,000 people daily. This is the first time that a campaign of this size has ever been undertaken by a radio station.

"Art Hellyer, who has been doing freelance work for WCFL for several years is a local boy who has made good. Not unlike Arthur Godfrey, he combines wit, charm and an amazing sense of humor on his daily shows, creating an alive, bubbling three hours of entertainment."

The reviews, and the listeners may have found me combining "wit, charm and an amazing of humor" on my daily shows, but many of the sponsors were horrified when I deviated from the sacred words their copywriters had written. Moments after my March 31, 1954, show concluded, this WCFL inter-office memo was delivered to me as I was exiting the double sound-lock doors of the studio:

"WCFL   March 31, 1954
TO: Ronder, Hellyer
FROM: Leon Racusin
Re: Stineway Pgm

7:30-35AM

Monday-Friday

"Received a call this morning from the Advertising Manager for subject account who very strenuously objects to comedy on the Stineway portion of the Hellyer show. He INSISTS that the program be broadcast STRAIGHT—following the commercials EXACTLY. This is very important and this suggestion must go into effect as of Thursday morning, April 1st!

Thank you, Leon"

"ART: I dearly love the thought that a 'suggestion' MUST be followed, don't you? He did not say 'or else,' so I don't know what else there is. This account has been guilty of troublesome behavior in the past, and at this writing I have not been in contact with Marty Hogan regarding the commercial viewpoint on the account. Personally, I feel that if you sell the stuff honestly and thoroughly, the sponsor's sense of humor should not be cracked as wide open as this memo indicates. So I would advise you as of today to use your own judgment on how to handle it April 1st (what a day to start!) Lou Ronder..."

Over the many years I worked at WCFL, Bob Platt, the program director who first hired me and started my Chicago career, and the two program directors who followed him, Lou Ronder and Don McCarty, were very fair with me.

As a dedicated packrat, I save everything. This letter is dated December 14, 1955, from WCFL General Manager Marty Hogan to Mr. Mike Barkas....President Barlit Productions 225 N. Michigan Avenue, Chicago 1, Illinois:

"Dear Mike: As per our phone conversation of this date relative to the three hours in the morning presently occupied by The Art Hellyer Show in which your client expressed interest. It is impossible for me to consider the block sale of this time to one client because it is necessary to have segments of this time available for our national advertisers in order to give them a balanced schedule. Secondly, I feel that Art Hellyer has done a tremendous job in attracting listeners to WCFL as evidenced by an almost 400% increase in our Pulse rating the past year. I feel that Hellyer is the outstanding morning personality in the country today.

"In the event your client is interested, we would be happy to submit availabilities for you when there is an opening in The Art Hellyer Show. It is, at this time, sold out.

"Season's Greetings. Sincerely,

Marty Hogan   General Manager   WCFL Chicago"

In 1955, Cadillac went to huge bumpers and bumper-guards about the same time Coca Cola introduced the King-Size bottle. Coke was a sponsor of mine on my WCFL morning show. While doing the commercial one morning I said, "You know Coke introduced this new king-size bottle at exactly the right time. Cadillac has those new HUGE bumpers and over-riders so if yours have rusted out, a king-size bottle of Coke applied to a large bath towel should be able to get all that rust off....HEY!!! Imagine what coke does to your stomach." Well, the president of Coca Cola Midwest, Mr. Harry Kipke, former University of Michigan football coach was listening to me in his humble digs at the Drake Hotel, and he blew his stack. He phoned Mgr. Marty Hogan in HIS humble digs off Lake Shore Drive and Kipke told Hogan he was going to sue Hellyer for a million dollars.

The next day I said, "It has come to my attention that Coca Cola is going to sue me for a million dollars. If they will check my bank account they will find they might as well sue me for a BILLION dollars, because either way they won't get one red cent."

Now Mgr. Hogan was really mad at the guy he had told in

THE HELLYER SAY

1952 when I started the morning show, "Art, you have carte blanche to say or do anything you like, just keep it clean." I reminded him of that by saying, "I kept it clean Marty," and I remember him saying, "You get your ass over to Kipke's place and straighten this out NOW OR YOU DON'T WORK HERE ANYMORE!!!!!!!!!"

Well I did just that and found Coach Kipke to be a really nice guy. We talked about his legendary football career and how thrilled he was to be named an All-American player at Michigan and, as Michigan's head coach, how it was to be just one of three Big Ten coaches in history, to win 4 consecutive Big Ten football championships. We also talked about the Bears and my friend and dentist, the great Bill Osmanski, and our mutual friend, Bears founder and coach, George Halas. Then he said, "You know Art, I have met more people on the street and had more phone calls about your comment the other day....everyone seems to remember that Coke commercial more than any we've done over the past 20 years. I'll forget it this time, but don't ever say anything like that again." I promised him I would not, we shook hands and after that episode, I've always spoken of HARRY KIPKE AND COKE in glowing terms. What a fine man he was!!!

I have an extremely serious side too, and it was most evident the day after four teen-agers died in an Oldsmobile that skidded on a dark, lonely road in northern Illinois's lakes region. Since the late nineteen-forties I'd been campaigning on my shows for seat belts in all cars, and for better suspensions, and steering. In commenting about this terrible tragedy I talked about no seat belts in any cars, sloppy suspensions and steering. Then I said: "May the blood of these four young men forever be on the hands of the Chairman of the Board of General Motors Corporation."

Well, some General Motors official was listening to me as he drove to work in Detroit and within ten minutes Marty

Hogan, panic-stricken, his hands visibly shaking, came skidding into the studio shouting, "What the hell did you say about General Motors?" I told him verbatim exactly what I had said. I wasn't going to try to lie my way out of it. I deeply and passionately meant what I had said. Marty Hogan then told me an attorney had phoned from Detroit and informed him General Motors was going to sue WCFL and Martin J. Hogan and Art Hellyer, for a million dollars, EACH.

Marty had Howie Roberts take over my show, and he marched me into his office, slammed the door and said, "I've seen that little red shit-box (writer's note...I loved my little red 1952 MG TD, and Marty was hurting me, big time) you drive, but you have a wife and kids, so you must have a family car." I told him I also had a powder blue 1953 Cadillac. His eyes brightened, and he said, "Is it here, downtown?" I told him it was only thirteen miles away at my house in Skokie. He said, "OK...Here's what I want you to do. Get the Caddy, drive to Detroit, let GM brass see you driving it, feed some execs, and get this straightened out before it hits the papers, or we'll both be out of here. And if that happens, I promise you, you will never work on a radio station again as long as you live. I MEAN THAT, ART! Now get the hell out of here."

To make a long story short, a World War Two army buddy of mine, Arnie Weiman was high up in the GM corporate advertising department. I phoned him from the house, made a dinner date with him, and I added, "I'll be happy to pick you up at work." Right, I'd get him in my Caddy and let the conversation flow...our families, baseball, football, music, shows, then slide into an explanation of why I said what I did. "Often, Arnie I say things of a controversial nature because it builds the audience, and that pays off in a big way for me AND for my sponsors. At the same time Arnie I know that all the automotive engineers in Detroit are working on beefing up the suspensions and getting the number of lock to lock turns, down in the steering mechanisms, so I wasn't really knocking Detroit. I was just speaking aloud what all those fine engineers are thinking, and Arnie I wouldn't be driving a Caddy myself if I didn't firmly believe we build the greatest cars in the world, etc. etc.." We had dinner at the Book-Cadillac Hotel with some other GM execs, and Arnie insisted on paying the bill. Thank God!!!

After dinner I drove back to Chicago, slept soundly overnight at WCFL on a sofa, and then did my morning show.

We never ever heard another word about the lawsuit. And no one at General Motors ever knew that right after I bought the Caddy, I had the suspension beefed up by Andy Granatelli's race car team mechanics in his shop on North Broadway in Chicago. Andy agreed with me about the sloppy suspension and poor handling characteristics inherent in the great majority of automobiles in those days. He turned my Caddy with the sloppy "boulevard ride" into a beautiful road-locomotive that handled and held the road as though it were on rails.

I recall two other million-dollar-lawsuits which were threatened but never came to trial. I don't know if "Linco" is still in the marketplace. Elaine would use it in the clothes washer as a bleach, and after our complete cleansing of our sewer-filled flooded basement, Elaine and I would pour Linco on the concrete floor to sterilize the area.

Linco smelled just awful, and with all my allergies it caused me much discomfort. So when I delivered their commercials, I called it "STINKO." Unfortunately the Linco suits had no sense of humor, especially when thousands of housewives shopping in grocery stores started asking for "Stinko, please." The sponsor and his "Yes, sir" lackeys at the advertising agency had cardiac infarctions, and heated up the telephone lines into Marty Hogan's office, and sales manager Tom Haviland received the following memo from WCFL

Linco account salesman Leon Racusin:

"Date 3/13/56   Re: LINKO
"The 1st day this account started Hellyer made some reference
to STINKO in referring to this product. The agency people
heard it. Fortunately the client was out of town. Agency tells
me this client is very serious about his product. Is there
anything we can do to see that horseplay is eliminated in
connection with this account? The announcement is recorded.
Agency asks that if Hellyer wants to add to the effectiveness
of this schedule he should give the product some hard sell.
Thanks. REMEMBER...They are Listening!!!   LR."

This turned out to be another story like the Harry Kipke
one. So many, many thousands of additional customers bought
the smelly, but highly effective, product as a result of my
commercials, the company quietly called off the litigation,
saving all of us a major headache.

When the radio station sales people sold me in those days,
they not only cited the fact I was frequently number one, but
Marty Hogan had told them, "Tell the truth...Art Hellyer takes
a different approach to commercials than you are used to."
So they were forewarned, and though none of these threatened
lawsuits ever got before a judge, I feel we would have won
them all.

And then there was the sponsor's product I called "The
Yucky-looking Pink Stuff that works so well clearing up all
yours and my problems below the beltline. That yucky-
looking pink stuff curls itself around your messy abdominal
region and makes you forget you ever had an upset stomach.
Oh...yeah...if you had a dinner last night of greasy, mutton
pot pie, with a hard glaze of pure Vermont maple syrup,
topped with rich whipped cream, with walnuts and cherries on
top, and it didn't agree with you, then take a big, long slug of

The Yucky-Pink Stuff, and you'll feel a hundred percent better. Whether it's indigestion caused by your indiscretion, nausea, heartburn, or worst of all, flaming diarrhea, The Yucky-Pink Stuff....PEPTO-DISMAL will leave you feeling washed out, sure...but oh!!! YOU WILL FEEL SO MUCH BETTER!!! So pick up the Yucky-Pink Stuff at Walgreens, Rexall, Stineway-Ford-Hopkins, or your friendly local mom and pop drugstore TODAY. That's PEPTO-DISMAL."

Well, the corporate suits of this product too, fell over each other racing for the telephones. And then the whole thing quietly slipped into the background as sales were greater than ever. I don't think I was ever malicious. I had fun selling the clients' products. And the listeners loved it.

Somewhere back there in the early nineteen-fifties I started closing each show with: "This program has been a Work of Art." And it became one of my trademarks. In recent years I have heard other "Arts" saying that. Am I going to sue them? No way. Imitation is the sincerest form of flattery.

Reading author John Russell Ghrist's definitive history of Chicagoland radio, "Valley Voices: A Radio History" (Published by Crossroads Communications, 1996), helped me recall some things Dr. K and I did, in addition to the routine daily ad-lib comedy bits. He and I would select an extremely hot Chicago day, one over ninety-five and preferably over one hundred degrees. We would then play NOTHING but Christmas music for the entire show. I would read the lyrics of the songs, and I would in a deep voice portray Santa Claus, and in much higher falsetto voice Mrs. Santa Claus, always nagging the jolly one-night-per-year-world-wide traveler. The fact that the roly-poly old fat man in the red suit only worked one night in every three-hundred-sixty-five bugged the daylights out of Mrs. C. And the fact he wore that red suit didn't help his cause with her either. Dr. K would, of course add multitudinous voice tracks to these conversations.

On July 26, 1955, Herb Lyon in his extremely popular "Tower Ticker" column in the *Chicago Tribune* wrote, "DJ Art Hellyer played two solid hours of Christmas music on WCFL the other scorching morning and the switchboard lit up like a Yule tree. (Art, are you awright?)"

On November 10, 1950, "THE TOWN CRIER" Tony Weitzel wrote in the *Chicago Daily News*:

"The other midnight Art Hellyer deliberately perpetrated the silliest commercial in radio history. Art told his vast audience of listeners about a new, and non-existent product called 'SLURPO,' that was guaranteed to remove from your blood the rust caused by eating too much iron in your food. When your trial package of SLURPO arrives, Art said, you are supposed to feed two tablets to the postman. 'If rigor mortis sets in within three minutes you are to send the postman to us, express collect, and we will refund double the money you owe us.' What happened? So far more than a hundred eager listeners, from seven states have sent in their ORDERS."

Frankly, I never expected any mail, so I had to do something. I went to a stationery store and bought one hundred twenty-five very small boxes. I couldn't send any pills of course, so the Lovely Elaine came up with the answer to our problem. She was a wordsmith and also had superb executive-secretary skills, so she typed this message, and placed a copy in each box: "IMPORTANT NOTICE... PLEASE READ CAREFULLY!! The tablets herein must be taken within ten minutes of the United States Post Office postmark time on the box, or they will EVAPORATE!! No residue will remain in the box." Not one recipient complained!!!!

As I was driving into WCFL each morning I really believe the azure beauty of Lake Michigan just a few yards to the left of my little red 1952 MG TD, inspired my thoughts. It was a warm April Fool's Day in 1957 and I decided, without my making any reference to the significance of this day, until my closing bye-bye, I would announce the time one hour ahead throughout the four hours. Remember, this was Morning Drive Time, the most important radio show of the broadcast day.

Hundreds of thousands of people counted on me to give them the correct, on the nose time. From the time the alarm clock rang until they arrived at their place of work, these folks relied on me to get them to work ON TIME. Imagine the confusion in Chicago and the surrounding states...People going by my time checks. Bolting out of bed already running an hour late.

That show made "TOWER TICKER" too, when Herb Lyon, on April 3, 1957, wrote, "WCFL was in an uproar Monday morning when Art Hellyer perpetrated the zaniest April Fool's gag of all time. He kept announcing the time as one hour later than it was and the station switchboard is still blinking. Very funny."

The five o'clock network and local newscasts, the daily papers and the trade papers all picked it up too, and I still hear about it. Even hizzoner Richard J. Daley, The Mayor, himself had his secretary call the station to "PLEASE tell Hellyer his clock is off one hour." I needed a police escort when I left the studio that morning after my show.

But, the one Lenny Kaye...Dr. K...and I had the most fun with was the "Bomb Squad." That was the name I gave it the very first time we did it. The "Bomb Squad" started innocently enough one morning when a worried housewife called me to ask if there were some way I could help get her husband out of bed, so he could get off to work for the day. This was before telephone conversations were broadcast on the radio. So, I told Dr. K on the intercom, "Find a good LOUD bomb." Instantly, the good doctor's white-gloved hands flew through his stacks of voices and sounds, and he found just what I had

138

asked for, and he cued it up. I told the caller she should put the radio as close to her husband's ear as possible. Then I informed her I would start a countdown from ten, and when I said "three" she was to turn the volume knob on the radio all the way to the right producing full volume. She complied and I started my count...very softly, "ten, nine, eight, seven, six, five, four, THREE, two, one." Dr. K then "exploded" the bomb with a tremendous ROAR!!!!!! And I shouted so loud engineer Ernie Nottger, had to almost close the microphone pot to zero, "HARRY FINSTER—YOU LAZY NO GOOD FOR NOTHING LOUSY BUM—GET OUT OF BED AND GET TO WORK!"

I could hear all this on the lady's phone. Then she ran to another room and told me her husband flew up out of the bed, and was standing there, hair on end, with his entire body shaking. But, by God he was UP!!!!

That started frequent employment of the "Bomb Squad" for many years, and I could always envision our poor target standing, ashen-faced, in shock, wondering "what the hell was that?" It was probably the most effective waker-upper ever devised. Just another public service of "The Art Hellyer Show."

I have in my possession a letter written to me in 1955 from Mrs. Jerome Lazo of Burbank, Illinois, telling me her husband heard her calling me as he was in a semi-snoozing state, and he leaped out of bed and shouted to her, "June, for God's sake I'm UP. DON'T LET HELLYER FIRE THAT DAMN BOMB!"

In today's world climate would I or could I do that? Of course not, but life was quieter and, I do believe, more fun back in those wonderful days before "political correctness."

This was also back in the days when the "little woman" stayed at home doing the housework, and preparing nutritional meals for her working husband and family, BUT most important of all she was in the house. Unlike today when no one is in the house when the kids return from school. Add to that the garbage the kids see on TV and in the movies, and the awful video games they play, unsupervised, and the crude, vulgar, downright dirty lyrics of rock'n'roll, rap and hip-hop. Is it any wonder the kids of today are growing up in a morally decaying world? I liked our gentle, naive world of fifty years ago so much better.

Fortunately I have an excellent memory, but I still meet old listeners who recall additional things Dr. K TT and I did. So many of my listeners are dead now or in nursing homes, and are not available to say to me, as so often happened over the years, "Hey Art! Remember the time you did this or said that?" Well while I was writing this book it happened. But it was because of the internet. I had two e-mails in one day from gentlemen who were college roommates at Aurora College (Illinois) from 1953 to 1957. "Remember the day you gave the owner's phone number over the air?" Well I had completely forgotten it of course, but the listener's mind-jogger brought it back for me.

This man and his brother owned two of Chicago's most powerful radio stations, and I did freelance shows on their stations for various clients. I would run into the studio, sit down, do my fifteen-minute or thirty-minute show, then run out to another station to do another show. Well, these two brothers made life on their stations hell for me, and they harassed me in so many ways I found it difficult to do my shows. One of them even had his neurotic, tic-bedeviled son come into the city from their home in the western suburbs and TIME me with a stopwatch. He would sit right next to me, pulling at his right ear and twitching, and making strange little chuffing noises with his mouth. As I gave my deliveries, I would hear the soft click of the stopwatch as I started and ended each commercial for the client's product. When I concluded and introduced the next song and the engineer closed my microphone, the demonic timekeeper put his face right into mine, nose to nose, and said, "You ran sixty-one seconds on that one...do the next one in fifty-nine seconds."

This went on for months, then one Sunday he didn't appear, so I made an announcement to what was really in those days, before TV had made serious inroads, a vast audience: "Folks, at this very moment, there's an old man sitting by himself in his rocking chair, in his lonely mansion, probably gumming a bowl of gruel. I'd like you to bring a little sunshine into his life right now. You may phone him at this number and help to cheer his dismal existence." I then gave his phone number right there over HIS 50,000-watt powerhouse.

What happened? So many calls were made, the trunk line shut down, and a large area of the Midwest was without phone service. Fortunately, Illinois Bell and AT&T cleared the problem quickly, and I received a very serious phone call at the station from a bigwig at AT&T. I was to make an announcement and stop the calls. So I quickly thanked the listeners for phoning the lonely old man, and peace and quiet returned to the hinterland. I never ever did that again!!!!! I also was barred from both their stations, but did go back on them years later when they were sold to nicer people.

As fate would have it, some years later I became the radio spokesman for Illinois Bell. That also involved recording many of their commercials with the great Dick Marx and Johnny Frigo, and also with the finest quartet with whom I've ever worked, The Fabulous "Jamie and The Jays." Their harmonies, English madrigal style, on thirty-second and sixty-second spots enchanted me. They were recorded on sixteen inch, thirty-three-and-a-third RPM electrical transcriptions, but I found a few of them some years ago and had them transferred to cassette. If you'd like to hear just how great they were, drop me a line and I'll send you a tape of those beautiful commercials.

Jamie and The Jays guested on my WCFL morning show a number of times during those years that seemed to move soooooo slowly, and now fifty years later as I look back upon them I can't believe all I did. That must have been some other Art Hellyer. How in the world did I keep up the pace? I literally worked seven days AND nights year in and year out. One period of the Fifties I was on the air LIVE every day, and/or night of the week for over four-and-one-half years. People often asked me how I found time to father five wonderful children, much less spend any time with them. The truth of the matter is, I believe I spent far MORE time with my children than did most fathers. And I might add I made very little money. The biz did not pay well then, no matter how busy one was. Even today, I live as Elaine and I did over fifty years, from paycheck to paycheck. Elaine has been gone many years now and I wish so much I could have given her a better life. That dear, never-complaining woman deserved so much better.

I never drank hard liquor or smoked, so I didn't, as so many of my peers did, stop off somewhere on the way home. Our little post-war home at 3851 Harvard Terrace in Skokie, Illinois, was exactly thirteen miles from the Wrigley Building, and I would make the round-trip at least twice daily, sometimes three times a day. That way I could spend time with our five super children, Larry, Mike, Debbie, Vickie and Jeff.

And spend time I did. I cleared the Samuel Insull-owned property next door to our home, of taxes dating back to the late nineteen-twenties, and in the spring and summer we, and all the kids in the neighborhood, would play softball, or a great new thing called "WhiffleBall." For sometime I held the record for most WhiffleBall home runs hit over the garage, but as the kids grew larger they wrote me out of the record books. One of Larry's gargantuan drives over the garage is still spoken of in awe by those who gather in Skokie's watering holes.

In the fall we played football, and their mom, who would be my wife for fifty-one wonderful years, "The Lovely Elaine," more than once constructed a hockey rink in the wintertime. And of course, we played all the board games from Monopoly to Risk to Yahtzee. New Year's Day 1959 we had a five-hundred lap Aurora scale-model cars race on a huge four-lane racetrack we built in the basement. I don't recall who won, but I know who didn't win...ME.

To this day Mike carries an assortment of board games in the trunk of his car, always ready to get a game going, and his license number has for years been "PLAYME 1." My favorite game in recent years has been "Empire Builder," a coast-to-coast railroad game where each railroad owner attempts to pick up various cargoes in different cities, and transport enough bauxite or tourists, or whatever, to accumulate two hundred fifty million dollars and become the king of the railroad barons.

And now, as I do a rewrite and final edit on my book in 2008, we play a newer railroad game called "Ticket to Ride." A man named Allen Moon is gaining great fame for this game and others he has developed. We play it at home as a board game or on the internet, and we highly recommend both train games.

The stations at which I worked...WCFL (Furniture Mart), WIND and WBBM (Wrigley Building), WBBM-TV (Ice Arena Building on McClurg Ct.), WJJD (Carbide and Carbon Building), WLS (Stone Container Building), WGN (Tribune Tower), WAIT (Lincoln Tower Building), WMAQ, WNBQ-TV, WMAQ-TV (Merchandise Mart), and WBKB, WLS-TV (State-Lake Building) were all a stone's throw apart.

Chicago's Loop is the area bounded by the "EL" and only one of those locations, and just barely so, was in the loop: The State-Lake Building. It was because of the close proximity of all those buildings I was able to run back and forth, admittedly, like "The Wild Man of Borneo," and do over 100 quarter-hours on seven stations every weekend for over ten years.

Many of the major recording artists made the Saturday "Grand Tour" with me, Frankie Laine, Spike Jones, Patti Page, Harry Belafonte, Buddy Hackett, Jackie Gleason, Liberace, Doris Day, Les Paul and Mary Ford, Maurice Chevalier, Nick Lucas, Peggy Lee, George Gobel, Dorothy Collins, Rosemary Clooney, Gordon MacRae, Dinah Shore, Andy Griffith, The Ames Brothers, The Four Lads, The Four Aces, Vic Damone, Jerry Vale, Eartha Kitt, and Dean Martin and Jerry Lewis, when they were a team, to name a few.

But the one that stands out, because of what he said at the end of the long day, is Perry Como. I first met Perry in 1947, when Rocky Rolfe, the RCA Victor A&R rep for the Midwest, brought him into the WISN studio in Milwaukee, and I interviewed him on my late afternoon record show. It would be my pleasure to interview this fine gentleman many more times over the years. In fact, that meeting led to a lifelong friendship because Perry Como stayed in touch with me, I am proud to say, over the decades that followed.

He once spent one entire Saturday with me in the mid-fifties as my guest on all the stations, and we zipped from WIND to WMAQ to WGN to WLS to WAIT to WCFL and WJJD. We moved from taxicab to taxicab during my marathon, and from elevator to elevator and from studio to studio. And each cabbie and each elevator operator had the pleasure of shaking hands with Perry Como. At one point Perry pulled me off to the side and said, "Art, do you do this every day?" I replied, "No, just on Saturdays and Sundays."

Perry looked at me, made the Sign of the Cross, and said, "Oh, thank God."

And he meant it. He was a lovely man, who brought such great music to the world. I miss his heartwarming TV shows, especially at Christmas time. And most of all, I miss him.

Frankie Laine, whom I mentioned earlier, was another fine gentleman I knew for a long, long time. Our friendship started also in 1947, when one day Johnny O'Brien, A&R man for Art Talmadge's Chicago label, Mercury Records, walked in on one of my shows in Milwaukee, waving the country's hottest new release, Frankie Laine's "That's My Desire." I can hear Frankie's great voice now, "To spend one night with you, in our old rendezvous, and reminisce with you, that's my desire." This one song put Frankie Laine AND Mercury on the map to stay.

Since then Frankie was my guest on every station at which I've toiled, and in March of 2003 we spoke on his ninetieth birthday. Frankie recorded on everything except wax cylinders, from 78RPM to compact discs. As recently as 1998 his voice, great as "Mule Train" and "I Believe" days, starred on the CD "It Ain't Over 'til It's Over, A Celebration in Song of Life as a Super Senior," written and produced by Deane Hawley. The songs are fun, thought-provoking and poignant, and I, now well along as a senior citizen, am proud to have a personally autographed copy.

CHICAGO TRIBUNE....TOWER TICKER...11-3-56
"Radio's morning madcap, Art (WCFL) Hellyer is about to grab off the emcee job on a top network quiz show out of New York."

The show was "Name That Tune" and I had turned it down because our families were in Chicago, and my shows all seemed to be going well. Had I been able to see into the not-too-distant future, I would have "grabbed" the job.

All good things must come to an end, and so it was with our WCFL ART HELLYER MORNING SHOW. Just after the Fourth of July, 1957, the Chicago Trade Show opened on Navy Pier, and WCFL had their own Navy Pier broadcast studio opening night. Dr. K and I did a special four-hour "Art Hellyer and Dr. K From The Trade Show at Navy Pier show." And we had a ball! Huge crowds almost pushed the portable studio over a number of times, until finally Chicago's Finest were called to stand guard over us. The show was a tremendous success, and when we finished it, Don McCarty, WCFL's new program director told us we were to do the morning show from the Navy Pier studio each day the following week. I reminded Don our show was on the air weekday mornings from 6 AM to 10 AM and the Trade Show didn't open to the public each day until 11 AM, so it really didn't make sense.

Don McCarty said those were the orders, and I asked him if the Trade Show people had been alerted, so we could gain access to the building at 5:45AM on Monday. He said they would be informed.

WELL THEY WEREN'T INFORMED!!!!! The good Dr. K, our engineer Ernie Nottger and I were refused admittance. So we walked back to WCFL's Furniture Mart studios and did our show from there. After the show WCFL General Manager, Marty Hogan personally gave me a copy of a letter he was sending by messenger to the people at Navy Pier informing them we would be broadcasting from there the next four mornings.

Here is the letter that was sent to the constabulary at Navy Pier:

      "WCFL "THE VOICE OF LABOR"
          666 Lake Shore Drive
          Chicago 11, Illinois   Mohawk 4-2400
Mr. Jerry Flaherty

Chicagoland Fair
Navy Pier

"Dear Jerry:

Per our conversation, this will serve as identification for our announcer-personality, Mr. Art Hellyer. Art will be performing at the WCFL exhibit Wednesday July 10 during the evening hours, Saturday July 13 again during the evening hours and daily at 6:30 AM.

"As you have said, this letter will enable Art to obtain the assistance of your personnel re parking, transportation to the WCFL booth, etc.

Thank you.

Yours truly,
Bob Finnegan
Bob Finnegan
Program Director-WCFL

We arrived at the Navy Pier gate Tuesday morning at 5:45 AM, I showed the above letter and we gained immediate admittance and did our show with no problems whatsoever. Wednesday and Thursday also went just fine.

THEN CAME FRIDAY JULY 12, 1957

D-DAY..............DISASTER DAY

The Monday Navy Pier crew was back on duty, and refused to let us enter, claiming there was NO letter authorizing them to do so. Ten minutes of cajoling and arguing got us nowhere, so I did what had to be done. I picked up a large trashcan and in three or four whacks I broke a segment of the wire-reinforced glass door, and reaching through I managed to unbolt the door from the inside.

As Dr. K, Ernie Nottger, and I walked in, a guard carrying a 1927 Thompson sub-machine gun ran toward us. As he rapidly approached I waved my copy of the letter at him, and headed into the studio. I sat down at the microphone, cued Ernie for the mic, which he opened and I started talking, "Good morning This is Art Hellyer from WCFL's studios at Navy Pier. Dr. K and Ernie Nottger are here with me, and so is a guard from the First National Bank of Chicago's million-dollar exhibit here at the Trade Show. Folks, the guard has a 1927 Thompson submachine gun pointed at my right shoulder." At this point dear friend Howie Roberts, the announcer on duty at WCFL's studios in the Furniture Mart had engineer Ted Swanson open his microphone, and he was imploring me to not say anything that "will get you fired, pleeeeease Art, don't do this."

"Well I do know this," I continued on. "I learned 1927 Thompsons during the war, and if he pulls the trigger he won't hit me, because Thompsons always pull to the upper right, and the shells will go through the ceiling. I also know the problems I've had getting into this building to broadcast this week have been awful. I can understand the daytime and evening programs broadcasting from here, but my show goes off at ten o'clock, and the Trade Shows doors don't open until eleven o'clock. I'd like to strangle the mental midget who sent us out here."

Machine-Gun Kelly is still in back of me, and he would not even be here if the First National Bank didn't have one million dollars on display. Not one of us in a lifetime will earn the amount of money that's in that gold bucket out in the hall. First National Bank's exhibit is corrupting our morals, inviting greed and avarice into our souls, and helping to put larceny in our hearts."

Howie Roberts was now almost crying as he was begging me to stop. I continued my harangue: "Folks…I'm going to fix the First National Bank of Chicago. I'm sending this message to Bob Elson. Bob, be at the bank when they open at 9 o'clock this morning, withdraw all your money, and by 4 o'clock this afternoon the bank will be insolvent."

That was at 6:05 AM and somehow I completed my show at 10 AM. NO ONE FROM THE FRONT OFFICE CALLED ME. I went home for a few hours, played baseball with the boys, then went to Universal Recording Studios. I was recording commercials for Standard Oil when I was informed Elaine was on the phone. She told me a furious Marty Hogan wanted me in his office "NOW!!."

I phoned Marty whose voice was shaking with near-uncontrollable rage....."HELLYER, GET YOUR ASS OVER HERE NOW AND RECORD AN APOLOGY WE CAN PLAY EVERY HOUR OVER THE WEEKEND!!!!!!!!!"

I was shaking as I tried to sound unruffled: "I have more Standard Oil spots to record Marty. I'll get there when I'm through here." I hung up before he could scream at me again.

More than thirty minutes later, I ran through rain just starting to fall, to my little red MG-TD in a nearby parking lot, and drove to the Furniture Mart. When no parking was available, I was allowed to park on the city sidewalk. Mayor Richard J. Daley (I had been his personal announcer since his Cook County Clerk days in the early fifties) himself had authorized that, but if Officer Jack Muller was in the area he would have me towed to the city pound. Having been his victim more than once, I prayed he was off-duty.

I did my best to casually stroll into Manager Martin J. Hogan's office, when ALL HELL BUSTED LOOSE!!!!!!

"WHERE THE HELL HAVE YOU BEEN? I TALKED TO YOU OVER AN HOUR AGO. I'VE WRITTEN AN APOLOGY FOR YOU. GET YOUR ASS IN THE STUDIO AND RECORD THIS RIGHT NOW!!!!!!!!!!"

I reached for the telephone on Marty Hogan's desk as I told him I would have to call my dad, who was my attorney, and read the apology to him, and ask him if I should record it. Marty put his hand over the phone, looked straight into my

baby-blues, and very coldly said to me, "Look, you son-of-a -
bitch, you record this RIGHT NOW, or YOU DON'T WORK
HERE ANYMORE." I, very softly, and very sadly, said to
General Manager Martin J. Hogan, "I don't work here
anymore."

"In 1957 Hellyer was fired," Arnold Passman continued in
The DeeJays." "'It came at a time,' said Hellyer, who like
many a fiercely witty morning man, said nobody has had an
influence on him, 'when Howard Miller and I were jockeying
for the 1-2 position in the morning.'

"'One of my sponsors, the First National Bank, displayed a
million dollars at Navy Pier, where I was doing my morning
show. I said I thought it was wrong because it helped to build
avarice and greed in us. It bugged just one man in the bank's
ad agency and WCFL was forced to can me. But the First has
sponsored me since then.'"

Following my final meeting with Hogan, my little red 1952
MG TD was nearly submerged in rain as I opened the keyless
door. I sank slowly into the dyed-red kangaroo-leather bucket-
seat, fired up the engine, and double-clutched the non-
synchro-mesh first gear.

The little racer's engine roared in Hogan-hating fury as I
drove North on Chicago's heavily rain-drenched Lake Shore
Drive. I was number one in morning show ratings, and I was
praying another station in the city, which was growing smaller
in my rearview mirror, would remember me.

After my departure from WCFL I arrived at our Skokie
home in a torrential rain storm, about 7PM. Longtime fellow
radio broadcaster and friend Cy Nelson (he had among other
credentials been a member of Admiral Richard Byrd's crew on
one of his trips to Antarctica), and his wife Fran, had invited
us for dinner that night. Elaine and I drove over to their
apartment, less than two miles from our house, and were

enjoying the evening with our old friends when our longtime babysitter, Mrs. Llama phoned. "Mama Mia....Duh baysuhment, sheeezz alla fillup with a water....cumma hom." We loved Mrs. Llama, but when she became excited her Italian dialect was something else. Well, Elaine and I were the "King and Queen of Home basement floods and disasters." It was well known that if we lived there, THAT place would flood. Our floods didn't just cover the floor a few inches, our floods went up to the overhead joists, and the top of the basement stairs. And our floods weren't your everyday rainwater floods—our floods were full of All-American sewage.

Whereas the average flood-waters victim could possibly expect to have everything cleaned-up and sparkling within three to five days, it took us three to five MONTHS of washing, mopping, scrubbing, Lysoling and "Stinkoing," spreading everything out in the yard under the sun on nice days, plus many, many trips to the laundromat, because all the appliances...even the furnace, were wiped out. Elaine and I became mental cases every time the TV weatherman said, "we need RAIN you know, and there is a band of nice showers approaching us right out here where you see these isobars." HELP!!

Well...the day I was fired at WCFL...July 12, 1957, also went in the record books as Chicago's worst rainstorm. We had just recovered from the October 10, 1954, rain holocaust when this one struck. I always called our town "SOAKIE" on my shows. Skokie Mayor Wilson called me many times on that, but I stood my water-soaked ground. Skokie back in those days WAS "SOAKIE."

As I edit this in 2008, daughter Vickie and her husband Jon live perhaps ten blocks from the house we lived in, and they've not experienced any liquified disasters. So we can assume Skokie has installed much larger sewers than we had in the fifties. Let us hope so, because I would not wish on anyone but Adolph Hitler and Saddam Hussein the watery problems we had.

The day after I was fired, Saturday July 13, 1957, I was standing in hip high water…yes it was receding, wrestling with the freezer that had floated and bounced against the overhead joists all night, when Elaine, in her always cheery way, which though she's been gone nine years now, I still hear, said, "Honey, there's a reporter from the *Chicago Tribune* at the door." That was all I needed at this time, a police-reporter, which he was, interviewing me about the WCFL fiasco. I told him I couldn't care less about the WCFL story…the REAL story was my basement. Two other reporters showed up that day. I didn't have time to talk to them. My family's home was still under attack by the flowing, stinking waters. I told no one the biggest story, Bob Miller, the owner of WAIT contacted me the following week. I agreed to go to work for him, and Dr. K, bless him, would be joining me.

On Sunday, July 14, 1957, I made Herb Lyon's "Tower Ticker" in the *Chicago Tribune* once again, "Lots of calls as to why Art (Mr. Zany) Hellyer was fired as WCFL's AM disk jockey. Well, sir, Arthur rapped The First National Bank for the way the guards handled that million bucks on display at the Chicagoland Fair, (with tommy guns, etc.). This incensed WCFL Boss Marty Hogan, who prepared a retraction and insisted that Hellyer read it intact. Art wanted to do it his way. Impasse. So Marty said to Artie: 'OUT!' Two other radio stations are trying to hire Hellyer as of this morning."

Variety, "The Bible of Showbiz" ran this article… "Hellyer in WCFL to WAIT Shift

Chicago…..Art Hellyer, deejay specializing in wild humor, signed with WAIT less than a week after he was summarily fired by WCFL's manager, Marty Hogan. Hellyer was broadcasting his show from the Chicagoland Fair where the First National Bank attracted gaping crowds with an exhibit of a million dollars in cold cash. The deejay remarked, in a typical Hellyerism that the exhibit is 'corrupting public morals, inviting greed and avarice, helping to put larceny in our hearts.' Hogan demanded that Hellyer immediately tape an apology to the bank, which incidentally is not a WCFL advertiser.

The deejay says he was willing to do so, but wanted to consult with his father first, who doubles as Hellyer's attorney. Thereupon, according to Hellyer, Hogan bounced him. His time on WAIT will be identical to his hours on WCFL, which may encourage some of Hellyer's formidable audience to switch stations during those hours."

Our first morning on WAIT I announced a new club I was forming and I invited people to join. I called it, "Art Hellyer's Let Somebody Else Do It Club." I had the Gore Printing Company, longtime listeners, make up a business card size membership card. Fred Gore came up with some cute graphics, and Elaine wrote this copy which appeared on the cards: "This is to certify that the undersigned is a member in good standing of Art Hellyer's Let Somebody Else Do It Club, and is not required to do any menial 'Do it Yourself Task' in the house or in the yard on Saturday, Sunday or Weekdays."

I did this for a reason. I wanted to see how many listeners would write us the very first week of our switch to WAIT. Gore printed one thousand cards. We needed a few more. Over twenty thousand listeners flooded us with requests for membership cards. The owners Bob Miller and his wife Gen, and the rest of the Miller family involved with the station were babbling incoherently in astonishment. Of course they were thrilled with this showing, because rating services have always said you're doing a good job if one in a thousand listeners writes you. *Variety* was right! We did have a, to use their words, *"formidable audience."*

So Dr. K and I moved to WAIT where three years later we, and many other station people were the victims of bouncing checks. The good doctor continued his full time job at WBBM and I went back to free-lancing, and Casey went on dancing with the strawberry blonde.

During this period CBS West coast Exec William Thompson flew into Chicago, and wined and dined the Lovely Elaine and me at Fritzel's. We talked about our identical red 1952 MGs, and he offered me the morning drive show on CBS Hollywood. With Elaine right at my side, I very nicely turned it down, because our families were happy and settled in Chicagoland. We were native Chicagoans, and our children loved their schools, so Hollywood DJ Bob Crane got the call. I never regretted it, but I've often wondered HOW much it might have changed our lives. We were not paid big money in Chicago in those days. Network Announcers like me received $187.50 for a 45 hour week.

Elaine and I were always happy if we had enough to pay the mortgage, and as she always said, "enough food for the five children, a roof over our heads and warm clothing."

Elaine and I had been married just a little over one year when we had our first of many, many flooded basements with which to contend. In fact, my late father-in-law Erv Miller said more than once, "The government should subsidize you two, and build you a big home on the Mojave Desert."

The *Skokie Sun* agreed. Bob Moore, the owner and editor wrote in his column "Over Rollo's Desk: A week ago Wednesday we opened the office early in order to tabulate the election returns. Coming in, we were listening to Art Hellyer on his morning show and he suddenly announced, 'Now that the elections are over, I have a poem I would like to read.' It was written by a Chicago attorney, who told us later, 'My sense of humor is much like Art Hellyer's.'

The Art Hellyer Show...1950–1957

"It is impossible to print into this poem the feeling and impact Hellyer gave each word as he recited it and for this we are truly sorry.

"Art, his wife Elaine, and their children, Larry, Mike, Debbie and Vickie have owned their own home in the East Prairie school district for several years.

— The Editor."

ODE TO A STANDPIPE
By Raymond Lopatka

OH, to be in Skokie
Now that April's there.
With heavy rains and gushing drains
Flooding basements everywhere.

Going down those cellar stairs
Means taking quite a chance,
Of soaking shoes and stockings
Or worse, your underpants.

Sadie Thompson had her troubles
Caused by heavy monsoon rains!
But, brother, they were nothing like those
Downstairs floods in Skokie and Des Plaines.

'WE'RE LOST!' Art Hellyer shouted
As he staggered down the stairs,
Plunging headlong into swirling waters
High above his thinning hairs.

155

THE HELLYER SAY

In the laundry room he began to sink
Near the washer, clothes and things,
But saved himself in finding that size C
Made perfect water wings.

But Art and his beloved wife
On basement stairs side by side,
Romantically sit each passing day
Watching flowing basement tides.

And then Elaine leans toward her loving Art
And whispers, 'I must confess—
I'll pound your big fat head, you slob
If you try to leave me with this awful mess.'

But the kids, they have a picnic
Grabbing sheets for use as sails,
As gaily they keep floating by
Elaine, as she frantically bails.

And in going to the boat show
Art's thoughts are not of Northern lagoons,
Shucks, he's looking for an outboard
For waterskiing in his rumpus room.

In sloshing through those basement floods
And those furnace controls you splash to find,
It's hard when fumbling in the dark,
Prodded by standpipes from behind.

Ah, Yes, Art Carney should the builder be
In Skokieland, I'm sure—
Cause every doggoned house out there
Has its dependable backing-up sewer.

The Art Hellyer Show...1950–1957

And in flooded Skokie basement bars
Those toasts with glasses raised high,
Are really meant when shouted,
"Here's MUD right in your eye!"

And as the sun sinks slowly
O'er those swampy basement shores—
It's still your happy Home Sweet Home,
Even with flooded lower floors."

UNIQUE HAPPENINGS
ON THE AIR

* Essay 8 *

"CHANNEL SEVEN'S ART HELLYER CORRALLED TOP HONORS AT THE RECENT COPYWRITERS AWARD BANQUET. ART'S PERK DOG FOOD SPOT (THAT'S THE SIXTY SECONDS OF SILENCE IN WHICH THERE IS NO SILENCE COMMERCIAL) WON THE AWARD AS RADIO COMMERCIAL OF THE YEAR. CONGRATULATIONS, ART."
—*ABC-TV Chicago press release, May 23, 1966*

"In about 1957, after WBBM had moved from the Wrigley Building to McClurg Court, I went from writer to Creative Director. It was my job to develop new programs for the sales department to sell. There'd be musical programs like Luncheon With Billy Leach and The Supper Club with Art Hellyer. Art was incorrigible. I don't think he even knew what he would say on the air. He refused to read scripts as they were written, and he even tore up some of my scripts right on the air. He was always getting on bad paper with the manager of the station.

"You know, if he didn't like a guy, no matter what his rank was, he'd tell him off. He was a great guy, and I liked him. When I became Program Director, I was always going to bat for him in the front office, but management finally ran out of

patience. I thought he had great talent, but he was only with us
for a year or so. — Art Thorsen"
—WBBM RADIO...YESTERDAY & TODAY,
by Chuck Schaden, published by WBBM Newsradio 78, Chicago

Well, I was with WBBM longer than Art Thorsen
remembers. Mr. Thorsen sent me an inter-office memo dated
January 27, 1961, that I feel should be in The Inter-office
Memo Hall of Fame. I herewith quote it in its entirety:

"Whether you know it or not Art, you let me down again
last night. I am sure you are not aware of these minor
infractions, but they are always enough to make me reach for
the Rollaids.
"EXAMPLES:
"Thursday night you stepped on the COMMERCIAL by
referring to Columbia Phonographs as 'Columbia Phono-
giraffes.' Then before you even completed the commercial
you departed completely from it to have a conversation with
Bob Vegas before returning to the completion of the
COMMERCIAL. These things might be done over and over
again without anyone ever saying a word to you on some of
the TeaPot stations around town, but we just cannot have this
on WBBM. I again remind you of my position regarding this
and I am for you to use a little more tact with the very serious
side of our programming.
"The rest of your work is fine. The way you handle the
talent, the orchestra, the all around quarterbacking of the show
is very commendable, but it's just these picayunish things that
are enough to knock a hole in the boat. Please give me just a
little more cooperation. Art Thorsen"

Well on my Supper Club Show that night, with the live
orchestra I loved to work with, I, of course, read the memo on

the air for hundreds of thousands of listeners to hear. My grizzled former big-band musicians did not let me down. After the long pause, came the gasps, then a drum rimshot followed by uproarious laughter only great musicians can pour forth.

I, of course, was instantly hauled out of the studio by the CBS VP/GM, and by a trembling, barely able to speak, Art Thorsen. I wasn't fired this time, but I was suspended for two weeks without pay. Not a bad time to stay home in front of the fireplace with the Lovely Elaine and our wonderful children; the last week of January and the first week of February.

On a chilly day in October 1965, I received this message in my WBBM-CBS, Chicago mailbox:

"Dear Art: Next Tuesday we will be doing a remote at a bowling alley. You have been selected as the commentator. We will probably leave here about 11:30 AM, so I thought I would warn you so that you'll be available. I'll see you Monday and explain the format, the program, and the general gimmicks.

Ken Carbonel, Program director."

Well there were no "gimmicks," except the car we drove out there in. It was the producer's horrible DKW, a car from The Netherlands with a "sliding rubber-band transmission." As we were driving to the far southside of Chicago in this miserable Dutch excuse for a motorcar, the sounds coming from underneath the conveyance sounded like slingshots being pulled back, and then fired. Some of the good people of Amsterdam had better stick to prostitution and forget attempting to build automobiles on the banks of the Zuider Zee.

When we arrived at the bowling alley, just a few mid-day bowlers were there. Apparently no league bowlers had been notified, and even if they had been, they probably could not get off work to bowl at 1PM on a Tuesday afternoon. Or they all agreed with me. I told Ken Carbonel, the program producer, "WBBM is thirty years too late with a bowling show on RADIO." I never, ever again heard anything else about this birdbrain idea.

I hosted two weekend musical shows on WBBM, Saturday 1PM to 6PM and Sunday 6AM to noon. I also had a regular Monday through Friday shift of 2PM to 10PM, which included doing afternoon and evening newscasts, with a great live musical show I hosted daily at 6:30PM, The Supper Club.

The most exciting single experience I had at WBBM occurred on November 10, 1965, the night the entire east coast lost its electricity. There were constant news bulletins about the problem from WCBS, New York, until all New York State grids went dark. I had a frantic phone call from the WCBS, New York newsroom to: "Please do what you can covering this story from 800 miles away, so that millions of people on the east coast can be informed on their battery-powered radios."

It was standard procedure for only one newsman to be on duty during the night-time hours at WBBM, and five nights a week I was the guy. I had the engineer swing a boom mic over me as I grabbed a chair in front of the Associated Press and United Press International teletype machines, and I froze my eyes on the copy quickly rolling through the glass windows. For over four hours I did nothing but ad-lib information from those two roaring news machines. And for one of the rare times in my broadcast career, a station exec paid me a compliment. In my mailbox the next day was this message:

"To: Art Hellyer
November 11,1965
From: Len Schlosser   WBBM CBS Program Director
     Good work again on your newscasts Tuesday night.
     You are on the ball as a NEWSHAWK!   Len"

One of the things that always made my audience happy was when I would poke fun at my current radio station manager, something they would love to do to their bosses. Through me they lived vicariously. I recall one day referring to Marty Hogan, General Manager at WCFL as a very melancholy person, "Marty has a head like a melon and a face like a collie."

Another time I said to Dr. K on the two-way speaker, "Let's marry Marty and Adele Drasgoulis." So Dr. K popped on the wedding march, turned to his left to his stacks of 78, $33\frac{1}{3}$ and 45 rpm records from which he would in nanoseconds find and cue on his three turntables voices and sounds appropriate to the occasion, and I said in the proper somber (why do ministers, priests, rabbis and justices of the peace, always use somber voices as they unite the happy couple in holy headlock?) tone of voice…"Do you Adele Drasgoulis take this man…Martin J. Hogan…Beloved General manager of WCFL, to be your awfully married husband, to honor and obey, to cherish, and wash and iron his shirts, and to take his dictation and make his hourly cocktails, 'til death or worse than that, a firing, do you part?" Then I asked Marty Hogan, "Do you Martin J. Hogan, beloved Vice-President and General Manager of WCFL take this woman, Adele Drasgoulis, Executive Secretary to You, you bum….beloved general manager of WCFL, to be your lawfully wedded wife…..to cherish her and to endow her with everything that will make her happy, including a new Underwood Typewriter, and dictation pad, until death do you part?"

I then pronounced them man and wife. Dr. K had the crowds cheering and the organ playing as I described the happy newlyweds departure from the WCFL studio, and their long, long, long walk the length of the nineteenth floor of the Furniture Mart to the elevator. For their descent to the first floor Dr. K had a loud buzzing noise running on one of the turntables, and as the elevator sped toward the first floor, the listeners heard the buzzing noise getting louder and louder. Then as it reached the first floor, Dr. K turned on another turntable that had the sound of a terrible car crash. I burst in with, "Well, Marty and Adele are off to a bang up start." How was all this received by Marty Hogan?

Well, immediately at 9AM, "Beloved General Manager," Marty Hogan, alternately ashen faced and then blood red with FURY, popped into the studio shouting "WHAT THE HELL IS WRONG WITH YOU? I"VE BEEN MARRIED CLOSE TO 30 YEARS. THIS IS THE FINAL STRAW HELLYER. UNMARRY ME THIS INSTANT YOU SON OF A BITCH OR YOU ARE OUT OF HERE." My engineer Ernie Nottger opened the microphone and I annulled the marriage two seconds later.

I worked for some superb station managers over the years: the legendary Jules Herbeveaux (WMAQ–NBC Radio), Red Quinlan (WBKB/WLS-TV ABC), Harvey Wittenberg (WLS-FM), and Ralph Sherman (Satellite Music Network and WJOL, Joliet, Illinois), but most of the others were pompous jerks who didn't know a thing about radio or television.

Ernest (Ernie) Shomo Vice President and General Manager of the 50,000 watt Midwestern powerhouse WBBM–CBS, sat in an office that looked like a Hollywood set, with a beautiful blonde secretary, and a black waiter with a white towel over his arm, always at his beck and call.

In his home and private life I heard Ernie Shomo was really a nice guy, but as soon as he entered the work place he became a fire-breathing dragon. This nice guy turned VP/GM tyrant loved to roam the halls terrifying his serfs. One afternoon I was doing a two-person show with a fellow announcer. We were each clothed in the required station uniform: blue suit, white shirt, blue tie, black socks and shoes.

THE HELLYER SAY

Each of us reading words written by an authorized station scribe, and pre-approved by Art Thorsen, the Program Director, who was fully schooled in what was and what was not acceptable to the tyrant VP/ GM, who even now was swaying through the halls looking for someone to devour.

Somehow, with what must have been xray-vision, he saw through the walls and noted what my colleague across from me was wearing on his pedal extremities. The VP/GM pushed the extremely heavy sound-lock door to the control room, opened it, and entered, pushing his way between the seated people: the director, the assistant director, the writer reading aloud, along with us, every brilliant word she had written for us to enunciate through the microphone to our electrified audience. The record-turner, who had nothing to do during our talk show, was sitting, bored, smoking a cigarette. The engineer was really the ONLY person we needed in that overly-crowded control room.

The VP/GM pointed and crooked his finger at me through the soundproof control room window. I assumed he wanted me to leave the studio and come into the control room to be chewed out for my latest infraction, whatever the hell that could be. But…NO…he was pointing at my colleagues back. I couldn't believe it. Someone else, not I, had caused his latest ulcer attack, so I pointed at my fellow broadcaster, then I pointed to the control room. All this took only a few seconds and we both continued to flawlessly read our lines, something I'm sure the tyrant was not even aware of. My colleague turned around, not missing a beat on the air, and the tyrant indicated he was to leave our gem of a broadcast for me to handle it alone, which was simple, because the mindless copy could have been read by a chimpanzee for all the value it contained.

Well, to make a long story short, my fellow broadcaster quietly rose, and slipped through the heavy sound-lock door. I went on reading, and I never saw my reading partner again.

No, the tyrant VP/GM didn't take him to the bowels of the building and grind him into sausage, BUT he did FIRE him. For wearing white buck shoes.....ON RADIO!!!!!!

A few months later I broke the uniform code. I was caught heading for the first broadcast in my eight hour evening shift wearing my approved blue suit, approved black socks and approved black shoes, and a nice Marshall Field's maroon turtle neck sweater Elaine had given me for Christmas. I had a very sore throat, and the February temperature was below zero. Art Thorsen saw me in the hall and pulled me into an office. White faced and shaken, he put his index finger into the top of the turtle neck, pulled at it and said, "My God Art, if the old man sees you, he'll fire you." Well the old man somehow saw through Studio C's walls, and he charged through the heavy sound lock door, and he did indeed fire me on that subzero February night in the year of our Lord 1961.

Just ten years earlier, in 1952, on my very first Sunday afternoon appearance on WGN ("World's Greatest Newspaper") radio I clashed with another one of broadcasting's major typhoons, er, er tycoons. I opened my thirty-minute show with news headlines at 1PM, and followed that with a commercial for my freelance sponsor Downtown Nash, then I did a lead-in to a song. Colonel Robert R. McCormick, the ultraconservative, far-right-wing owner of the *Chicago Tribune* apparently had nothing to do on a Sunday afternoon, while sitting on his duff, surrounded by the splendor of his Wheaton estate, "Cantigny," and his remarkable World War One Museum.

What he was doing was monitoring the Fifty Thousand Watt radio colossus of the heartland which he also owned. And I was the lucky one to whom he was listening. He was frowning. I had just introduced myself to the vast WGN audience, and the colonel was hearing me for the very first time and there was something about me he didn't like. The red light on the telephone started flashing in the studio. The engineer pointed to it and me, so I picked it up, and said: "This is Art Hellyer," after which a voice barked at me, "This is Colonel McCormick. CHANGE YOUR NAME!" There was a click on the phone and the line buzzed. If that really was the Colonel, and I doubted it, he certainly was brief and to the point.

I ad-libbed a commercial for Downtown Nash, introduced a song, which the American Federation of Musician's Union record-turner started spinning, as the control-board operator member of the Radio Engineer's Union closed the switch on my microphone and opened the switch that put the record-playing-turntable on the air. All this was done in a moment, and then I walked into the control room and asked the program-producer who had been the first person to answer the phone, "Who was that I just talked to?" He replied: "That was the Colonel himself. He hates your name. You'd better change it." So it was no joke. I finished the show for Downtown Nash, and took off for my next show at WIND in the Wrigley Building, just across Michigan Boulevard. At 3 PM I was back at the WGN microphone, news copy in front of me. When the red light came on I said, "Good afternoon. This is Headlines and Music brought to you by Downtown Nash. Now first with the news headlines I am your announcer, Ambassador Drake."

I thought that sounded pretty classy. I had named myself after Chicago's two finest hotels. If the Colonel was still listening he should like that. There was much laughter in the control room. And that was the end of that episode. After that thirty-minute show I never again used the nom de plume, and only once more did I receive a call from the WGN owner.

The Colonel died in April of 1955, but he took one more shot at me shortly before he went to the big broadcast studio in the sky. Once again it was a Sunday afternoon. I opened the mailbag, as I frequently did on my shows, and I read the letter on the air. I said, "This is a letter from a young man in Naperville, Illinois, named Steven Hyett. He writes, 'Dear Art Hellyer. What is the dirtiest thing in the world?'" I answered, "A horse with a buggy behind." The Colonel was listening. He had heard my innocent answer. He phoned me, and he threw me off his station.

Marina City wasn't always a Chicago landmark on the Chicago River. The property upon which it would rise was for many, many years an open-air, city parking lot. It was nestled against the banks of the river and the girders of the State Street bridge, and many of the over four hundred employees of Channel 7/WBKB, now WLS-TV, parked their cars, for a fee—one dollar a day—on this windblown, very dusty and ugly piece of terra-firma.

Two afternoons each week I started my nine hour WBKB shift at three-fifty-eight-forty-seven, NOT FOUR O'CLOCK, but THREE-FIFTY-EIGHT-FORTY-SEVEN. In those halcyon days, ABC-TV Chicago was the flagship station of the ABC Television Network and we announced all the network system cues, and many of the international and national news stories.

"We" being Charles Homer Bill, Fred Kasper, Wayne Atkinson, Al Parker, Don Ferris, Bob Rhodes, Tom Mercein (with whom I had worked in Milwaukee in the late forties and, though a very fine broadcaster, is best remembered as the man who did not have a Christmas tree for his family one Christmas Eve and so, after work, stopped at a store just closing for the holiday and purchased a gorgeous, completely decorated tree...including all the lights...dragged it onto a streetcar for the long ride home, and took the now-frazzled, needleless tree in the door to his long suffering wife Mary, sans even the ornaments and lights) and Art Hellyer (who never brought a Christmas tree home on a streetcar, but did a lot of other strange things).

I must explain something else at this point. For many years, from the late fifties until 1979 (when ABC-TV, in its infinite wisdom, installed automated voices in a filthy, rat-infested building in Union City, New Jersey, where taxes were cheaper than in Chicago, and put all of us here on the unemployment line), every program except the first live network newscast each evening came out of ABC-TV Chicago. And each show was fed at YOUR local time so no matter where you lived in the United States of America you knew exactly when each network show was on. In other words, let's say you lived in Portland, Maine and you watched Lawrence Welk at 8PM on Saturday Night.

Now let's say your Uncle Arnie Peterson lived in Portland, Oregon, and he's looking forward to Norma Zimmer flashing her pearly whites at him on the Welk show, well, Uncle Arnie tunes in at the same time as you tune in, in Portland, Maine, 8PM, but Pacific Coast time. Because all the ABC-TV network shows were fed into a myriad of two-inch videotape-recorder machines on the 11th floor of the non-rat-infested State-Lake Building in Chicago, and then fed to each time zone in the USA, so no matter where you were when an ABC-TV NETWORK show came on, you saw it LOCAL TIME at the same time you saw it in your time zone. It sounds nuts, but it worked and only ABC-TV did it and we were the lucky broadcasters you heard. You could not hide anywhere in the fifty states from our dulcet tones. One hundred eighty engineers and we EIGHT (I never did figure out this ratio disparity, 180-8) announcers would handle introducing the shows, system IDs and cues, sometimes inserts in the network shows, latest news stories etc. Example: Two afternoons each week I was the network announcer on, among many shows, "Rocky and Bullwinkle"...a fun show I loved. Often the network log would indicate I was to read a live spot. I remember reading a Chevrolet thirty second commercial (not 29 4/5ths, but 30 straight up….on the nose…..PERIOD). One day it just happened to be my daughter Vickie's birthday, so in the middle of the Chevrolet commercial I wished Vickie a "Happy Birthday" coast to coast.

How did I do that in a split-second, 30-second commercial? I sped up my reading of the commercial verbiage, then softened my voice and more slowly delivered my birthday message, then poured it on for Chevy down the stretch and came in at thirty on the nose. I remember director Richie Victor's words to me on the intercom after the spot was over, "Hey Guy!!!! You did it again. Wish Vickie a happy birthday for me, WHEN YOU GET HOME TONIGHT."

I remember one of the tens of thousands of local IDs I delivered because the same Richie Victor, this time directing from the local control room, not a network control room, was rapidly shouting on the intercom, "HEY GUY, MAKE THE ID SHORT!!!" In other words do not do the usual seven-second local station identification, "This is Channel 7, WLS-TV, ABC, CHICAGO, the time 8 PM." So when the red light flashed on I just shouted "SEVEN." Richie told me some years ago this was his all-time favorite station break and he told that story thousands of times.

Richie and Johnny Harkins and Herbie Cunniff, and Howie Shapiro and George Paul, who now, in the year 2008, is Barbara Walters' director on "20/20," were all so much fun to work with. They made a nerve-wracking, cardiac-arrest-causing, everything timed to the thousandth of a second existence, tolerable, and frequently enjoyable. I miss working with those real pros.

We announced from one local booth, Studio C, and two other booths, Studio H and Studio N for network announcements. Local announcements ran from 3 seconds to 7 seconds to 15 seconds to 20 seconds to 30 seconds (all on the nose).

Network system cues in Studios H and N ran from 3 seconds to 10 seconds to 15 seconds to 17 seconds to 20 and 30 seconds (all, of course, on the nose).

Because our announce staff was so small we each often would be on duty alone. So alone in fact that one night I was doing the local IDs in Studio C; announcing the opening to, and the guests on, the "Kup's Show" program; recording IDs in another studio for the following day; and running down the hall to studios H and N to do the network (full country) announcements.

Another night I recall vividly an episode I shall not forget as long as I live. The twelfth floor at 190 N. State Street was our main studios floor. Studios A, B, C, D, H & N were all on twelve and were always being walked by everyone important in the world—JFK, RFK, Hubert Humphrey, Adlai Stevenson, Richard Nixon (whom I interviewed for the ABC-TV Network, right there in Studio B), movie and TV stars, great sports figures and more.

I had the usual three-studio announcement break coming up. I would be required to run from local studio C to studio H and do a ten second announcement to the East Coast, then I would run next door to studio N for a seventeen-second announcement, when the red light came on for the West Coast. Then I'd have thirteen seconds to sprint the length of the building, with a ninety-degree left turn halfway in the run, back to Studio C for a thirty-second local announcement.

This particular night I had completed the first two announcements and was roaring down the hall in my thirteen-second dash for studio C's local message. I was doing fine until I made the ninety-degree left turn and barreled full-bore into a soft pile of pink fluff. It was a gorgeous blonde woman who at my impact hit the floor in one bounce, while at the same time a pink poodle came flying through the air yipping and yapping. MY GOD I HAD CREAMED JAYNE MANSFIELD!!!!! I grabbed one of her arms as I kept moving toward Studio C. Apologizing profusely I pulled her to her pink encrusted feet, then I dropped her in a chair in the Studio C control Room as I roared through it, past the seated technicians, and on into the Studio C announce booth. I leaned over into the arc of the microphone in Studio C as the red light came on. I made the announcement and thirty seconds later I helped a disheveled Jayne Mansfield down the hall to Studio B where Irv Kupcinet was waiting for her to tape record his "Kup's Show." I couldn't give him an explanation at this time, but I shouted to him, "I'll be back in C to intro your show in ten seconds." And I was. It was a tough job, but guys and girls I wish it was still then and I was still working with all those fine people, many now gone forever.

But now let us return to the parking lot I was just getting ready to depart when I decided it might be wise to explain how we operated at WLS ABC-TV. I parked my car and had to merely walk across the State Street Bridge as I had done thousands of times, stroll leisurely south one block on State Street to the State-Lake Building where WLS-TV occupied the top four floors, and start my late-afternoon-evening announcing duties.

As I got out of my parked car I heard the bridge bells start to toll. Ye Gods, the damn thing was going up. Well, even if it took ten minutes to go up and down. I would calmly wait. Most boats they raised it for were small craft with a single much too-tall mast. The bridge started down in plenty of time for me, BUT somehow it jammed. Well folks, many times in my career I had to break some minor law to be to work on time. So I walked up the bit of an incline and looked the situation over. There was approximately a three-foot gap through which I could see the condom-filled river rapidly flowing.

I looked at my watch and noted, three-fifty-eight-forty-seven was quickly approaching. So I did the only thing a red-blooded ABC-TV broadcaster could do. I backed up a few feet, took a running jump, and I leaped the Chicago River. I then ran down the slope, ducked under the gate, AND A COP GRABBED ME BY THE ARM. I had to give him my driver's license, believe it or not, and he was going to call a paddy wagon. I showed him my ABC-TV card and police department press pass and told him my predicament and then invited him to come the one block with me to the ABC-TV studios and see what I meant. Well, he did. He came right up in the elevator with me.

We turned to the right, went into network Studio H.....The director shouted, in his usual cadence, "Art stand by............ ANNNNNNOOOOUUUUNNNNCCCCEEEEE!!!!!!!" And at three-fifty-eight-forty-seven I made the announcement that got me back my driver's license and an apology as the cop said, "I never saw anything like this!" Before he left he asked me for a note and my autograph so his wife would believe him when he told his story over the dinner table that night.

A woman who was an internationally-known personality was seated with her skirt pulled up high, and her nylon-hose-clad feet were on the table that held the TV monitors and the microphone in Network Studio N as I roared in from the adjacent Network Studio H, to do a thirteen-second announcement to the East Coast. I quickly informed the imposter she would have to leave "RIGHT NOW." She hiked her skirt up further on her spindly legs, and told me what I could do. It was not complimentary and it was not clean. I then warned this bleached-blonde she was to keep her mouth shut, and told her this was a network broadcast studio, and I was about to make a live network announcement.

At that very moment the cue came from the director,

Unique Happenings on the Air

"ART...ANNNNOOOOOOOUUUUUNNNNNNCCCCE!!!"
With trepidation I spoke the words, fearing any moment foul words just might be shouted over my voice. The big star did not open her mouth, and without another word I started my mad dash to Studio C for the local seven-second message. Shortly thereafter, director Johnny Harkins cued me to introduce "The Kup Show" which was being recorded down the hall in Studio B. The blonde with whom I'd had the unpleasant encounter was the featured guest that night and it was my duty to introduce her. And I did so, reading the copy just the way it had been written by the Channel 7 staff copywriter, "Kup's featured guest tonight is Joan Rivers." I did not ad-lib the thought I had in my mind, "and she looks like she's had a zillion face-lifts."

Channel Seven was involved in many of my strange schedules, but the one most difficult to explain without a blackboard and chalk is the one that involved my daily show at WOPA-FM in the mid to late Sixties. I continued to work my nine hours a day, five days a week at WLS-TV Ch.7 in the State-Lake Building, but I also did an eight hour DJ show Monday through Saturday, 8AM to 4PM on WOPA-FM, which was atop the Oak Park Arms Hotel.

How did we do it (see table next page)? Sid Schneider, WOPA's superb chief engineer would record all eight hours everyday, then he would put four recorded hours here and there to cover when I was on at Channel 7. I've made it sound very simple. Believe me, it wasn't. Here's how we did it:

THE HELLYER SAY

	WBKB Ch.7 Chicago	WOPA-FM Oak Park	Freelance
SUN	6AM-3PM	OFF	
MON	Noon-9PM Midnight-12:15AM (VIDEOTAPE Midnight news)	LIVE 8AM-11:30AM 11:30AM-4PM ON AUDIO TAPE	Limo to O'Hare. Fly to Minneapolis on 10:10PM UAL. Stay at Radisson Hotel Midnight to 6:30AM
TUES	OFF Midnight-12:15AM (Midnight news)	8AM-Noon On Tape.... LIVE Noon-4PM	7AM WCCO Tape National Food Store Commercials. Fly UAL Back to Chicago Limo to WOPA-FM
WED	5PM-4AM Midnight-12:15AM (Midnight news)	8AM-4PM LIVE	
THUR	5PM-4AM Midnight-12:15AM (Midnight news)	8AM-4PM LIVE	
FRI	Noon-9PM Midnight-12:15AM (Midnight news)	8AM-11:30AM LIVE.. ON Tape 11:30-4PM	
SAT	5AM-3PM	ON TAPE 8AM-4PM	

Unique Happenings on the Air

Whether or not it was true, by order of Egmont Sonderling, a nice gentleman and owner of WOPA-FM and his program director Al Michel, I was to say on every station break, "This is One Hundred Thousand Watts, WOPA-FM....America's most powerful FM station.....with studios in Oak Park, Illinois, and Chicago, Illinois." WOPA-FM was indeed a 100,000 watt station, with a very, very powerful signal, and I know I had tons of mail from all the Midwestern states, but I also know we did not have studios in Chicago.

"OUR TOWN" Column, Chicago Sunday *Tribune* 1966: "No doubt you know of Art Hellyer's Memory Lane, broadcast daily from 8 a.m. to 4 p.m. Monday through Saturday over WOPA-FM, Oak Park. Eight hours each day of old-time records, classified and commented upon, make for very interesting listening."

You will note there are shifts that end and start three or four hours apart. No way could I drive the 40 miles from the loop to my home in Naperville, and return to get a few hours of sleep, so I would nap either on the Bob Newhart cot at Ch.7, or the sofa in the entrance hall at WOPA-FM.

Newhart had a show, with Tom Mercein from 8AM until 8:30AM, five days a week in 1958 on WBKB Ch.7, and he purchased a war-surplus army cot to nap on before other daily assignments, and/or talent agency visits. For example, he like all of us in the Chicago talent pool, called on super agents Shirley Hamilton, Sabie, Tweet Hogan, and Amelia Lorance, frequently, and Tweet became Bob's agent for years. These calls were the lifeblood of our business, and the auditions we would win kept the wolf from the door. When Newhart went to Hollywood, and super-fame, our legacy was his cot. It really wasn't very comfortable, but it beat sleeping on the studio floor.

Like Marty Hogan and his Program Director Bob Platt at WCFL in the Fifties, Mr. Sonderling and Al Michel in the nineteen-sixties, granted me carte blanche with my programs. Listener Marilyn Strorigl recently reminded me that every time General Manager Al Michel came into the studio while I was broadcasting, he did so on a very noisy pogo stick. (A sound effect I would play). Refreshing because most managers and program directors wanted complete control of me, and my show. I certainly could not and would not allow that to happen, and this stance cost me many jobs. I used to say to managers and program directors, "Just leave me alone...let me do my show, my way. I know what I'm doing." And as the years rolled by, more quickly than I at this time can believe, I proved myself right saying that. The proof is in the highly rated shows I produced, and the millions of dollars in gross revenue the Art Hellyer shows brought the stations. I am fiercely proud of my track record.

Al Michel even provided me with two outstanding guests I'd never have had on the air except for him, "The Queen of The Jazz Age" Ruth Etting and the biggest recording star of the Roaring Twenties, Nick Lucas. Lucas even sang his signature song "Tip Toe Through the Tulips," which sold over TWO MILLION copies in the twenties, live on my show, and he presented me with a one-of-a-kind special Nick Lucas tie, which I regret to say, I have somehow lost.

Ruth Etting told me LIVE her tragic, ill-fated story. Seventeen-year old farm girl from Nebraska comes to Chicago to become a star. She makes the chorus line at Marigold Gardens in the early nineteen-twenties. Business-man with underworld connections, Martin "The Gimp" Snyder, comes into her life. She marries him in 1922...he becomes her manager. She signs recording contract with Columbia records and has SIXTY hit recordings. Ruth joins Ziegfeld Follies of 1927, then radio and Hollywood stardom. Everything seems rosy for Ruth Etting Snyder but Ruth divorces The Gimp in 1937.

Unique Happenings on the Air

She had fallen in love with a piano player named Myrl Alderman. She wants to marry Myrl. The Gimp is not happy. The Gimp shoots Myrl who survives the brutal attack, and the Gimp is convicted of attempted murder.

Ruth, the "Sweetheart of Columbia Records" and "America's Radio Sweetheart" and Myrl are married. I'd tell you more but rent the video "Love Me or Leave Me" and Jimmy Cagney and Doris Day will verify it all. In fact on one of my interviews with Doris in 1955 she told me all about the film, and she declared it to be an extremely accurate portrayal of the sordid events.

Snyder was still alive and well and once again a free man walking his old haunts, the streets of Chicago's famed loop in the Fifties, and I often saw him gimping into Henrici's on Randolph Street mid-mornings for breakfast. He refused my many requests for him to appear on my show. He was a pal of Bob Elson, but never appeared on one of Bob's great shows from the "Pump Room" of The Ambassador East Hotel either. The Gimp was a very special character who added much color to the history of Chicago in the Twenties, Thirties, Forties, and Fifties.

Early one morning, Lucille Lawrence, WOPA-FM's office manager, who knew more about running WOPA-FM than all the other employees combined, came running into the studio completely out of breath, "Art, Art.....Mr. Durante is on the phone. I can't believe it Art, I just talked to Jimmy Durante!"

Another day Lucille stood in the studio door just staring blankly at me. When she had regained her composure, she said softly, trying to control her emotions, "Art, Nelson Eddy is here for your show. Mr. Michel saw him and practically pulled him into his office. I'll bring him in here when he comes out of Mr. Michel's office. Art, I can't believe Nelson Eddy is right here in our station. I'm shaking all over. Oh! Art, I saw every one of his movies with Jeannette McDonald. I think 'Maytime' is my favorite. Remember how they sang? OOOOH! Mr. Eddy I didn't know you were in back of me. Art, this is Eddy Nelson, I mean oh! My, I am flustered....

Nelson Eddy then spoke to Lucille, thanking her in that magnificent voice we all loved, and she swooned herself out the door, red-faced and stammering. That scene will live vividly with me until the day I die. Lucille had never met this Hollywood kind of personality before. She was accustomed to greeting Frank Yankovic, "King of the Polka Bands," and Louie Bashell, the "Silk Umbrella Man," and "Whoopie John Wilfarht, all the Way From Minneapolis," and "Norbie and Gillie." All nice polka people with whom I had worked earlier in my crazy career, during my broadcasting days in Milwaukee.

But now people from Hollywood were stopping at the WOPA studios to guest on my shows. Poor, dear Lucille almost fainted the day Dean Martin and Jerry Lewis strolled in and literally took over the place. Residents of the hotel were told by the dazed doorman that "Martin and Lewis are on the ninth floor in the studio with Art Hellyer," and before the interview was half over, hundreds of Oak Park residents were milling around in the major intersection of Washington Boulevard and Oak Park Avenue. Many more were jammed in the ninth floor hallway trying to get a glimpse of Martin and Lewis. While I was interviewing them, the police were devising a plan to sneak the two of them down the hotel freight elevator so they could slip out of the hotels back door, and board a Village of Oak Park garbage truck that would take them to their suites at The Ambassador East Hotel. My sister Irene, who was a PR person for Bing Crosby Productions and The Ambassador East, came up with this idea. And it worked.

The following year, Irene worked out the same means of escape when word spread like wildfire that I had Perry Como, Bing Crosby, Dorothy Lamour, and Julie London and her husband, "Dragnet's Sgt. Friday," Jack Webb, as my guests. This was known by we who were involved, as "Operation TWO Garbage Trucks." The good people of Oak Park were wrong though about who my guests were. Jack Webb had a bad cold and couldn't make the festivities. A wonderful by-product of being a broadcaster is the lifetime friends one makes. Of course, the great majority of listeners, unfortunately, we would never meet.

In the sixties I represented Van Heusen Menswear in Chicago, and conducted once-monthly interviews with primarily Chicago sports figures. I would appear at Carson, Pirie Scott and Company, and Marshall Field Stores with people such as Ernie Banks, Sid Luckman, Gayle Sayers, Billy Williams, Stan Musial, and George Halas.

On November 4TH, 1965, at Carson, Pirie, Scott and Company in Evergreen Park, Illinois, a voice piped up from the audience with a question for my guest, Dick Butkus, "What size shirt do you wear?" The voice belonged to Henry Strorigl of Chicago, who was with his beautiful wife Marilyn. I don't recall Butkus's answer. Seems he said "twenty-two collar," and after our one-hour question-answer session I shook hands with the Strorigls and we've been good friends ever since.

In fact, I would do a German dialect and call him "Heinrich Stroweagle" (correct pronunciation of their last name), and play his favorite recording by "The Old Philosopher" Eddie Lawrence, "Old, Old Vienna." "Every May the Zecond, the people of Old Vienna would eat schtrudel and dance in the streets," Eddie Lawrence would sing on his Coral 45, and the Strorigls in their home and I in the studio would split our sides laughing.

At another of these Van Heusen get-togethers I met Mr. and Mrs. Tom Waterloo, quiet, gentle people whose lives were changed forever when they lost their beloved son Michael to a landmine in Vietnam. They, too, have been close friends for almost forty years, and I always found warm pleasure in playing one of Nelson Eddy and Jeannette MacDonald's beautiful duets for them.

UNIQUE HAPPENINGS
ON THE AIR 2

* Essay 9 *

"The first thing you notice is the Voice. It's smooth and deep and somewhat growly, kind of like honey mixed with gravel. It's calm and soothing yet authoritative-the kind of tone and bedside manner you'd want a doctor to have, telling you that everything's okay, and you're going to pull through. And it's folksy and friendly, like your best friend sitting and talking to you over a cup of coffee at the kitchen table. This distinctive voice belongs to radio personality Art Hellyer, and millions of people are intimately familiar with it." *CHICAGO SUNDAY TRIBUNE, May 19, 1996. By Nancy Stetson, Feature Writer*

There is much more to this item in the Chicago Sun-Times' "Kup's Column" of Wednesday, September 10, 1969, than meets the eye. Kup wrote, "THERE'S A TRAITOR in our midst-WLS-FM's ART HELLYER. He's sporting a N.Y. Mets hard hat and he is pulling for the New Yorkers over our Cubs (Hi ya, Benedict Arnold!)..."

Over the summer of 1969 I had taken Elaine and our five children to 4 or 5 Cubs games at Wrigley Field, and they had spent another Cubs evening with me as I hosted a Beckert-Kessinger autograph party at sponsor Mike Moore's "Townhouse TV." The Cubs' second baseman and shortstop asked me to tell the blocks long lines of fans they would not sign baseballs, only flat objects. Turned out their "tools of the trade," their hands, were warn out from the all the appearances the Cubs had lined up for the players on this club that had seemed pennant-bound. But now in September, after leading most of the summer, overwork—on and off the playing field—was catching up with them, and the team's lead was fast fading.

On September 9th I did my daily WLS-FM morning show from the front window of sponsor Phil Rosten's Camera Exchange store on Dearborn Street in the heart of Chicago's loop. Thousands of listeners had come downtown to watch the broadcast and they mingled with daily loop office-workers threading their way through the crowds on their way to work.

I sat prominently displayed among the Eastman Kodak, Minolta, Canon and Polaroid cameras, surrounded by plate glass windows. The morning was rolling rapidly along with Dr. K back in the studio playing the music I would introduce and also throwing his famous voice tracks at me.

Things were going just fine until I commented about the Cubs apparently falling apart, and I predicted The New York Mets would shortly leave the Cubs in the dust. As I was making this announcement I placed on my head a blue Mets batting helmet I had very recently purchased at Wrigley Field.

Well, many of the "Bleacher Bums" were standing in front of the store and suddenly a riot broke out. The plate glass windows were smashed to smithereens, and my engineer Ralph Davis and I fled for our lives to the interior of the store. I might add we never missed a beat and the show went on, BUT Dearborn Street became a combat zone. "Bums" were fighting the police, and barricades were set up and the street was closed to all traffic, including city buses.

Television trucks arrived and TV cameras were whirring and reporters were rushing into the store. One station was interviewing Phil Rosten, and I saw the Ch.7 microphone shoved under Phil's son Mitch Rosten's nose. A number of salespeople were getting on TV for the first time, which was a nice touch I thought. In fact, the story made all 5PM and 10PM local newscasts, and ABC-TV carried the story on the 5:30PM network news.

I said nothing of an anti-Cubs nature. I even said many times, "although I grew up a Sox fan, I have always pulled for the Chicago teams in all sports events." Needless to say, the next morning I was thrilled to return to the quiet WLS-FM studio on the third floor of the Stone Container Corporation Building at Michigan Boulevard and Wacker Drive.

On October 23, 1969, WLS-FM fired Mike Rapchak, Steve Hodges, myself, and our terrific manager, Harvey Wittenberg. The broadcast geniuses at ABC New York announced we were being replaced by automated programming. Harvey asked us to each finish the next two weeks, then quietly disappear from the airwaves. That is the way it almost always happens and the faithful listeners are left in the dark wondering what happened. Well needless to say I pointed to my engineer Ralph Davis, he opened my mic, and I was fired INSTANTLY!!! The headline atop page three of the *Chicago Sun-Times* the very next morning proclaimed in huge bold type, "WLS-FM's HELLYER HASTENS OWN FIRING." And future Pulitzer Prize-winning author Ron Powers wrote, "WLS-FM personality Art Hellyer put on an Al Martino record, and by the time the song was finished, so was Hellyer. He was dismissed immediately after making a series of on-the-air comments critical of WLS, which had announced it would release virtually its entire performing staff, including Hellyer.

"The station had said that it would implement a new format called 'Love' to attract a younger audience. In reply, WLS-FM General Manager, Harvey Wittenberg released a memo, 'To whom it may concern, I can highly recommend Art Hellyer as an outstanding radio personality. In a year and a half at WLS-FM, due to Mr. Hellyer's efforts, WLS-FM moved from fifth in the American Research Bureau ratings to the number one position among Chicago FM stations in reaching adults 18-49.'"

When one works in radio and television as a broadcaster, one must not go to pieces when one gets fired. It is part of the business. Each time it happened to me, and it happened many, many times, I would pick up the latest local paper and read the "door-to-door salesmen" ads. I would always come up with something that paid me more than the broadcast business did. So when another station eventually called and offered me a job, why did I go back? Lots of reasons: I am a naturally shy, introverted person who likes to hide, and I could hide in a broadcast booth, yet still be working at something I loved to do. All I ever asked was that THE MANAGER AND PROGRAM DIRECTOR AND OWNERS AND SPONSORS AND AD AGENCIES WOULD JUST LEAVE ME ALONE. And selling door to door is often done in inclement weather and most broadcast studios and booths had heat and air-conditioning in them. (Please see my "Door To Door" Essay in this book.)

I was not fired from my very first job in 1947 at WKNA, Charleston, West Virginia, for concluding a program on the South-Eastern leg of the ABC Radio Network saying, "From the Union Carbide and Carbon Building in Charleston, West Virginia, this is Art Hellyer inviting you to join us again tomorrow at this time for Tea Time at the Terrace. This is ABC...The American Broad-chasing Company."

I had also survived the Auto Snooper Show on WKNA, Monday through Friday, from 5PM to 5:05PM for which I received a talent fee of five-dollars and fifty cents per week. That included the nickel each way bus fare. One afternoon, I introduced the show and myself. Then, as I did on each show, I introduced Mr. Birdsey Hughes the owner of the car dealership, with whom I worked this daily radio gem. But this day, I did the unthinkable. I deviated from the norm and everyone from Birdsey Hughes to the people back at the studio went to pieces. I pretended to open the left front door of "this beautiful like new 1947 Ford V-Eight car of the day, completely equipped with two doors cleverly hinged to each side, a lighted dashboard, and front and back seats, so you won't fall through to the street." I fully described on the air what I was supposedly doing. But, at the same time I emptied a full trash can of metal parts all over the microphone, and I said, "Oh my gosh folks, the driver's side DOOR JUST FELL OFF."

Mr. Hughes couldn't believe what he was hearing, because he was standing right across from me, and indeed the car door had not fallen off. At the same moment there was panic at the studio downtown. No one had ever heard such a thing described on radio before. I was later told by Fred Scott, the station's chief announcer, who was on duty, that everyone from Jack Gelder the manager and Harold Shaffer the program director to the engineer on duty were bouncing off each other, and hysterically shouting orders to anyone who would listen. Well the engineer did what all engineers in those early years after the war had been trained to do. He closed my line down from the disaster-area and I was off the air and Myrtle Blosser at the keyboard of the Hammond organ was playing "Liebestraum" faster than the manager could say "FIRE ART."

But believe it or not, friends in radio-land, I was not fired, though I was thoroughly chewed out by every suit in the front office, and I was warned by program director Shaffer: "If you EVER do anything like that again, you will NEVER EVER work on another radio station in this entire country. THAT WAS REPREHENSIBLE!!! Do you know, we here at the station, and listeners who phoned in, actually believed that car door fell off!!!" Goody!! That was what I wanted them to believe.

Nor was I fired for saying on "Art Hellyer's How-to-Build-a-Model-Airplane Show" one Saturday morning, "Folks, this is the dumbest show yet! I'd like to know who the birdbrain was who thought this one up. How in the world can I teach kids to build model airplanes ON RADIO?" I was reprimanded soundly for that. But please think about that statement. It was true, I was on radio. All I could do was describe over a small, tinny loud-speaker in the kid's home how to cut each wing rib, for example, so it was in the Clark Airfoil shape. Then, on radio, I would tell them to cover "a very old table, first with an old newspaper, then with wax paper. Now boys and girls lay your yardstick flat on the table, press down hard to hold the wax paper in place, and now with a nice sharp pointed black crayon pressed against the yardstick draw a straight line about two feet long on the wax paper. Now place your balsa-wood wing leading edge, which we talked about earlier, along the line you've just drawn, and gently push a number of straight pins through the balsa wood to secure it to the table. Now I want you to take the twenty-four ribs we formed out of balsa wood last week as I was winding up the show, and lay them equi-distance apart, at a ninety-degree angle to the wing's leading edge.

"Next, take the cap off your tube of Testor's airplane cement, and place a dab on the front edge of each rib, and place them, each standing in a row, again equi-distant from each other, against the leading edge. Now take one straight pin for each rib and push the pin gently through the rib so it attaches itself to the table. And now you see why I told you, you must use wax paper. That's so the airplane cement will not fasten the balsa wood to the newspaper.

"Well kids, that's all the time we have for today, so leave today's work fastened to the table until we meet again next

Saturday morning at nine-thirty, here on WKNA 950, on your radio dial for 'Art Hellyer's How-to-Build-a-Model-Airplane Show,' when I will teach you how to build and attach the wing's trailing edge, and how to cover the entire wing with airplane paper. Keep 'em flying, gang. This is WKNA, Charleston's Personality Station."

I was read the riot act for this, too: I introduced the number one song of the day, "I Love You For Sentimental Reasons" as "I Love You For Seventy Mental Reasons." This dreadful indiscretion, on my part, called for a full-scale meeting of all station personnel.

Nineteen years later Ernie Shomo the Vice-President of CBS Radio and WBBM, Chicago, would send the program director, Art Thorsen, a note I still have in my possession as I write this in 2007, telling him to warn Hellyer:

"This sort of thing will not be tolerated at WBBM....This is not some hillbilly station in the sticks.....last night on Supper Club I almost had a stroke when Hellyer introduced the song 'I've Grown Accustomed to Your Face' as 'I've Got a Customer For Your Face'—Art Thorsen, what is wrong with Hellyer? I believe he is totally incorrigible. You are the program director. PLEASE CONTROL HIM!!, or FIRE HIM!!! All employees must always remember...THIS IS WBBM, CHICAGO!!!"

UNIQUE HAPPENINGS ON THE AIR 3

* Essay 10 *

"His irreverence made him popular with listeners, who never knew what to expect."
—*Amanda Nielsen,*
Columbia College "Echo" magazine, Summer/Fall 2008

Having been warned at Radio Institute of Chicago by instructor and super-announcer Paul Barnes that announcers were looked on as dime-a-dozen commodities and were fired frequently I was preparing for the inevitable, and I had been mailing transcriptions of my unappreciated endeavors to other stations, so when WKNA axed me I had WOWO in Fort Wayne, Indiana, salivating to hire me. I jumped from a thousand-watter to a fifty-thousand-watter over night, and my pay LEAPED from $17.95 a week to $29.50 a week. I knew much about the city. During World War Two, I had become an Air Force weatherman, learning it on-the-line while stationed at Baer Field in Fort Wayne. I had also had my sergeant stripes torn off my sleeves at Baer Field for calling my commanding officer Second Lieutenant Don Meyers "a little tin demi-god, ninety-day wonder," which also resulted in the Air Force flying a special C69 in from Wright-Patterson Field Weather Headquarters, for the Air Force to pick me and my barracks bags up and fly me to Dayton, Ohio, for my punishment, which was meted out by a 45-year-old Sgt.

Fitzpatrick, who told me that if I had the guts to talk that way to Lieutenant Meyers, I was a good guy in his opinion. And he assigned me to a very cushy job. I would be the center fielder on the Wright-Patterson baseball team. I loved Sgt. Fitzpatrick and I have never forgotten that wonderful man.

So I knew all about Fort Wayne when I reported to WOWO with my just newly-minted bride, the former Elaine Miller of Elmhurst, Illinois, my hometown, at my side. Poor dear, beautiful child. If only she knew what was ahead of her, being the wife of a broadcaster, she would have married steady Al Swanson, a carpenter with a steady job, and my final competitor for her hand, and the beautiful rest of her.

We arrived in Fort Wayne on the Pennsylvania Railroad's crack train, the Broadway Limited, out of Chicago, bound for the Big Apple. We stepped off the train on the very station platform I had stood many, many lonely vigils on frigid winter nights waiting for trains to take me home to Chicago on weekend passes from Baer Field. This time I had my gorgeous bride with me, the weather was pleasant, but we had no place to stay. The stuffy program director who had hired me had recommended we take a room at the Hotel Indiana. Fine hotel, but we couldn't afford to pay $2.50 a night to live in the lap of luxury, so I bought a paper and looked under "Rooms for Rent." After phoning probably ten of them, and finding them all spoken for, we lucked out on one, hopped a bus, saw the room and rented it on a day-to-day basis. There were a few problems though. Our postage stamp-sized room was on the first floor, the community bathroom was on the second floor, and the one shower in the building was on the third floor. Elaine was pregnant with Larry, there was no elevator in the building, and all residents had to be out of the post-world-war-two, flophouse, normal working hours, 9 to 5 daily.

I did not, by any stretch of the imagination, work normal hours. To add to our problems, there was no place to cook or eat in the dump. But Elaine reminded me, this was right after the war, we had just arrived in town, and we were lucky to have found these charming quarters. The rules and regulations hit us the very next day when I got up at 4AM to prepare for my first day on the air at "THIS IS FIFTY THOUSAND WATT, WESTINGHOUSE OWNED AND OPERATED WOWO, FORT WAYNE, INDIANA...THE MIGHTY VOICE OF AMERICA'S HEARTLAND." Yes, this was BIGTIME POWER in a very nice small American city.

My shift three days each week was 5AM to 2PM, with my lunch hour from 10AM to 11AM. These hours did not exactly conform to the house rule of 9AM to 5PM, which meant I couldn't come back into our room until after 5PM, and Elaine would have to find somewhere to go from 9AM until 5PM. Elaine tried to find a job in Fort Wayne, but had no luck, even with her fine office skills honed for four years at Commonwealth Edison in Chicago where she was secretary to Mr. Plumly, head of purchasing, whose wife made him sit in the basement of their home when he smoked a cigar. Elaine also made a little extra money as the model in Commonwealth Edison's Chicago newspaper ads, and she gave up a job that paid her more money for a five-day week than I was getting for working a six day week on radio.

My WOWO morning shift for three days was bad enough, but my shift for the other three days was even worse, 3PM to Midnight. This really meant I had to be out of our room from 9AM these three days until 1AM the next day. Needless to say these strange hours made it totally impossible for us to explore other digs, if available. And it was most difficult for Elaine to properly nourish herself with the baby on the way, no job possibilities, and for her to abide by the house fuhrer's orders. Elaine would on nice days sit in the park across the street and read a book from the library, and on inclement days she would just stay at the library, which thankfully was only a few blocks from our flophouse.

I daily announced live shows with Nancy Lee and The Hilltoppers, a great yodeler named Jimmy Roberts, and others from either the WOWO studios or Buck Lake Ranch, which the station owned 40 miles away at Angola, Indiana. It was fast becoming apparent we could not put up with this situation, and something or somebody would have to give.

Thankfully I was FIRED!!!!! This is how it happened. WOWO-FM went on the air, but why I will never know. Not one single (or married, for that matter) person in Fort Wayne and environs owned an FM receiver EXCEPT our manager and program director. They, in the infinite wisdom found only in front office suits, decided WOWO-FM would broadcast two hours a day, from 7PM until 9PM, and the lucky announcer assigned to the late afternoon WOWO-AM shift would read those two hours on FM from a book selected by these two front-office mental midgets.

My first night on FM the book they selected for me to read was "Robinson Crusoe." I spiced the story up a bit by having a number of voluptuous females on the island with Mr. Crusoe, and a chef and servants who served Robinson "and his harem of gorgeous broads" fantastic French, Italian, German and Oriental dinners. I would pour water from a large pitcher into a smaller pitcher, right in front of the microphone, as I described the sound to my two listeners and their families, as Friday poured rare French and Italian wines. All the while I was playing exotic hip-swaying, Polynesian music softly in the background on one of the two 78rpm RCA Victor turntables that were standard equipment in all broadcast studios at that time.

When my shift ended at midnight that night I had the next day off, so Elaine was waiting for me at the Pennsylvania Railroad station and we grabbed the next rattler for Chicago. Then, we did one of my army stunts, hitchhiking a ride in a truck from the loop to the Borden Milk Company distribution center in Oak Park, Illinois. Once there it was easy to bum a ride to my folks house in Elmhurst on one of the milk trucks delivering there that day. THAT DAY was August 7, 1947, MY 24th BIRTHDAY!!!!! A day that President Franklin Delano Roosevelt, I am sure, would have described as "A day of Infamy."

It was during my party that sunny afternoon in my parent's solarium, overlooking their beautiful formal gardens, and the family maze, that the WOWO program director's secretary phoned me to tell me I would not start work the next morning at 5AM. Instead, she told me "you need not be here for your 5AM shift, but you are to report to Mr. Carl Van Degriff at 9AM instead."

This was indeed great news, another wonderful birthday present. Elaine and I were thrilled. We would not have to take the 9PM Pennsylvania Railroad "Nighthawk" train back to Fort Wayne as we had planned. We would instead, the next morning, ride the Chicago Aurora and Elgin electric railroad from Elmhurst to the loop at 4:35AM, then catch the 6AM Pennsy Flyer to Fort Wayne. I would report to the program director and find he was assigning me to a decent shift. Then we could find a better place to live where we would have a nice little apartment with our rooms all on the same floor, and no 9AM to 5PM house rules to abide by. Happy days were finally just ahead of us!! It was about time something good happened in my professional life. Things were indeed looking up!! I reported to the program director at 9AM as he had requested. He read me the riot act for "Robinson Crusoe" and then he FIRED me!!

Move ahead eleven years as the dreary March weather of 1959 found me virtually unemployed. I now had, not only my lovely wife, but also 5 wonderful young children to feed, clothe and educate. And financially, things were not looking up. I had been selling door-to-door for the Encyclopaedia Britannica, and the raw winter weather had taken its toll. For the fourth or fifth time in my lifetime I had contracted pneumonia, which had hospitalized me for 10 days, and I was in no condition to go into strangers' homes. I did have a few television commercials running...voice-overs, in Chicago for The National Food Stores, and Walgreens Drugstores, but those paid me only a one-time (no matter how many times they were aired) very small stipend every thirteen weeks.

The much better-paying commercials were those that ran on the three major networks, NBC, CBS, and ABC. Just as with local spots I was paid a recording session fee, but also a fee EACH time the spot ran on the networks. But I only had two of those at the time. One was an on-camera spot where I was standing in the middle of a Sears Auto Center, dressed in a mechanic's coveralls, explaining why Sears Diehard batteries were the greatest invention since chicken soup. The other network TV commercial of mine running at that time was for a major, major bread company, which unfortunately was very, very tardy in their payments, and my friend Jeannine Spangler at the AFTRA-SAG office was forever going to the mat with their ad agency, attempting to collect for me the monies I was due. Unfortunately many, many advertisers figured they spoke with their mouths, just as I did, so what was the big deal about paying broadcast talent for doing something that was a natural part of everyone's daily life? I always felt sorry for poor sweet Jeannine as she would explain over and over again that we (talent) do this for our livings, and we are highly skilled at what we do. One of the things she would say that I liked was, "Listen to those car dealers who do their own commercials, and then listen to Art Hellyer for Downtown Nash. The difference is night and day; the car dealer may be the best in his showroom one on one with his customer, but he is a rank amateur, with the exception of Jim Moran, when he is standing before that camera. People like Art Hellyer, Bill O'Connor, Mal Bellairs, Howard Miller, and Al Parker are skilled professional broadcasters who have a long track record of great success representing their clients on television and radio. Now please send Mr. Hellyer the check he has earned selling your product for you."

Sometimes they would and sometimes they would not. But if they did not they would be informed that no members of AFTRA-SAG would be allowed to work for them, and that meant their commercials would not be played on "signatory stations," stations on NBC, CBS, ABC, MUTUAL and local stations like WGN, WBBM, WMAQ, WLS, WCFL, WJJD, WENR, and WIND. Rarely did we not eventually get paid, but we and our families, could starve while waiting.

I have been told by those who know, whomever they are, that I, not having a personal agent EVER, made some dumbbell moves that cost me dearly. There is an old saying, "He who has himself as his attorney, has a fool for his attorney." I guess the same rule can be applied to talent: "He who has himself as his agent has a fool for his agent." I turned down at least three MAJOR offers from Los Angeles, and two biggies, including an iron-clad guarantee from Alan Ludden, CBS program director in New York. I never made big money, but I stayed in Chicago because it was my home town, and Elaine's entire family, and my entire family all lived within a few miles of each other. I have always been a family man. When people ask "Why aren't you in the Radio Hall of Fame?" I answer: "Because I always went straight home to my wife and family after my shows, and after my long shifts on ABC-TV. I never stopped off at "The Boul Mich" or any other watering holes for drinks with all the RIGHT people. (I could never understand why people with just one human body per person would inject it with alcohol, which Webster describes as "any member of a group of organic chemical compounds which form esters with acids." The main uses of alcohols are as solvents, for gums, for resins, lacquers, and varnishes; in the making of dyes and perfumes; and for alcoholic beverages. Alcohol as ethanol is consumed as part of the alcoholic beverage.) I went home after my shows and played games with my five children, or with Elaine, I helped them on homework projects. Almost every time Elaine and I went anywhere, we took the children with us. I did no political type mixing with the RIGHT people. I just didn't schmooze the people who counted, I guess. I preferred spending my precious time away from the daily grind with my most precious possessions, my family. Even today as I write this tome at age 83, with two or three exceptions, the only people I spend time with are my family members. I am not about to change now.

So when I had these offers others would have given the world for, I quickly turned them down. When Joe Pyne, the man who told callers-in, "Why don't you go gargle with razor blades?" was fired from his Los Angeles daily TV show, Alex Dreier phoned me and said, "I recommended you today for the Joe Pyne job." I thanked him and turned it down. Alex gave me only one more chance, and people say I made a terrible mistake on this one. When Bob Crane gave up his morning drive time show on KNX, Hollywood, to devote all his time to "Hogan's Heroes," Alex told me the stations reps were already flying to Chicago, and they would meet me for dinner that night at Fritzel's, contract in hand. As I look back, my not signing that contract was the most stupid thing I ever did. I was frightened. I did not believe I had the talent or the ability to do a daily show in Hollywood where the Jack Benny's and Bob Hope's would be hearing me in their homes. When George Gobel read in Irv Kupcinet's West Coast column I had turned it down, he phoned me at my home in Skokie, Illinois and pleaded with me to take it. When I told him of my fears he said, "Art, you've already been Number One in Chicago in the morning. You'll do it in Hollywood too, and everyone who lives here will hear you and guest on your show, and in return you will guest on their network television shows. ...ART, YOU ARE GOOD!!!!! Don't pass up your golden chance of a lifetime." George even pleaded with Elaine, who said it was entirely up to me. I turned it down. I was frightened out of my mind, and I suffered many panic and anxiety attacks. The same attacks I still suffer today.

And I just didn't blow my career on the West Coast. May 10, 1956, when I was a mere child of 32 years, Herb Lyon said in his *Chicago Tribune* "Tower Ticker" column, "Radio's morning madcap Art Hellyer (WCFL) is about to grab off the emcee job on the top network quiz show out of New York, "Name That Tune.""

Harry Salter, the show's orchestra leader, had been in Chicago appearing at the Chicago Theatre, and had guested on my WCFL morning show. Shortly after Maestro Salter got back to New York, Bill Cullen, the host on the show, gave it up because he had so many shows going he couldn't find time to sleep, so Harry Salter recommended me. Another dinner at Fritzel's and "Name That Tune" was offered to me. I remember I was actually shaking uncontrollably all over inside my body. I thanked them and said I would phone them the next morning with my decision. It was all I could do to drive my little red MG TD home that night. Elaine called Dr. Kokotek when I staggered in the door and fell on the bed shaking so violently the bed was vibrating. And I remember my teeth were banging each other so hard Elaine could hear the chattering across the bedroom.

The next morning Elaine phoned CBS in New York and told them my decision. I couldn't do so myself. Dr. Kokotek was at my bedside and I was having what was called in those days "a nervous breakdown." The good doctor told Elaine I nearly died of fright. I was Woody Allen before Woody Allen, was Woody Allen. Or as daughter Debbie said to me as I was writing this, "Dad, you would have left your comfort zone." I like that Deb. Thank you, Hon.

I have said this many, many times…The only times in my life I've been able to totally relax are when the mic's red light goes on. My sister Irene once remarked, "Why don't you get yourself one of those baby-totes, and hang it on your chest with a microphone in it?" Might not be a bad idea Irene, thank you.

Well, I was in another low period…I was getting over another battle with pneumonia. I had a few more days to take my antibiotic and, I needed a steady job, so I contacted some of the agents I knew in New York and Los Angeles. One in New York called me immediately…a man named Jack Masla. Mr. Masla was a well-meaning man who was quite familiar with my work. In fact, in 1955 after Elaine and I visited with the people at WINS New York, where Bob and Ray were the biggest radio show on the eastern seaboard, and after being wined and dined, and even being driven around in a station limo with a realtor showing us homes in the Hamptons and New Rochelle, we had decided to stay in Chicago, our hometown. Jack Masla told us, "I'm not going to give up on getting you into the New York City market." So in 1959 Jack answered my letter immediately and phoned me with a New York offer—BUFFALO, New York.

Mr. Masla had spoken to the general manager at WBNY, a Buffalo 5000 watt station. They needed a new morning man. How soon? "YESTERDAY, Art. I'd like very much for you to take this job. Will you do it?" I asked him if he'd give me a few hours to talk it over with Elaine and our five children and then I'd get back to him. He had told me what the pay would be. It wasn't great, but they would give me a 13 week contract. That did it….the family agreed with me…take it. See how it works out. Would we happy making this huge downward move from the nation's number-two market, at that time, to a far smaller city? Well, to make a long story short, I called Jack Masla and asked him, "When do I start?"

The very next day, a Sunday I hopped in my car, drove to O'Hare Airport, took a Chicago Helicopter Airways flight to Midway Airport, boarded an American Airlines twin-engine Convair at 1:10PM with a Buffalo ETA of 5PM. After all this activity, and still on an antibiotic, I was already exhausted as I settled into my seat awaiting the takeoff. The crew came aboard, the pilot, co-pilot and one stewardess. They welcomed us aboard, and gave us our various instructions, in case of a disaster. She also informed us of the planes Estimated Times of Arrival (ETAs) in Detroit, Buffalo, and New York City and how to put on our oxygen masks, if needed. Then, almost coinciding with our seat belt buckles clicks, we were airborne. I was seated on the aisle, with an elderly lady as my seat companion. We spoke briefly, then she pointed out to me, the window beside her was icing up. That made me even more shaky than I had been, in fact, had I suspected the kind of day that I was going to have, believe me I would never have left the warmth of our fireplace in Skokie, Illinois. The Convair was indeed icing up, and hitting large pockets of turbulence. The nice elderly lady next to me was clicking her Rosary beads, and apparently whispering prayers under her breath. But the most demoralizing of all was yet to come. Our friendly stewardess started reeling in the aisle and vomiting. She fell into the seat against the bulkhead and just sat staring into space as the co-pilot came running up the aisle with a paper cup of water, which she gratefully accepted and started to sip very slowly. Now, the co-pilot was holding onto a seatback and explaining on the tinny microphone that this turbulence would be our traveling companion the remaining twenty minutes it would take us to get to Detroit's Metropolitan airport, "but, just relax folks, everything will be just fine. This is just a little bit of turbulence. It will smooth out shortly."

Well it didn't "smooth out shortly." It got a helluva lot worse, and I felt like I was on "The Bobs" at Chicago's Riverview Park the night my eyeglasses flew off my face and were never seen again. The plane bucked and clawed its way through the gray skies and my stomach felt like it had rocks in it. Now passengers were joining the stewardess in a chorale of vomiting, and our stew couldn't care less. She was sitting with her legs stretched forward as she slumped in her seat, her little white cap askew and she looked generally disheveled and beat. She couldn't care less. We were on a roller-coaster ride to Detroit, when the pilot laid a cheery announcement on us, "Folks, this is your pilot...I am happy to report that everything is going well, but we have been told that Romulus (Detroit airport location) will be closed for approximately one hour, so we will go to Cleveland for fuel, and then return to Detroit so the fifteen passengers we have for there can get home...then we will proceed to Buffalo and our final destination today, New York City. Thank you for your patience and understanding."

So we veered out over Lake Erie which twice appeared very close to us as we quickly dropped a few thousand feet before the pilot saved us. Now we were in a full-blown, white-out blizzard. The lady next to me was loudly saying "Jesus, Mary and Joseph   SAVE US, DEAR GOD...SAVE US!!!" The plane smelled putrid, like a cow barn and I was drenched from all the antibiotics I'd been on. By now I was convinced we would sometime years from now be the subject of a country-western song: "Oh this is the story of an American Airlines Convair that on a Sunday afternoon in '59 dropped from the turbulent wintry skies and quietly slipped deep into the murky dark waters of the lake called Erie taking a hundred and twenty souls to their eternal watery grave only an hour from where the Edmund Fitzgerald and its brave crew lies forever moldering." I could hear Kris Kristofferson, Willie Nelson, and Waylon Jennings singing of our demise.

Shortly afterward we plopped onto Cleveland's tarmac, and skidded a few times. Then suddenly a red and yellow Shell fuel truck came through the flying snow and stopped under our right wing. Our pilot and co-pilot staggered bleary-eyed through the cockpit door and informed us that after the plane was refueled, we would take off in a few minutes and go back to Detroit so we could deliver the Michigan residents to their anxious families. Then the two intrepid flyers strode through the plane, took the fallen stewardess by her pale arms and dragged her off the plane. Almost immediately a sullen crew in overalls, entered with mops and buckets of water and spray bombs and, I use the word very loosely, proceeded to "sanitize" our flying stink bomb.

Our Sunday afternoon calamity then continued as a fresh new crew wearing big smiles on their faces came aboard. Ye Gods…it was now well past 5PM, the hour we were due to be in Buffalo, and I had a radio show tomorrow from 5AM until 9AM, and I'm sitting in a smelly Convair with a hundred or so people I will never know, on the tarmac of the airport in Cleveland, Ohio. Mercifully we were airborne 10 minutes later on our way back to Detroit at which time, the pilot announced the Detroit landing field was still closed, but would reopen shortly. The twin-engined plane took a few wide circles around Detroit, then the pilot gave us the good news, "Folks, this is your captain. We are sorry for the inconvenience, but we are now landing at Romulus, Michigan…our fifteen Detroit passengers will be leaving us, and we will then proceed to Buffalo and New York City. Thank you for your patience." When we were safely on the ground SIXTEEN passengers disembarked….fifteen for Detroit AND ME!!!

I left my bags on the plane. They held many of my personally treasured LPs and 45s and discs containing many of the voice tracks Dr. K and I had used on our shows just a few years ago. Frankly, at this point I wasn't going to lug them with me. I turned my ticket in at the American Airlines desk, and walked out to a Greyhound bus that said "DETROIT" on its destination placard. I paid my fare and began the 15-mile ride to, hopefully, the Michigan Central Railroad station. As I sat by myself in a rear seat I thought back over the day to this point. I had driven my car to O'Hare Airport, flown on a helicopter to Midway Airport, hopped a CONVAIR for Buffalo, and I had been in Cleveland, and now in Detroit I was on a bus hoping I could connect with a train heading to Buffalo. I could think of only one form of transport I had not been involved with...a submarine. But the day was not over. As we drove up Gratiot or Woodward or whatever, I must have been confused, because I stepped off the bus into the blizzard at the wrong corner and a completely empty downtown Detroit. It reminded me of when Orson Welles strolled into Manhattan devoid of a living soul in "War of the Worlds" back in 1938.

I had checked a Detroit map at the airport and thought I knew where the station should be, so I trudged my way in a northerly direction, I hoped, with not another human-being in sight. Was this Manhattan in 1938? I remember Orson's great voice booming out "Where Are The People?" A few minutes later I saw the huge station looking down at me through the swirling snow. Inside the station were a few people, all looking as tired and beat as I felt. I went to the ticket window and asked when the next train would be "Shuffling Off To Buffalo," and the ticket agent anxiously said "Now." I repeated it as a question-"NOW?" "Yes sir, RIGHT NOW." I bought my ticket, and ran up the steps to "The Wolverine." The steam whistle hooted and I was on the last lap, I hoped, of my latest odyssey.

The train with very few passengers aboard, smoothly glided toward Buffalo on the Canadian side, swiftly flashing through towering trees and tiny towns. Then at 1:30AM I was standing in a line at The Hilton Hotel, always my favorite hotel chain, waiting to pick up the room reservation WBNY had for me. That done, I ran out to the street, jumped in a yellow cab and headed for the Buffalo airport. I very much needed my luggage, and hoped it would be there. Without it I would not have my music and voice tracks for my first show which would start about three hours from now.

As we drove to the airport, whose beacon I could see flashing, I noted the snow on either side of the road was even with the bottom of the cab's windows. The driver drove me right up to the American Airlines terminal. The beacon was my Star of Bethlehem, but unlike that most famous night in the history of the world, there were no people. The stable, I mean the airport, was empty—brilliantly lighted, but empty, and there, on a counter, like the Blessed Babe in the manger, were my blessed two bags. The cabdriver got them, put them in the trunk, and drove me back to the Hilton. I paid him, went up to my room, and phoned the desk for a wakeup call two hours later. Charleston, West Virginia, New Year's Day 1947 all over again. I, exhausted, dropped into the outstretched arms of Morpheus.

When the phone wakened me at 4:30AM I must have looked like the Wild Man of Borneo. I sure felt like him. After a quick shower and shave, my face covered with little pieces of toilet paper to cover bleeding nicks and scratches of my lower facial terrain caused by my erratic facial tonsorial attempt, I now looked as if King Kong had torn into me. Hauling my overly large bag of morning show props I staggered to the elevator, then wobbled through the lobby, out the door, into a yellow cab which carried me less than two blocks to the WBNY studios. The all-night man let me in. I had a glass of Buffalo water, and sat down in studio A waiting for the network 5AM news to conclude. Then the bleary-eyed all night man gave me a hearty on-the-air welcome to Buffalo. I opened my microphone, thanked him, and I slip-faded up from background a piece of music already cued on the turntable by my predecessor.

Hey Buffalo I'm under way!!!!! BUT WHAT IS THIS? I WAS PLAYING A ROCK 'n' ROLL SONG, not a good rock 'n' roll song, but a noisychungachungachungachung nothing in just three monotonous chords—C, G7 and F. I don't play stuff like that. I assumed Jack Masla had told the Manager, Charley What's-His-Name, I played ballads and instrumentals primarily, with two or three COMEDY records each hour, and I was rumored to be the DJ who first started using voice tracks speaking pithy sayings at the proper time. Something was terribly wrong!!! So I cued up one of the gems in my magical bag of GOOD music and I faded out the ear shattering, air-polluting noise. I recited, *"Mona Lisa, Mona Lisa, Men have named you...You're so like the lady with the mystic smile..is it only cause you are lonely, they have blamed you, for that Mona Lisa strangeness in your smile?"* Then I brought up from the background the soft-as-velvet voice of Nat "King" Cole, singing this fabulous song the way Jay Livingston and Ray Evans had written it to be sung. The day after Vickie was born, Livingston and Evans, who wrote some of our greatest songs, sent Elaine the largest floral tribute the nurses at Elmhurst Hospital had ever seen. I actually borrowed Paul Hackert's pickup truck to haul it home.

As I cued the next song from my bag of <u>good</u> music on turntable number two, the private booth telephone we all never want to see ringing, was madly flashing its red lights and practically leaping off the console in front of me. I picked it up and heard an apoplectically-hysterical voice screaming at me,

"HELLYER...HAVE YOU GONE MAD??????? GOOD GOD MAN...WHAT ARE YOU DOING???...YOU ARE TO PLAY ONLY THE TOP FORTY 45s in the file to your right! NOTHING ELSE!!!"

I hung the phone up without speaking a word, and ignoring the red lights once again flashing I opened the microphone and spoke, "Good morning Buffalo. My name is Art Hellyer, and I was hired by WBNY, THE VOICE OF BUFFALO to entertain you in the morning, but I have just this moment had a phone call on our private studio line from a highly irritated person, quite possibly from WBNY's beloved manager himself, objecting to my choice of music. I am looking through the top forty 45s this voice told me I was only to play. Good people of Buffalo, please phone me right this moment and give me your input." I gave the regular studio line number.... AND IT WENT WILD. Most of the callers-in said it was refreshing to hear GOOD music again. In all fairness a few pimply-sounding voices said they wanted the rock music. So while the phone was still ringing off the hook I said, "My new friends, I will now open the front window of the WBNY studio. I am looking down four stories and I see your main street, Broadway, and into your main street I am throwing these awful Top Forty 45s. I will continue to play from my personal library the GOOD music I have brought with me at great personal expense, so you fine folks here in beautiful upper New York State, in the shadow of Niagara Falls, may once again enjoy it. This day will go down in the history books as the day GOOD music returned to Buffalo."

Only the roofs of a few busses were visible on the main street of Buffalo, New York as I sailed the evil music out of the stations front window. It was fascinating watching the discs weaving back and forth, in and out and through each others path, almost like 40 fighter pilots locked in combat.

Having disposed of the menace to our morals, and pollution

to our tympanic membranes, I sat down, and continued doing my type show.....Frank Sinatra, Doris Day, Tony Bennett, Vic Damone, Dinah Shore, Frankie Laine, Liberace, Dean Martin, Margaret Whiting, Peggy Lee, Perry Como.....comedy by Andy Griffith, Buddy Hackett, Jackie Gleason, George Gobel, and of course my voice tracks, supposedly the voices of the station's general manager, whom I still hadn't met, and the Mayor of Buffalo supposedly in the studio speaking the same words Dr. K used on my Chicago shows when Mayor Daley supposedly was in the studio. I asked "Mr. Mayor how do you like our facilities?" The Mayor (a voice track) shouted "There's no light in the men's room!!" A phrase I still hear from listeners when I first meet them at Senior Citizens' events I attend.

So it went on like that until 9AM. I got all the local commercials on so the station would make its money, and the clients would sell their products in their shops, and I did not hear from the hysterical voice again. Many listeners called to welcome me to their fair city. A few suggested I would get the same treatment Jack Paar got when he worked at WBNY. They said I would be fired. A newspaper reporter stopped in to talk to me, but I had the studio door locked.

I ended the show exactly at 8:59AM, punched up the 10-second ID, and got out of the chair as the next broadcaster slipped into the studio. I have never forgotten his words as he looked at me with an ashen face, "Man, if you repeat this I'll deny I ever said this to you. You did the best damn radio show in the history of this town, but I'll bet you will never do another show here." He then shook my hand, and said, "write when you get located. Good luck." I never saw him again.

I got off WBNY's premises like a rocket ship, and ran back to The Hilton. I knew the station manager, who ever the hell he was, would fire me, so I left word at the desk for no phone calls until 4:30PM. I called Elaine, and after many "Oh!!

My!!s" from my dear, long-suffering wife I jumped into bed and slept until the phone rang exactly at 4:30PM. It was the manager's secretary telling me to come directly to payroll and pick up my check covering the remainder of our agreed-upon thirteen-week contract. She also told me I was not to talk to anyone, and after receiving my check I was to quickly and quietly leave the building. As fast as I could move I did as instructed. I never met the manager...probably just as well.

As soon as I had the largest check I'd ever had in my life in my pocket, I realized I'd better cash it before word about my firing got around town, so I went to the Hilton Hotel manager and told a big lie. I said I loved the hotel and would probably be arranging to stay in it for some time, and I mentioned the station had given me an advance on my salary and I'd like to cash it and could he recommend a good bank? He did just that, and he told me how much he had enjoyed my "unique show" that morning and he wished me great success in Buffalo. I needed that right now, because I went straight to the bank, and collected my One Hundred Fifty Dollars times thirteen weeks, in cash. I put the wad in my right pants pocket and I did not let go of it for the next fifteen hours.

It was now approaching 5PM in Buffalo so I slipped into a phone booth. I sat on the hard wooden seat, and turned up my coat collar. I felt like Art Hellyer, Private Eye, as I fixed my gaze on the hotel manager's office door. This scene called for a lighted cigarette dangling out of a corner of my mouth, but having not ever smoked I was forced to dispense with that as part of my disguise. Shortly after 5PM the manager's office door opened, and he appeared, putting on his hat and coat. He walked to the front desk, and said something to the desk clerk. There was soft laughter behind him as he crossed the large, ornate lobby, and headed out the front door presumably bound for his home.

Waiting a few more minutes to make sure he didn't return,

I then left the phone booth, pulled down my coat collar and walked to the front desk. I paid my bill with some WBNY cash, then went to my room as rapidly as I could and got my bags. A few minutes later I hopped into a cab to the railroad station. And I bought a one-way coach seat on the next New York Central train to Chicago. I phoned the Lovely Elaine, and filled her in on my day's highly unusual activities. Elaine had never learned to drive, so I asked her to please phone her dad to be at LaSalle Street Station in Chicago the next morning when I would arrive at 9:55AM. I sat up all night with my right-hand guarding all that cash, and I never have been back to Buffalo, New York.

I have never forgotten my late father-in-law's first words to me as I got in his car that morning, "Art, Elaine can never say I didn't warn her about you. You live one helluva strange life." I could not disagree with him, as I thought to myself, "What next?"

UNIQUE HAPPENINGS ON THE AIR 4

* Essay 11 *

**"If Art Hellyer had a theme song, it might
well be Sinatra's 'My Way.' "**
—Nancy Stetson, Chicago Tribune

The show that almost finished me for good was the one I hosted on New Year's Eve 1965. It was on the coast-to-coast ABC-TV Network from their flagship station, WBKB ("Balaban and Katz Broadcasting"), now WLS-TV (my primary employer FOR thirty years) at the corner of State and Lake Streets in Chicago.

My "Midnight News" was cancelled that night for the big New Year's Eve event, so I left the comfort of the announce booth, where I was working the 5PM to 4:05AM shift, and ventured into the masses, which the police estimated at 200,000, flowing from the corner of State and Lake to the corner of State and Randolph. There was not a policeman in sight, and that was not good. At ten minutes to midnight the crowds were already jostling me and shouting their welcomes to the New Year and I kept trying to be heard as I would shout "NOT YET!!!!"

My producer on the street with me was an old pro with whom I had worked thousands of times, Sid Field, but he was being badly roughed up by the unruly masses and we were not yet on the air.

Unique Happenings on the Air 4

Just when I needed Sid most, at 11:59 I last saw him being swept past me by the now very unruly mob. So I watched Duke Dukevitch's camera above me on the theatre marquee. When the red light popped on I knew Dick Clark had completed his introduction to me from New York and I was now on the full ABC-TV network with Chicago's greeting to the baby in the diaper.

I said, "Thank you New York, and now it's our turn here in the great heartland of America to welcome in the New Year. I'm Art Hellyer." And as I introduced myself to the world I heard a loud, gruff voice yell, "GET ART." I was instantly slugged in my upper left shoulder by a right fist that broke a disc, I later learned, and I was shoved down to the State Street pavement as others pounced on my back. Someone kneed me in the lower spine and that shot herniated three discs, and crippled me for the rest of my life. I did not know the extent of my injuries and I never stopped talking into the microphone. More thugs lifted me, and the pain in my lower back was terrifying, yet I continued to talk. Then I was deposited on the hood of a Corvette in the middle of State Street midway between two Balaban and Katz movies palaces, The Chicago Theatre and The State-Lake Theatre. A superb newsman Joel Daly had recently joined Ch.7, and he was now assisting me voice-over from his perch atop the Walgreens Drugstore on the Northeast corner of State and Randolph, and Sid Field had reappeared with his blue ABC-TV blazer almost ripped to shreds. He quickly gave me the FIST, meaning, "WRAP THIS THING UP." I did so immediately, as the first police officer I had seen helped me off the hood of the Corvette and assisted me back into the State-Lake Building. He rode the elevator with me to the 12th floor and walked me into the men's washroom-dressing room and helped me compose myself. I still had to go back into the local announce booth "Studio C" and complete the remaining four hours of my announcing shift. I have no idea how I did that, but everyone told me I did a good job, and I signed Ch.7 off the air at 4:05AM. Then, thank God, engineer and long-time close friend Jack Signorelli drove me the 42 miles to my home. No way could I have driven my car home after that beating.

Al Parker, bless him, worked my New Year's Day 1965 shift for me. I was in such pain I could not have gone back into the loop. That night, the ABC-TV 5:30PM CST Newscast and 10PM News ran my episode on the network news to show those who had missed it, that a broadcaster's life is not all peaches and cream.

The years from then until now have been spent in almost constant pain, and I spent hundreds of days in University of Illinois Hospital under the ministrations of famed doctors Oscar Sugar and Caesar Alvarez, and, in a wheelchair himself, Dr. Alon Winnie, whose dad Russ had been the Green Bay Packers' announcer in the halcyon days of Cecil Isbell, Don Hutson and "Buckets" Goldenberg.

Alex Dreier recommended I see a clinical psychologist who worked with people who had my type of problems. So it was I started meeting with Dr. Thomas Henschen at Resurrection Hospital on the northwest side of Chicago. After a series of tests and discussions over a number of months, Dr. Henschen wrote me this letter......

"Dear Mr. Hellyer: I would like to share my impressions with you. You are to be commended, after the violent incident which you experienced a few years ago, for intensifying your will to live. Your fierce desire to maintain your health as opposed to becoming self-neglectful demonstrates your strong motive to survive. After an experience like yours, you could have wondered what it would be like to be totally helpless, and what that could mean as far as pain is concerned. Your self-reliance and bravery seem to be an important means of fighting your pain. People who have had experiences such as yours often wonder about what will happen to their jobs and their family relationships. They, like you, seem to dwell a great deal on the past.

"I would like to make the following suggestion: To assure that you maintain your health, keep focusing on your body. Attend to as many sensations as possible. Talk to others as much as possible, without going to extremes, about how you feel.

"I look forward to continue working with you.

Sincerely,
Thomas Henschen
Clinical Psychologist"

Dr. Henschen and Dr. Robert Small, the director of the pain clinic at Resurrection Hospital helped me enormously mentally, as did Elaine and Larry, Mike, Debbie, Vickie and Jeff. I would spend years in and out of a wheelchair and on crutches and have my radio-TV schedule cut to a minimum. Driving was excruciatingly painful and I would call to strangers from my car to help me park on the street. They would lean in the window and assist me with the steering wheel. On Sunday, September 23, 1984, I announced on my 6PM to Midnight show on WJJD I could never and would never drive to the loop again. The pain was just too bad. September 2004 was twenty years since I left the city I worked in seven days and nights a week for over forty years and I have never returned. So many people have asked why I never sued ABC-TV for not providing me with protection that night. I simply tell them I couldn't sue the hand that fed my family and me for over 30 years. But now as I look back over forty years, I realize those serious injuries badly hampered my career, and I probably should have brought a lawsuit.

Over the years I tried many forms of therapy. None really helped until in the summer of 2003 I started treatments at

Patrick Chapman's SRI Physical Therapy in Naperville, Illinois. Patrick has a master's degree in kinesiology from the University of Illinois, and he and Sally Markelz, a licensed massage therapist and member of the Associated Bodywork and Massage Professionals worked out a program of therapy including massage and Myofascial Release that has seen me once again able to walk without any means of support other than my two legs. It's been a long haul, and without the mental and physical assistance of great professionals and the never-ending encouragement of my dear family I'm sure I long ago would have withered away. Thank you all from the bottom of my heart.

Thursday, June 3, 2004—Charlie Gibson and Diane Sawyer, two great broadcasters, on "Good Morning America" made a boo-boo. Back when I was Art Hellyer and worked for ABC's then flagship station WBKB, now WLS-TV, Chicago, I did many news stories as a correspondent for ABC-TV. Some of them were part of the show Charlie and Diane now superbly anchor. Why am I making this point? Because these people, for whom I have the highest respect, did not research the information they disseminated. They declared 2004 to be the Twentieth Anniversary of the Infomercial. They Were Wrong!!!!!

If indeed that were true, then what the heck was I doing on TV in 1952? And what the heck were Bill O'Connor, Marty Faye, Mal Bellairs, Linn Burton, Al Parker and Howard Miller doing on TV? And what the heck was Ron Popiel doing on TV? What we were doing were FIFTEEN-minute "infomercials"!!!!!

I hosted four to five TV movies per week on WBBM-TV, WBKB (now WLS-TV), WNBQ (now WMAQ-TV), and WGN-TV in Chicago, WTMJ in Milwaukee, and a brand-new TV station in Rockford, Illinois. I don't recall its call letters, but it was in the middle of a cornfield, and the men's room was an outhouse. The director of each show was the person (whether he or she worked for the station or didn't work for the station) who sold the account. This could lead to unmitigated chaos! Wrong slides would appear, the camera would be pointing at a blank wall as I was giving that all important phone number to call, and once I saw myself in the studio's overhead monitor, standing upside down.

We had no interstates in those days, so I would drive my little red 1952 MG TD with the terrible two-inch coil electric heater throwing no heat on the coldest winter nights, on two-lane Route 20 from Chicago to the second stoplight southwest of downtown Rockford. I can still see the area, nothing but cornfields in the dark of night, and in the distance the lighted tower light that would guide me to the TV station. On the kangaroo leather seat to my right I had the three FIFTEEN MINUTES EACH commercials in my brief case. Finally arriving at the station, I would look around me at the vast horizons, and feel I had landed somewhere in outer space. I'd pound like hell on the TV station's door, and hope the two-man crew would hear me. Usually they didn't so I would hope one of them would require the use of the "men's room." Since those days I have stayed away from corn on the cob, which I love dearly. Why? Because the all-male crew did not walk all the way back to the outhouse, if all they had to do was alleviate themselves frontally. They just peed on the corn. In Rockford I pitched "The Parliament food freezer plan." They weren't called "Infomercials" in those early Neanderthal days of television...They were called "Pitches," and I would work in front of a giant freezer that you the viewer would receive "ABSOLUTELY FREE....I REPEAT FRIENDS. YOU WILL RECEIVE THIS MAGNIFICENT FREEZER (I would now be opening the door and pointing to the dozens of frozen food packages inside the freezer), WHEN YOU CALL RIGHT NOW TO PLACE YOUR FIRST ORDER FOR

YOUR FROZEN FOODS. YES, YOU HEARD ME RIGHT FRIENDS...THIS FREEZER WILL BE YOURS FREE....DELIVERED TO YOUR VERY OWN KITCHEN ABSOLUTELY FREE OF CHARGE WHEN YOU PHONE RIGHT NOW!!!!! OUR OPERATORS ARE STANDING BY RIGHT NOW WAITING FOR YOUR CALL TO JOIN AMERICA'S NUMBER ONE FOOD PLAN....THE PARLIAMENT FOOD PLAN!!!!! SO FRIENDS, GO TO YOUR PHONE RIGHT NOW AND CALL 555-5555. THAT PHONE NUMBER AGAIN, ESPECIALLY FOR YOU GOOD FOLKS HERE IN ROCKFORD IS FIVE-FIVE-FIVE FIVE-FIVE-FIVE-FIVE.   PLEASE PHONE US RIGHT NOW!!!!!!!"

Yes indeed, Diane and Charlie, we were delivering "INFOMERCIALS" fifty years ago. And Diane, please say "Hi" for me, to your husband, Mike Nichols. He and his equally hilarious partner, Elaine May, were guests on my shows when they first started playing the Marienthal brothers clubs in Chicago, and I still play their great ad-lib skits for enthralled listeners.

This essay is titled "Unique Things on the Air." As I continue to write this never-ending book in 2008 I believe this item belongs. This is an amazing story. It concerns my beautiful friend Jane Peterson, her son Harold Peterson, Jr., and Volney Lamb, Jr., or VLJ as his friends call him.

VLJ and I first met in 1956 shortly after Bill O'Connor and I purchased, with financial assistance (a long term loan) from The First National Bank of Terre Haute, Indiana, radio station WBOW. At the time of the purchase it was an NBC affiliate. When that contract expired early in our ownership we did not renew it. That way we divested ourselves of many, many hours of their programming so we could really live up to the true meaning of radio station ownership, and that is, serving the local community. It also meant we would have to add more people, and a young man with a fantastic radio voice, Volney Lamb, Jr., was one of the first new additions to our announcing staff. VLJ did a wonderful job for us and why he was fired I still don't know. But then why have I been fired fourteen times over my 55 years on the air, and why was Sally Jesse Raphael fired FORTY-FOUR times? The answer is, it is a precarious business, and if you (A) roll your eyes in the manager's presence or (B) wear a turtle-neck sweater to work on the coldest below zero night in February or (C) wear white buck shoes on radio, you could be fired. In fact I was fired for A and B. And a man I worked with at WBBM was fired for C.

We all land somewhere else after being fired, and as the years rolled by VLJ and I worked together at three or four more stations. Our final togetherness was in the nineteen-eighties when we were featured program hosts on the original Satellite Music Network. I was fired there too, because I received too much mail from listeners across the five time zones we covered. VLJ was not fired, he quit, so he and his lovely wife could move to a warmer climate. They chose Las Vegas and VLJ landed a job with Harrah's Casino. Which brings us to the astounding part of this narrative.

Jane Peterson's son Harold, a California rancher and construction-engineer, spent an evening at Harrah's enjoying the cultural environment. Upon his return to California he realized his wallet was no longer part of his attire. Meanwhile an employee at Harrah's found Harold Peterson's wallet, saw Jane Peterson's name and phone number in Chicago written in the wallet, and the employee phoned her to tell her he had found the wallet. Jane fully identified herself as Harold's mother, thanked the caller, and said she would phone her son in California and give him the good news. Jane then phoned Harold and told him of the phone call. So Harold phoned Harrah's. He identified his wallet, and profusely thanked the man from Harrah's Casino in Las Vegas. Oh, the man from

Harrah's name? Volney Lamb, Jr., the same man Bill O'Connor and I had hired 50 years earlier at radio station WBOW in Terre Haute, Indiana.

Jane Peterson's son Harold had his wallet returned to him by my friend of over 50 years, Volney Lamb, Jr., VLJ.

And Jane Peterson said, "It is indeed a small world."

REMEMBERING SOME NICE FOLKS WHO CHATTED WITH ME

* Essay 12 *

"Naperville residents never fail to amaze me. Right here in town we have a legend in Chicago radio, Art Hellyer. As host of the number one-rated morning show in the city in the 1950s, Hellyer interviewed the biggest stars in show biz.

"How did he manage the switch from being with celebrities in the city to living in a suburban town? 'Once I got back with my family in Naperville at night, I never gave a thought to who I was with that day.'"
— Susan Blake, Naperville Sun

"For President Johnson and myself, I want to also commend you and thank you for all you've done on your radio shows over the years to further the manufacture of safer automobiles.
— Robert F. Kennedy, U.S. Senator, New York"

One of my favorite radio programs back in the nineteen-thirties was "The WLS National Barn Dance." I've always loved country-western music, and except for Henry Burr and Grace Wilson, who beautifully sang hymns, The Barn Dance performers sang lots of country songs and performed funny and not-so-funny humor. I loved listening to them all...Patsy Montana and the Prairie Ramblers, Louis Massey and The

217

Westerners, featuring her brother Curt, who crooned amazingly like Bing Crosby himself, and Arkie, the Arkansas Woodchopper, Lulubelle and Scotty, Homer and Jethro, and a 12-year-old native Chicagoan, George Gobel. Eight years later Gobel was teaching US Air Corps pilots how to fly the tricky B-26 bomber. There was also a terrific occasional guest guitar player, "Rhubarb Red," who had played with an early Fred Waring orchestra. This young man, who was born Lester Polfus on June 9, 1915, in Waukesha, Wisconsin, self-taught himself the guitar in the early nineteen-twenties, and by the time he was 12 years of age he was highly knowledgeable in electronics, before there was such a word.

I learned all this when I first interviewed this guitar-genius in 1953 on my "Morning Madcap" show on WCFL. I also did not call him Lester or Red, but rather "Les." Les Paul, and his wife Mary Ford, who was sitting alongside him, were chatting with me on the RCA 44 microphone that was on the table between us.

On the wall behind me in "Studio H" in my home, where I am placing this information on material which just a short while ago was a tree in a Green Bay, Wisconsin, forest, is a picture of fellow announcer and dear friend Bill O'Connor and me standing, with Les and Mary snuggled between us.

Les, since childhood had worked on multi-voicing on his guitar and in 1946 Capitol Records invited him to their fabulous tower in Hollywood to record his first six-layered offering. It was a 78rpm single with "Lover" the "A" side backed by "Brazil" on the "B" side, and both sides were tremendous sellers.

Les Paul and singer Mary Ford, nee Colleen Somerset, were married in 1949 and in the short period of time between that event and their first appearance on my show, they had produced some of the biggest song hits in musical history. In the early fifties, coinciding with my Chicago radio debut, Les

Paul's guitar overdubs with Mary doing the vocals enjoyed multi-million sales, and I was one of the major-market DJs who was playing them daily to huge audiences.

1951 saw Les and Mary roar to the top of the charts with "Mockin' Bird Hill," "How High the Moon," and "The World is Waiting for the Sunrise." Then in 1953 their recording of "Vaya con Dios" was the number one hit of the year. I opened the WCFL microphone and harmonized with Mary on the chorus, and I continued to do so for fifty more years. It is one of my all-time favorite recordings.

1953 found Dr. K and me riding the crest of the wave. Our Art Hellyer Show on WCFL would alternate the number one spot in the ratings with Howard Miller's morning show on WIND. I also continued to build my freelancing base and I had over 180 quarter-hours weekly for Downtown Nash and Walgreens Drug Stores on Chicago stations. I would often be heard on seven stations at the same time so I was required to record many, many shows.

I would frequently see Howard Miller in the studio at WIND, where he was also the program director. I remember Howard saying to me one Sunday afternoon as we were both running between shows, "Art, there is no back-stabbing in Chicago. There is plenty of work for all of us; you, me, Bill O'Connor, Mal Bellairs, Marty Faye, Linn Burton, Bill Hamilton, Al Parker. We each have our own sponsors, and we respect each others work. It's fun."

It was true. I loved it. And I would never ever think of taking someone else's show away from him. I was offered shows others were doing but always turned them down.

In addition I was doing shows live on Chicago TV three nights a week, Milwaukee TV one night a week and Rockford TV, at a station out in the middle of a cornfield, where the bathroom facility was an outhouse, and the salesman who sold the show, was, because he sold it, the director and cameraman.

And I can't forget the quick trip to New York on a United Airlines DC6B Sunday evenings to do the sixty-second commercial, for, as I would proudly proclaim "Stoppette, the FIRST ROLL-ON Deodorant" LIVE on "What's My Line?" People would ask me what John Daly, the host, Arlene Francis, Bennett Cerf, Dorothy Kilgallen, Fred Allen, Hal Block, and Steve Allen and the other famous guests were like, and I'd tell them I really didn't know. I just ran into the small offstage announce booth, read the voice-over commercial when the director cued me, and ran out to the elevator and headed for the street.

Then I'd jump into my waiting limo for a quick trip to Newark and the return plane trip to O'Hare arriving approximately 2AM. I'd drive my car to The Furniture Mart where I would grab two hours of shuteye on a sofa in the WCFL lobby. Then I'd start my weekly early morning show all over again on WCFL with Dr. K. Hectic times, frantic times, but fun times, because I loved my work.

I must admit, even though I was in my late twenties and early thirties, my schedule took its toll. There were times when I was in the NBC limo to and/or from Newark Airport to Radio City the chauffeur would pretend to not notice my uncontrollable crying spells.

In Chicago's loop I had a monthly paid-in-advance parking spot in the garage across the street from ABC. But often my spot would be taken by some rude person who couldn't, or wouldn't read the "RESERVED" sign, so I would circle around and around the loop. At times like this, my body would shake all over, inside my skin from head to toe, a problem that returned in 1998 as I helplessly watched Elaine daily, dying of breast cancer, and it remains a major problem to this day.

Broadcasting was always fun for me and a challenge I looked forward to. Getting to and from the broadcasts was the

BIG problem. Driving in from our home was bad enough, but arriving at the gates to the loop and finding a raised bridge was a HORROR. Usually all one could see of the boat was a tiny mast, just tall enough to require bridge tenders like Mike Decina, and his fellow lifters to bring on my tremors. Trembling that would feel so intense and large inside my body I often wondered if I would shake the bridge down. Only we who suffer from anxiety attacks, and panic attacks know how powerful these feelings are.

The average age of death for a broadcaster in our two unions, The American Federation of Television and Radio Artists (AFTRA), and Screen Actors Guild (SAG) during those frantic years, was forty-eight. How I've survived the tension, OUTSIDE the broadcast booth is beyond me. Inside the broadcast booth I would be on edge until the microphone's red light came on. Then a sudden, wonderfully warm feeling came over me.

That is why I loved it most of all when the entire ABC-TV NETWORK COAST TO COAST collapsed in front of my very eyes, and the director was screaming in my ear "Art....do it again...save the GD network." And I would. That was the challenge I waited for. I LOVED IT!! Ask directors, Richie Victor, Johnny Harkins, Herb Cunniff. Johnnie Kern, Howie Shapiro, George Paul (who is now Barbara Walters director on her ABC-TV Network shows)...they remember.

This is not bragging, this is fact. Truth be known, I needed that bolstering because never once during those very busy years did I believe I was any good at my trade. I thought I was (and I would say this on my shows) very lucky to be employed. I always knew I would be fired, wherever I was working, AND I WAS, EVENTUALLY.

Much later the shakes would hit me big time. And, no, they were not the "DTs." I did not drink in those days. I was a teetotaler until my doctor, James Seubold said to me when I was in my mid seventies, "Art, it won't hurt you to have a glass of red wine with your dinner. In fact, it could be good for you." So I now enjoy a goblet or two of Merlot (it sounds romantic, to me), or a Door County, Wisconsin wine.

It was in 1954 that I met the first man in the movies and music I truly idolized, Harry Lillis Crosby, "der Bingo." He was the most popular radio and movie star of the first fifty years of The Twentieth Century, and he sold over half a billion records.

Bing was doing something exceedingly rare for him. He was making a whirlwind national tour promoting his latest movie. And he would grant interviews to only two morning personalities per market, and the interviews "MUST be AFTER 9 AM." The afternoon and evening people were the lucky ones. He would see all of them.

Well, Howard Miller and I often traded places in the ratings for number one in morning drive time, so we would be the ones honored by his august presence. Howard and I actually flipped a coin to see who got him first. I won the toss, so I would have my visitation from 9 to 9:25 AM.

HA!! Mr. Crosby and his entourage of movie and record promotion men, body-guards and hangers-on, showed up at 9:30AM, so I got him for ten minutes, then he was limo'd over to WIND for Howard to have him for maybe ten minutes.

In my allotted time, during which I was blinded by ten minutes of flash bulbs popping, and off-mic comments from his entourage, I managed to ask, maybe three or four questions. Unfortunately the reel-to-reel tape of that event was lost in our massive SOAKIE (Skokie, Illlinois) flood of July 12, 1957, because I would love to refresh my memory of what actually transpired.

I do remember he talked about his new movie, Irving Berlin's "White Christmas," and he talked about his boys on the ranch he owned in Nevada. He also told us he was very strict with his sons. It wasn't until years later we learned just how strict he had been.

But he sure could sing, everything from jazz and country-western to patriotic songs, hymns, show tunes, and pop and Irish ballads. And he was a wonderful Father O'Malley in "Going My Way." And, of course, he was the star of The Kraft Music Hall for ten years in the thirties and forties, when his wonderful sense of humor and his songs, helped get us through the Great Depression and World War Two.

And he loved baseball. For a time Bing was part owner of the Pittsburgh Pirates and Santa Anita Race Track, and he sponsored the Bing Crosby Golf Open, on which my sister Irene was one of the producers in the mid nineteen-fifties. And fittingly, I guess, it was on a golf course in Spain, Harry Lillis (Bing) Crosby died on October 14, 1977.

In his seventy-four years his accomplishments in the musical world and the movies will, in all probability, never again be equaled. Bing was one of a kind, the absolute greatest in his field. Aren't we lucky he lived during our lifetimes?

I emceed the opening of, and I had the pleasure of interviewing two of the stars of the 1956 movie "Around the World in 80 Days," David Niven and Shirley MacLaine and the Academy Award-winning composer of the film's music, Victor Young. It was just Shirley's third movie, in what would blossom into a fantastic career for her.

Shirley's folks named her after Shirley Temple, so she was born to be in show business. She was just twenty-two years old when her gorgeous legs thrilled Broadway show-goers as she flashed them in "The Pajama Game" as the understudy to the lead, Carol Haney. When Carol Haney broke a leg, literally, Shirley took over and endeared herself to the audiences.

I had read that Shirley not only loved baseball, but that she had played baseball and also had been a cheerleader at Washington–Lee High school in Arlington, Virginia, in the late nineteen-forties.

So, with my love for baseball, I started our talk not in a showbiz vein, but rather about our favorite game. Shirley knew not only the names of all the major leaguers in the mid-fifties, but quoted batting and pitching averages, and she told my radio audience and me, Willie Mays was her favorite player. I, of course, told her I had five favorite baseball players: the Chicago White Sox great batsman and shortstop Luke Appling, who won two batting titles during his twenty years with the "Palehose"; Billy Pierce, the classy left-hander of the Sox; and Chicago Cubs third baseman Stan Hack, who always seemed to have a smile on his face no matter what disasters befell the Cubs. And, of course, "The Yankee Clipper," Joe DiMaggio, and the Boston Red Sox' "Splendid Splinter," Ted Williams.

She was married to Steve Parker at that time, and I must say theirs was a strange union. Shirley lived in the Los Angeles area and her husband lived in Tokyo, Japan. I much preferred my marriage where I went home each night to my beautiful wife and children. In fact, in the summertime I would run home between shows and play baseball with Larry and Mike and their friends on the lot I bought next to our home in "Soakie."

Shirley MacLaine's career was in the same stage my broadcast career was in. We were both just getting off the ground. Ahead of her were great successes in movies like "Some Came Running" (1958) for which she received her first Academy Award nomination. In "Ocean's Eleven" (1960), she first appeared with and became an official member of "The Rat Pack" along with Frank Sinatra, Dean Martin, and Sammy Davis, Jr. In "Can-Can" (1960) movie audiences got to see her great dancing legs for the first time. Also in 1960, for "The Apartment" she received her second "Oscar" nomination.

"Irma La Douce" (1963) reunited her with director Billy Wilder and her costar from "The Apartment," Jack Lemmon. This comedy brought her another Academy Award nomination. One of my favorite Shirley MacLaine films would be filmed in 1964, "The Yellow Rolls Royce."

She didn't just play frothy roles. In "The Children's Hour" in 1962, for example, she played a lesbian school teacher. And it was in 1969 she gained a theme song that henceforth would be played every time she would appear on a talk show. The movie was "Sweet Charity." The song was, "If My Friends Could See Me Now." In 1983 she did win the Academy Award for Best Actress, playing Aurora Greenway in "Terms of Endearment."

What do I remember most from our chat that day so many years ago? It was our discussion of her belief in reincarnation, and my remark that wound up our chat. I said, "Shirley, I know my wife Elaine believes reincarnation is highly possible. I don't know if I do or not, but I do know that if there is such a thing, I want to come back as a bull in Montana." As Milton Berle once said to me, "Art, always leave them laughing." Shirley MacLaine left the studio laughing.

George Shearing shared the WCFL microphone with me one morning, and as we ended our most enjoyable get-together he invited me to attend his concert that night at The Civic Opera House. I was to bring Elaine with me and the great jazz pianist who of course was blind, would leave a pass for us at the stage door.

Everything went gloriously, the concert was fabulous, he was gracious in all his comments, he even introduced me to the audience, and he talked about each piece he played and thoroughly charmed the over-flowing house.

When the Chicago Civic Opera House had pretty well

emptied following his brilliant performance, Elaine and I climbed the five or six steps stage right and walked diagonally across the stage to where George Shearing was still seated on the piano bench, chatting with a few admirers.

We were approximately ten feet from the piano when he startled us with, "Hi Art Hellyer, and I assume that is Elaine with you." I must have been stammering in amazement as I said, "Yes, it is I, but how in the world did you know?" George Shearing replied, "I recognized your footsteps from when I heard you walking at the studio this morning. It also helps that you are pigeon-toed."

Years later in the late sixties I was driving my red Volkswagen sunroof sedan home from work in the loop, when I saw a large RV, with the name Fred Lowrey and musical instruments painted on it, parked on the side of the East-West toll road. I had to stop, of course to see if the world-famous blind whistler needed help.

We had never met and as I knocked on the door and asked if the two occupants needed assistance, the tall stocky man said, "Yes, Art, we do, thank you." We had never met but he had heard me on radio and knew my voice.

He and his wife, who was also his driver, had indeed broken down, so I told them I'd send my mechanic, Bob Brinkman, out to the RV, and they could rest at our house. So Mrs. Lowrey sat in back and Fred up front with me. As we drove the ten more miles to my house some interesting things, in addition to his recognizing my voice, occurred.

Fred said to me, "I like your red VW sunroof." I asked how he knew that. He replied, "Well, I can hear the air-cooled engine in the rear, I can feel the breeze and the sun on my head, and I've heard you enough to know a man with your personality would drive a red car." Wow!!! But the best was yet to come.

We were now driving through downtown Naperville,

Illinois, our home since 1962, when Fred startled me big time, saying, "Art I just love those girls in their miniskirts at Burger King."

Most of the girls were wearing miniskirts in those days, but how did he know we were passing a Burger King? "The smell of the burgers. They smell differently than McDonalds and Wendy's." Again WOW!!!

The final straw was when he wanted to buy something at Ace Hardware. The aisles were very narrow, and we also went up and down a long, thin stairway, and he negotiated everything with ease.

I introduced him to the owners Clarence and Jesse Buikema, and they told Fred Lowery how they listened to his remarkable whistling way back in the nineteen thirties when he was featured with "Horace Heidt and his Musical Knights." Art Carney (who later enjoyed tremendous popularity as Jackie Gleason's friend in the sewer, Ed Norton) was a vocalist with Heidt's band. The Buikemas talked about the day I brought Fred Lowery into their hardware store every time I saw them the rest of their lives.

Mr. and Mrs. Fred Lowery stayed at our house that night and he had many calls from NBC in Hollywood, and Chicago. He would call them, and give them our number and have them call back. And he would go up and down our difficult stairwell to the second floor to take the calls. Amazing.

Fred had an icebox full of his favorite Lone Star Beer in the RV, which Bob Brinkman had repaired and driven to our house. He flawlessly kept going out to the RV, and back into the house. He got around much better than I.

Elaine cooked up one of her fabulous steak dinners for the Lowerys and Fred fascinated all of us with a short concert. None of us will ever forget his visit, and his triple-tongued whistling of "Listen to the Mockingbird." and as son Michael just reminded me, "Yellow Bird." Fred Lowery was truly one of a kind…a remarkable virtuoso.

I left the house for my morning show before they were up, and Fred called me during the show to thank me. Then they continued on their cross-country college concert tour.

After that, until his death, Fred Lowery wrote us many nice letters from his home in Palestine (I learned from him, pronounced "Palesteen"), Texas. A chance meeting turned into a longtime friendship.

Back in the very early nineteen-twenties when dance orchestras, later they would be called big bands, were first heard on crystal radio receivers, Paul Whiteman and Ben Pollack became household names. At the same time a young man named Irving Berlin, who was born in Siberia, was making a name for himself as a songwriter. Eventually he would become the greatest popular songwriter who ever lived. Berlin had already had success with songs sung in vaudeville, but now he had a new medium that would present his music to the world…radio AND the dance orchestras.

Irving Berlin was a walking file cabinet of music, and he wrote songs in his head. While dining in a posh New York Restaurant, he would scribble lyrics on the tablecloth and on menus. When he traveled from California to New York and back on trains, he would write songs on Santa Fe and New York Central ticket folders or club car note paper, and when there was no paper available his shirt cuffs would become his writing pad. Queen Elizabeth once whispered to Berlin how much she enjoyed a particular song he had written. After thanking her, he confided, "I wrote that one in the bathtub."

Irving Berlin told me these choice morsels of information on my radio show on WMAQ, NBC Chicago, one Sunday morning in the mid nineteen-fifties.

Hugh Downs was my announcer in those days just before he took his career East. I recall it was a Sunday in 1954 when Hugh told me he was flying to New York that afternoon, and he would be working one week on "The Arlene Francis Radio Show." He'd be back with us the following Sunday. He WAS back the following Sunday, but not at WMAQ, NBC Chicago. He was at his suburban home, winding up all the things one must wind up when one is moving to New York. NBC brass in New York loved him, and hired him, and the rest is history.

May I further digress before getting back to Irving Berlin? Thank you. 1954 found me in my fifth year as a Chicago broadcaster. I was thirty years old, but I was still walking on air. As a child growing up in Chicago and its environs I had dreamed of being a baseball player (every young boys dream), a broadcaster, or a college professor, teaching American history on a small town college campus.

I played baseball while in the Air Force in the Forties, and in the seventies and eighties I would teach on a city campus and a small town campus. Columbia College, Chicago had a HUGE campus... Michigan Boulevard! St. Francis University in Joliet, Illinois fulfilled my boyhood dream of a small college campus.

Elsewhere in this book I talked of my start in radio, so you already know how thrilled and astounded I was to find myself toiling in Chicago radio. And being one of just two freelancers (the other was my dear friend, Bill O'Connor) who passed the AWESOME NBC AUDITION, and was allowed to walk the hallowed halls of NBC, and tap the three metal bars with the special mallet...bong-BONG-bong, and speak the magic words, "This is NBC...the NATIONAL BROADCASTING COMPANY" was almost more than my quivering nervous system could take.

Imagine then how I felt sitting in the, as the sign over the shrines door proclaimed, "NBC ANNOUNCERS ONLY" lounge, talking, as though I belonged there, with Mike Wallace, Dave Garroway, Norman Ross Sr. and other NBC luminaries, and having a very young Hugh Downs as MY

NBC announcer on MY OWN NBC "ART HELLYER SHOW." I am surprised, as I look back, I could even stammer my name each time the engineer opened my microphone.

Now the NBC red light was on and I was chatting one on one with, MY guest, Irving Berlin. AMAZING!!!! ASTOUNDING!!!!!

I recall telling Mr. Berlin I believed "White Christmas" to be the most beautiful song ever written. To which he replied, "I agree. I believe it is the best song ever written by any songwriter." I don't call that ego, I call it stating an irrefutable fact.

And now, Mr. Berlin was inviting me to bring my wife to dinner with him in his suite that very Sunday night, at The Ambassador East Hotel. How did I do these shows without fainting dead away?

It is most unfortunate that I lost the tape of that show, and so many other shows, and pictures (Bob Hope, Dinah Shore, Bing Crosby, Rosemary Clooney, and Milton Berle, who recorded personalized introductions for my shows) in the catastrophic basement flood in our Soakie (Skokie), Illinois home July 12, 1957.

Fortunately the picture of the Lovely Elaine and me with Irving Berlin was not among those destroyed on the wall in our basement family room. That picture was hanging with a small group in our living room, which the filthy seven feet deep waters didn't quite reach.

I don't recall whether or not the visit with Irving Berlin would rank with my better interviews, but I vividly recall the one with a top-ten woman singer, "Her Nibs, Miss Georgia Gibbs."

"Dr. K, TT (Turntable Technician)" would interject voices and sounds liberally throughout the Art Hellyer Show, and the record company reps would duly apprise their expensive artists of this fact before they'd appear on my shows.

Remembering Some Nice Folks Who Chatted with Me

It was not unusual for a woman to shout "Get your dirty, filthy hands off me" or a man to proclaim, "There's no light in the men's room" in between words of a Frank Sinatra song or a Rosemary Clooney song. And Dr. K was a genius at properly placing those voice tracks. I called him "Doctor" because he did his work with a brain surgeon's deft touch.

Well the lady-singer didn't hear it or see it that way when the good doctor operated on her latest release. She let loose a tirade in some language, which I didn't understand. Then she swooped up her mink coat and hurled herself through the door, still shouting. Well, you can't win them all. I never heard from her again.

But I did hear from "My Little Margie," Gale Storm, who appeared on my show the very next day. She wrote,

"Dear Art: I was warned in advance by Dick LaPalm what could and DID happen on your great show. Unlike your guest, Georgia, the day before my appearance, I loved it!!! Keep it up.

"With warm affection, Gale."

Spike Jones made many personal appearances on my show, and each time, he was ready for us. He would bring a HUGE wooden hammer into the studio...you've seen it on his television shows, and he would laugh maniacally while pounding the hammer on the table at which we were seated. Needless to say Dr. K didn't add any of his sounds or voices to Spike's recordings. They were already loaded with them.

My last interview with Jackie Gleason was low-key and poignant. Jackie was appearing in a play at the Blackstone Theatre, and he invited me to have dinner with him, Irv Kupcinet, and a few other Chicago "Pals" in his palatial trailer which was docked behind The Blackstone Hotel. It was a very quiet evening. Drinks were offered, but Jackie had NONE, and he did not look well, nor did he talk much. He was very, very quiet that evening...not the Jackie Gleason we all knew so well. "The Great One" died just a few weeks later.

Jackie Gleason first appeared with me on one of my WCFL shows in the fifties. I was one of the stops on his record-promoting cross-country tour. And it wasn't a comedy album he brought me, but a Capitol 45rpm, Number 4704, "single" recording of his beautiful theme song, which he wrote, "Melancholy Serenade." It was backed with a sentimental narration he also wrote, "Apology at Bedtime." Of course I played his theme song first, and I remember remarking when it ended, "Jackie, I saw 'The Poor Soul' [a Gleason "sadsack" character] in my mind's-eye when I heard that," and he didn't say a word, but gave me that "Poor Soul" look and shrug we all loved so well.

Jackie Gleason on his early 1950s television show not only did a "Honeymooners" skit, but he also portrayed other characters: the afore-mentioned "Poor Soul," "Joe the Bartender," "The Loudmouth," "Fenwick Babbitt," "Rudy the Repairman," and my favorite, "Reggie Van Gleason III."

Reggie would semi-stagger into his parents fancy drawing room attired in formal dress, donned in a large top-hat, while twirling his walking-stick. Lionel train tracks ran the length of the rear wall of the room and Reggie would push a button. A Lionel 4-6-4 Hudson steam locomotive would chug into the room, pulling a string of gondola freight cars. The gondolas each contained a whiskey bottle.

Reggie would select a bottle, take a drinking glass from another freight car, and then pour himself a long one. I loved to watch Reggie's facial expressions as he poured, then took a long sip followed by the words we all were waiting for, "Mmmmm!! That's Good Booze!!"

Needless to say, "Apology at Bedtime" became over the years one of my most-played on the air recordings. And I had many heated discussions with managers and program directors who objected to my playing it, because "It's not music.

Listeners turn the station off when they don't hear music," or "That thing is too sentimental." My answer always was, "The world needs more heartwarming sentimentality."

I am holding in my hand, as I write this, a beautiful portrait of Jackie in a gray jacket with a gorgeous red carnation in its buttonhole. He is leaning forward deep in thought, with his left hand curved against his chin. He wrote on it, "To Art—Thanks, Pal, for everything. My Best Wishes, Jackie Gleason." The world lost the greatest when he left us.

8 AM, June 8, 1966, I opened my daily show that ran to 4PM announcing to the large, Midwestern-states audience we had on one-hundred-thousand-watt WOPA-FM, that Jimmy Durante would be my guest. "The Lovely Elaine" and I had been his guests the preceding night at his delightful show in The Empire Room of The Palmer House.

At 8:03AM Lucille Lawrence waved to me from the other side of the control room window to pick up the phone. I did so, and I heard Jimmy Durante's most distinctively recognizable in the world voice, and we started talking as though we'd always been talking. The way old friends who haven't seen each other in years talk, yet this was our first ever on-the-air conversation. Only a few people I talked to over my fifty-five years on the air had that rare quality Jimmy Durante was blessed with. Perry Como had it, Spike Jones had it, Dinah Shore, Nat "King" Cole, George Gobel, Dean Martin, Bing Crosby and Harry Truman had it too. And my best friends in broadcasting, Dr. Lenny Kaye, Bill O'Connor, Al Parker, Chuck Schaden, John Russell Ghrist and Ralph Sherman had/have that rare talent too, of making me feel I had never been away from them. Sitting and talking with those wonderful people was as though we'd always been sitting there and talking.

First, of course, I thanked Jimmy Durante, after having done two full shows the prior night, for coming on my show so early in the morning. His reply was, as I'm listening to the tape in my headphones as I write this in June 2007, "Oh! Art I promised you I would call you right at eight o'clock, and I always keep my promises."

Then he went into an almost melancholy rendition of his theme song, "Inka-Dinka-Doo." I asked why he had sung it that way, and he just quietly said, "I don't know Art. I guess because it's early in the morning, and it got me remembering what it was like a long, long time ago, a time Art when 'The Schnozzola' was a very young man. You know, Art, those were tough times. I didn't know from day to day if I'd have any food to eat, and some days I didn't. But you know Art, I wouldn't trade those days for all the gold in Fort Knox." My next question was about Jimmy Durante's formidable proboscis. "Jimmy, is it true your nose is insured?" Jimmy, always very modest, answered me: "Oh! Art, you know how it is in Hollywood. Back in 1930 or 1931 I was making my second movie, 'The New Adventures of Get-Rich-Quick Wallingford' and the director Sam Wood, you remember him Art, heard someone call me 'Schnozzola,' and he asked me if my nose was insured. Well, Art, I barely had enough money in those days to insure the rest of my body. So I told him I did not have my nose insured. Then a few days later I read in one of the Hollywood columns that my nose was insured with, was insured with, Oh Art, a big London insurance company, I can't think of the name now. That was a long time ago." I said, "Lloyds of London, Jim?" Jimmy Durante softly replied, "Yeah Art, that was it. Can you imagine the studio insured my nose for a million dollars (long pause). They insured my nose for a million."

Jimmy Durante was on the verge of tears as he remembered Lou Clayton, and Eddie Jackson, who teamed with Durante as a vaudeville team that was formed in the mid-nineteen twenties, and then starred on Broadway during the early years of the Great Depression.

For those approximately forty-five minutes or so I had the nicest chat I ever had with a major celebrity. Jimmy Durante was sentimental. He talked about everything, beginning with his days in vaudeville when he was billed as "Ragtime Jimmy" for his piano-playing style, and his very early recordings as World War One was ending, with Jimmy Durante's Jazz Band. He was a jazz pioneer, one of the very first to record jazz music.

Jimmy had worked very late the prior night, and he was not a young man, so I decided to wind things up by asking him about his signature close on his night club, radio and television shows, "Goodnight, Mrs. Calabash." I had heard him asked this question many times on programs, and I often heard different answers. This is how Jimmy Durante answered me, "Well, Art I had just finished an engagement at The Chez Paree in Chicago, and my wife and I were driving back to California, when in western Illinois we saw this sign on a pretty little town called 'Calabash' and I decided right then to say goodnight on all my shows to 'Mrs. Calabash.'"

That's the way my interview with Jimmy Durante concluded, and to this day I've never found "Calabash, Illinois" on any Illinois roadmap.

The pleasant-faced man with a friendly smile was waving an LP in his right hand as he tapped gently on the inner sound lock door of my WCFL morning show studio. I peered through the small glass window in the door at a face I did not recognize. I pulled the door open, and a voice from behind the young man in the gray suit, white shirt and tie, greeted me. It was one of the free lance Chicago song-pluggers, Paul Gallis (who is Chicago's last song-plugger as I write this in the year 2007). This was a scene that was reenacted hundreds of times over the fifty-five years I was a broadcasting personality (I've never liked being called a DeeJay, remember). In a moment

Paul would introduce us, "Art Hellyer shake hands with Deacon Andy...we hope you'll play his first album."

I invited the "Deacon" to sit on the chair right across from me with the RCA microphone hanging down between us from the overhead boom. I welcomed him, at the same time, taking from him the vinyl LP in its colorful jacket.

The song playing on the air was ending. I gave Dr. K and Ernie the "fade to background and open the mic" hand signals. After I backsold (gave the title) the prior song and gave the time and temperature, A MUST ON MORNING DRIVE TIME SHOWS, and gave the station's call letters and spot on the dial, a station requirement, and ANOTHER MUST ON MORNING DRIVE TIME SHOWS, I turned to my guest.

I asked the good Deacon if he had a last name. This is what he actually said, in a very pleasant country voice, "Ah do sir, yes indeedy sir, ah do ...last name's Griffith....Full name sir, is Andy Griffith." Meeting him for the first time and hearing him speak, I had no idea he had a degree in music from The University of North Carolina at Chapel Hill.

I am looking at a picture that was taken of us at that moment. I was born August 7, 1923, and I would later discover Andrew Samuel Griffith first appeared on the world scene on June 1, 1926, so he was just three years younger than I. We were really just two kids meeting for the first, but certainly not, the last time, on a 50,000-watt station in what was then the nation's number two market.

Dr. K was, as always rummaging through stacks of records, and engineer Ernie Nottger to my right, behind the control room glass, was munching on a doughnut and reading the morning paper. Hellyer was about to play a song by another song-pluggers guest, another guy we never heard of. Big deal!

Well, friends in radio-land it WAS a "big deal." Dr. K smiled, always a good sign, and Ernie put the sports section down and we had a wonderful time listening to, for the first time on Chicago radio, Andy Griffith's "What it Was, Was Football." But the biggest indication of having discovered a real winner was when Dr. K did not embellish it with a single burp or voice track.

There were other comedy bits Deacon Andy Griffith had also written for this first album. His countrified version of Shakespeare's "Romeo and Juliet" for example, but the hit was definitely "What it Was, Was Football."

Just three years later the former "Deacon" became the Toast of Broadway as he starred in the play, "No Time for Sergeants," for which he received a Tony nomination. In 1957 Andy Griffith stunned movie viewers in his very first movie "A Face in the Crowd," a role for which I felt he should have won the "Best Actor Oscar." No one has ever done a better job portraying a despicable human-being. If you've not seen this film, put my book down right this moment, and run out and rent it. I consider it one of Hollywood's classics.

As the years following our meeting that day in 1952 rapidly flew by, Andy Griffith became one of the most beloved stars in television history. I am thrilled to have had him on my show before he burst on the national scene.

For years I received a Christmas card from the "Deacon," but these stopped after he contracted Guillain-Barre Syndrome, a most debilitating illness, in 1983. I continue to send him a card each Christmas at his home in Manteo, North Carolina, and wish him many, many more years. In 2007 Andy played an important role in the poignant movie "Waitress" and I feel he should have been nominated for "Best Supporting Actor." I am sure "The Andy Griffith Show" and his "Matlock" shows will be seen in reruns for centuries to come.

Late in the sixties I was driving home alone from Branson, Missouri, where over the years we had purchased some acreage, and as I neared Kansas City, Missouri, I thought it would be nice to stop at The Truman Museum in Independence. The size of it surprised me as I drove into the parking lot, and once inside I noticed that Captain Harry S Truman's 1903 Springfield rifle had no bayonet. I had one hanging on a wall at home, so I thought I should offer to donate it to the museum. Then LIGHTBULB! Why not drive over to his home and present the idea to someone, hopefully, the President himself? Well, I can dream can't I?

I drove past the big old Truman house at 219 N. Delaware and decided to look for a parking spot in the next block. As I sat thinking about how I should do this, a four-door Chrysler pulled in the drive in back of the house. I expected to see a chauffeur and secret service people alight, but my goodness, Bess Truman, the Presidents wife stepped out of the drivers seat. As she started pulling bags of groceries from the car...Another LIGHTBULB!!!! I would offer to assist her and perhaps gain entrance to the house.

I half ran up Delaware Street. I didn't want to frighten her or seem too anxious. Then I slowly walked up the drive waving my ABC-TV press pass. I introduced myself and found myself offering to help her carry in the TRUMAN groceries. I amazed even myself. What was I doing? This was my favorite PRESIDENT'S WIFE! Ye Gods! This was the wife of the man who succeeded President Franklin Delano Roosevelt, the man who guided us through World War Two, and then died in his fourth term on April 12, 1945 as the beloved leader of the Free World, just a bit too early to share with us the winning of the war that saved the world.

My knees were shaking. I'm sure I stammered as I assured Mrs. Truman, in answer to her question, I had no recording equipment with me. Thank goodness, I had left them back in my station wagon. I also told her of the 1903 Springfield Rifle bayonet I had at home and how I'd like to

Remembering Some Nice Folks Who Chatted with Me

tell the President I would like to donate it to his museum, and how I would love to shake the President's hand. I must have been babbling. Even with all my years on radio and TV I was still awestruck in the presence of great people.

I was shaky and babbling in 1965 in Robert Kennedy's inner office when he was showing Elaine and me his brother's Presidential desk, and his and Ethel's children's homework on his office walls, and my hands were shaking as I took a picture of Elaine and him. I was shaking now as Mrs. Truman and I ascended the three or four steps to the back door.

I couldn't help but note this was just like tens of thousands of middle-class American homes—wooden outer door, then a vestibule with coats and hats hanging on hooks, boots on the floor, a broom, a mop, etc. Then I looked through the glass of the inner door, into a typical American kitchen...and, I couldn't believe it, I was putting two bags of groceries on President Truman's.....YES, PRESIDENT HARRY S TRUMAN'S...kitchen table, and helping Mrs. Truman with her bags.

Then I heard a familiar voice saying, "Who's that with you?" And Bess Truman replied, "This young man is from ABC in Chicago and he'd like to make a donation to the museum." Now I was in BIG trouble. The President would now be expecting a monetary endowment. All I was going to offer him was an old bayonet.

He stepped into the hallway I had seen as I came into the kitchen, and invited me to come forward to his small den on the side of the hallway. He had a nice friendly smile on his face as HE extended his right hand. In HIS home I was shaking hands with the 33rd President of the United States, who then invited me to sit with him and chat for awhile.

I told him about the bayonet, talked about the newspapers he had on his desk. "Each day I read three newspapers, the *New York Times* for the Liberal side, the *Chicago Tribune* for the Conservative side, and the *Oakland Tribune* for down-the-middle news."

The atomic bombing of Japan? "I prayed over this...I talked with all our military leaders...with the other leaders of the Free World, and we were all in agreement...we dropped millions of leaflets on Japan....we did everything we could to end the war without atomic bombs....Japan refused to surrender, and our studies showed that if we invaded Japan, another million to two million American and Japanese lives could be lost, so we had no choice."

I asked him how he must have felt, assuming the presidency following the death of President Franklin Delano Roosevelt, "I felt as if the sun, the moon and all the stars had fallen on me."

"What was the toughest decision you ever had to make Mr. President?" Without a moments hesitation, President Truman replied, "Korea."

The last question I asked him was about the Truman family departure from Washington. Why, in the world did they drive back to Independence? President Harry S Truman's reply, "We didn't have much money, so Bess, Margaret and I climbed into our car and drove home. It was that simple." Truth is the only income the Truman's had was his Army pension of $112.00 per month. I told Mr. Truman I found that amazing, and he said, "One has to do what one has to do."

Looking back on his administration in those months following the war I realized that it was that philosophy that got him, the United States of America and the world through that most turbulent time in the history of the world.

Those, and the man's high degree of integrity, are just some of the reasons Harry Truman is my all-time favorite president of my lifetime.

I did not ask Mr. Truman about a story I had heard years earlier: The President and Mrs. Truman were at an important state dinner, and one of the wives in attendance said to Mrs. Truman, "Can you get the president to STOP using the word manure so much?" Mrs. Truman replied, "You don't know how long it took me to make him START saying it."

I wanted to ask him if that was a true story, but our conversation was of a very serious nature, and I just didn't feel it would be appropriate.

I asked him if I might have a personally autographed picture. He said he had no pictures there, but would mail one to me. It arrived shortly after I arrived home.

As I was taking my leave, something extremely poignant happened as the President and I went out on his front porch together. After I called a heartfelt "Thank you" to Mrs. Truman, and as I started down the steps, Mr. Truman said to me, "Watch out for that third step...we must get that fixed." Then as I walked up Delaware Street to my car I turned around to look one last time back at the house, and there was President Harry S Truman, leaning with his left hand on his cane...WAVING TO ME!!!

If I live to be one hundred years old, I shall never forget that moment.

It was because of Mr. Truman's plight, the Congress voted to begin presidential pensions. This information spurred me to dig out my high school American History books, and check presidents prior to Mr. Truman to see how they fared.

When "The Father of Our Country," George Washington, left office, he commanded the army. James Monroe, whose law office I've been in with my family, in Fredericksburg, Virginia, sold books door-to-door, which puts me in good company. I sold Encyclopaedia Britannica door-to-door.

Millard Fillmore had the strangest job of all the former presidents. The only employment he could get was reading Shakespeare aloud to the workers in a New York shoe factory. Why in the world, the owners of a shoe factory would want someone to read The Bards words to the workers my history book didn't say. There were no loud-speaker systems then, so how did Mr. Fillmore project his voice? Perhaps he just strolled up and down the aisles as he read, and perhaps portrayed "Hamlet," "Shylock," and "Romeo and Juliet." It certainly gives us something to think about, doesn't it? At least they had jobs.

The victorious leader of the Union Army in the U.S. Civil War, and then, President of the United States of America, Ulysses Simpson Grant, declared bankruptcy when he left office.

Some time later, I had a presidential interview on my home grounds at WLS-TV Chicago. It was with Richard Milhous Nixon, and the Ch.7 crew and half a hundred or so secret service men gathered in Studio B at 3:30PM.

I've always preferred to ad-lib interviews, but two members of the news writers union had prepared some questions, so when they handed them to me I read them, then dropped them in one of the waste baskets in the corner.

At that very moment the President entered the studio surrounded by another half hundred or so secret service men. Mr. Nixon brushed against me just as I was dropping the news writers papers in the basket, and when we sat down across the table from each other, he leaned forward and softly said to me, "I know you threw out some papers about me. What did they say?" I told him they were questions written by the news department, and I preferred not to use them. He whispered "Why?" I softly replied, "I prefer to ask my own questions?" He looked at me, with the quizzical expression we all remember so well, and then said "Oh." That was it…"Oh."

For a few moments before we started the interview I thought about what he said, and decided all the things I had read about him must be true. He must be haunted day and night thinking everyone is talking about him. He must be as insecure as many writers and broadcasters say he is, and as most broadcasters are too.

Now the tape was rolling, "Standby Art...Five, Four, Three, Two, One." I took the cue from Jerry Kupcinet, the stage manager. The President and I had exchanged no more than three questions and answers when he leaned forward, wrapped his hand tightly around my left wrist and said softly to me..."I have to take a _ _ _ _. Where's the men's room?" I have a picture that was taken of us the moment he finished the last word of his question, and you can see he has just sounded the "T" at the end of the word.

When he finally came out it was too late to finish our interview because he was scheduled someplace else and was already late. So what was quite possibly the shortest sit-down studio presidential interview in history didn't take up much time on the ABC-TV Network 5:30PM CST newscast that day.

I wrote Mr. Nixon a personal note in 1985 following surgery he had, and received this interesting and most informative answer:

"RICHARD NIXON
26 Federal Plaza
New York City

August 20, 1985

"Dear Mr. Hellyer:

It was most thoughtful of you to remember me as you did with regard to news reports of my well-publicized operation.

"A skin tumor is nothing to get particularly excited about except that in this case it was behind the ear and was extremely large. Now that it has been removed there are no after effects whatever except for a rather prominent scar.

"The doctor tells me that he would like to graft some skin on it so that it would look better but I vetoed that idea since most people will see me from the front and not from the back.

"Mrs. Nixon joins me in sending you our very best wishes.

Sincerely,
Richard Nixon"

Fred Kasper, Charles Homer Bill, Wayne Atkinson and I were, over a period of some eight years, the ABC RADIO NETWORK announcers on Paul Harvey's various daily shows.

On one occasion Chuck Bill broke himself up right at the top of a thirty-second network promo, and as he got deeper into the announcement, he struggled even more, until finally, this possessor of one of the greatest laughs in broadcast history just broke wide open, and if I recall it correctly, he finally blurted out for all fifty states, and Canada and Mexico to hear, "Mother warned me there would be days like this."

Paul Harvey, who always maintained that stentorian, dignified, super-cool manner almost came unstrung himself as he watched Chuck, convulsing with laughter at the upright RCA microphone. I've always liked Mr. Harvey and certainly enjoyed working alongside him on his shows.

The thing I most like about Paul Harvey is his complete devotion to his lovely wife, Angel. On one occasion she was in the studio with him as I walked in at 10:58 AM for the daily 11:00 AM broadcast. Paul had to leave for the airport immediately after the program, so he turned to Angel and asked, "Would you rather have a two minute kiss now, or a ten second one after the show?" She, obviously just as devoted to him, chose the former.

One warm Spring day in 1969, song-plugger Dick LaPalm

knocked on the window glass in Studio B at WLS-FM, and pointed at the young couple standing alongside him, a smiling young man with a black Poncho Villa mustache, and a dour, hawk-faced young woman.

I waved to Dick to come into the studio and he introduced me to Sonny and Cher. They spent the better part of two hours seated across from me at the small table the station had deemed "The Interview Table." In fact we were in such close proximity that I found Cher constantly playing "kneesy" with me. Sonny didn't seem the least bit aware of the game going on beneath the table and I enjoyed his witty and casual style far more than I enjoyed Cher's bony knees.

Her answers to my questions left much to be desired. She didn't seem the least bit interested, and I just assumed my questions were boring her. Sonny's self-deprecating replies were refreshing. He certainly was not your typical shallow celebrity. He was very, very interesting and a really nice guy. Salvatore Bono was born February 16, 1935, of poor Sicilian immigrants, in Detroit, Michigan. His family moved to Los Angeles when Sonny was seven, and he admitted he hated school, and dropped out when in high school. He worked as a construction worker and a truck driver, and he would frequently pull the huge truck he was driving over to the side of the road, and he would write songs. He said that in his early twenties song-writing became his all-consuming passion, so he talked himself into a low paying job with Specialty Records where he met famed record-producer Phil Spector, and sang as a back up singer with the Righteous Brothers, Little Richard and Sam Cooke.

The low-paying job was about to pay-off. It was there he met a teenager named Cherilyn Sarkisian. She called herself "Cher" and they recorded songs like "Just You" and "Needles and Pins," and others that had modest success. In 1965 Sonny wrote a love song, "I Got You Babe" and they had a monstrous hit. Sonny told me he wrote that song because he was inspired by his love for Cher. This was still very early in their careers, and Dr. K cued up the one song they brought me, and then played "I Got You Babe." Sonny looked at Ralph Davis, my WLS-FM engineer, and pointed his cue-finger at the microphone. Ralph opened the mic and Cher really came to life. She jumped up, then Sonny joined her, and they sang a duet with themselves right there on my show.

That was the high spot of the interview, and as we wound it up I asked them if they would send each of our five children an autographed picture. They assured me they would and Sonny, in his bell-bottom pants, left the studio. He was followed by Cher in very high heels, and a very short mini-skirt wiggling its way through the door. The kids never did get their Sonny and Cher pictures, but many years later I received, out of the blue, an autographed picture from Sonny when he was a United States congressman from California. I believe anyone who ever met Sonny Bono would say he was a very nice person. A very decent human being. The sad way his life ended touched me deeply.

Rocky Rolf, RCA Victor's Midwest A&R man appeared at the door. With him was Freddy Martin's featured vocalist, Merv Griffin. I was doing my afternoon show at WMIL ("WMIL Means Milwaukee") in early 1950. I shook hands with Merv, and Rocky handed me a 78rpm copy of "I've Got a Loverly Bunch of Coconuts," Martins latest recording with Merv's vocal in a cockney accent. Merv's nightly appearances with Martin's band were rarely in the same city two nights in a row, and it was a tough job. I, of course got some background information from Merv. Where was he born, how did it all start, and so on?

Merv was born in San Mateo, California and entered many local talent shows as a teenager. Some he won and some he lost, but one of them landed him a job at radio station

Remembering Some Nice Folks Who Chatted with Me

KFRC in San Francisco as the male staff vocalist. Back then, most larger stations had a house orchestra. I was the announcer with Jack Kelly's house orchestra in late-1950 to 1955 at WCFL, Chicago, for example.

A strange thing happened during our visit. A young lady called the station and asked to speak to me. This was 15 years before two-way radio-telephone conversations were put on the airwaves. While Merv's newest tune was playing I picked up the phone and heard, "Art, I'm engaged to Merv, I'd like to speak to him." I covered the phone with my hand and gave Merv the message. When he whispered to me he certainly was NOT engaged to anyone from Milwaukee, rather than get caught in the middle of who knows what, I said he had gone to the men's room.

Since I interviewed Merv Griffin in 1950, among other things he has: syndicated the two most successful game shows in television history, "Jeopardy" and "Wheel of Fortune," hosted his multi-Emmy award winning "Merv Griffin Show," and sold his production company to Coca-Cola for two hundred fifty million dollars.

And there's more. He owns the Beverly Hilton Hotel in Hollywood, and the Hilton Scottsdale Resort, and St. Clerans Manor in Galway, Ireland, and Merv Griffin's Resort Hotel and Givenchy Spa in Palm Springs, and....Well, there's so much more it would fill a book.

Suffice it to say, Merv Griffin has done quite well since he appeared as a low-paid big band singer on my show in early 1950. In fact, today, he is a multi-billionaire. Which gets me thinking: All the people who appeared on my shows over the years are now enormously wealthy. Maybe I should send them each a small bill for my promotional efforts. Nope, I'm not that way. God Bless them all for their great achievements and for all the happiness they've brought into hundreds of millions of lives.

DOOR-TO-DOOR
SELLING

* Essay 13 *

"Can you imagine opening your front door and seeing Art Hellyer standing there holding a Fuller Brush in his hand? Well, he was a great salesman on radio and television, and I'm sure he did very well door to door."
— *Shirley Hamilton,*
President of Chicago's number-one talent agency

"My compliments to you Art, for sending such wonderful students to our Atlantic Airline Schools. You have done a fine job in enrolling only the best students available. Believe me, your efforts are greatly appreciated.   Sincerely,
Dr. Eugene Auerbach, Director of Education, Atlantic Schools"

"Dear Art: Just a line to welcome you to the Britannica organization and congratulate you on your initial sales.
I am one of your many television admirers and have enjoyed many a chuckle over your plugs describing, in your special double-talk, some of the various and obscure portions of an automobiles anatomy. Cordially,
Dr. J. C. Bradley, President, Chicago EB Region, 11/25/58"

Having been unemployed many times in my chosen field of work, Radio and Television broadcasting, early on, I realized if I were to keep the wolf from the door, I'd best develop myself in a second field. It could not be any field of permanency, because I loved broadcasting, I just didn't like the pompous jerks who ran it.

As early as age twelve I was a salesman in a small privately owned sporting goods store in my hometown Elmhurst, Illinois. I felt I could meet people well, talk knowledgably about the sports most people followed in the thirties....Babe Ruth, Lou Gehrig and baseball, the Bears, Green Bay and Washington, Red Grange, Knute Rockne in football, and the great Joe Louis who for years after he defeated Jimmy Braddock WAS boxing. Bowling was the most popular community sport in the thirties, and the two Willies, Hoppe and Mosconi ruled in billiards. The Kentucky Derby, The Preakness, The Santa Anita Handicap, Seabiscuit and War Admiral were the biggest names in horseracing,

I discovered as a young kid if I could sell *myself*, selling the product would be a breeze, so I just talked sports, and sold more bats, balls, gloves, wooden shaft golf clubs, and 8- to 16-pound bowling balls than the store owner did. In fact, I didn't know if he meant it or not, but more than once he offered to sell me the store on any terms I could handle. Big Deal!! I never had enough money as a kid to buy ten Penny baseball card gum packs at one time.

So the first time I was fired by a radio station in Milwaukee I decided to put this selling ability I believed I had, to work. I looked through the Milwaukee newspapers "Help Wanted. Door to Door Salesmen" ads. Back in 1948 this was an equal opportunity field, perhaps the first, and women sold door to door too, AND received the same pay as did the men. Oh! This is important. Never sell on a set weekly pay basis. And don't take a draw. Always work for COMMISSION ONLY. You will find this is the way to really make money in sales.

And remember there are a lot of write-offs at income tax

time: gasoline costs, toll-road fees, motel costs, postage, and automobile wear and tear. And there is a great deal of that. One year I drove 129,000 miles and never left Illinois, Indiana, Wisconsin and Michigan.

I answered an ad for THE COLUMBIA SCHOOL OF MUSIC with their offices and classrooms in a small building on the far west side of Milwaukee. I had a short talk with Mrs. Gill, the dean. I filled out some papers and I was given a kit with my sales materials. I would start work at 8 AM the next morning.

So help me! Promptly at 8 AM the next morning, the sales staff (about ten of us), the dean and her office staff (two young ladies), and two music instructors stood in a semi-circle around the school's beat-up, upright piano, and as Dean Gill tickled the ivories, we sang The Columbia School of Music FIGHT song. And then the Alma Mater...the former to the tune of "Go You Northwestern" the latter to the tune of the Yale University "Whiffenpoof Song."

Then the hard stuff started. Each salesperson would purchase "Leads" from Dean Gill. Each lead cost ten cents and was nothing more than a phone number the dean copied at random from the Milwaukee phone book. She recommended we each purchase FIFTY LEADS each day. This not only lined her purse early each day, but we really needed to make fifty phone calls each to tackle phase two of operation "Sell Accordion Lessons" as I dubbed it. Each phone call was very brief. "Good Morning, Mrs. Mosakowalski, my name is Art Hellyer. I am calling you to ask if there are any children of school age in your home. Ah...three...that's fine...may I have their ages please? Nine, eleven, and thirteen...excellent. And do they have an interest in music? Fine, fine. Now Mrs. Mosakowalski I have been asked by Dean Gill of the Columbia School of Music to select just three children from your area for musical training at our famous school right here in Milwaukee. I must meet with and test your children to see if they meet our extremely high standards and I will be in your area this evening. Now what time do you folks finish eating dinner? Six-Thirty…that's just fine…I am looking forward to meeting you and your fine family at six-thirty this evening, and I will do my very best to help them qualify for our superb musical training. Thank you! Goodbye." And the dean and her staff called that "A qualified lead." Yeah!

It took the rest of the morning to phone my "leads," and if I were lucky I would have three to four appointments set up for that evening with "Qualified Leads." The appointments would start as early as 3 or 3:30PM, and could run as late as 10:30 or 11PM. Some nights I came home with two to four sales, many nights the houses were all dark (they were there, but hiding), and other nights I would just want to hang myself. It was a tough job!!!!!

Upon arriving at the "Qualified Lead" I would go to the door, introduce myself and show my State of Wisconsin school representative license. Then I would quickly walk into the living room and place my hat, coat and bags where I did not want my hosts sitting, and I would make sure everyone in the house was present. This is crucial because many a promising sale has been lost when Uncle Barney comes up from the basement halfway through the presentation, and not knowing a thing about the subject, says, "That's no good. Say goodnite girls and go to bed." Sometimes the spoiler will remain, but often he will move on, firing one last shot. "Franny you remember the Thompsons? A slick talker like this guy cost them their life's savings."

I've even gone into the kitchen when grandma's been washing the dishes, and I've dried those dishes, then conducted her into the living room telling everyone, "We don't want grandma to miss a word Mary Ann, because this is a big moment in your life. We could be determining your entire future here tonight. Don't you agree, grandma?" And she always says "Yes" which very much helps my cause. They all listen to grandma.

Many times when well into my presentation, whether it was music lessons, the airline training school I repped, the Encyclopaedia Britannica, the Winfield China Company of California, or International Correspondence Schools, if the telephone would ring I, yes, I would answer it, and explain to the caller, in the case of the schools or Britannica, "We are determining Mary Ann's future RIGHT NOW. She would like you to call back in about an hour. Thank you. Goodbye." If I picked up the phone while doing the china presentation I would explain I was helping the family beautify the house, and especially the dinner table and the folks would call back after I had left their dining facilities the nicest in the area with the South Pacific blue china.

I also made sure that somewhere in my Winfield China presentation I would "accidentally" drop two or three plates on the floor, then bounce them off each other as I clumsily picked them up. The women, in particular would be horrified, until I assured them. "because only Winfield, among the world's finest bone china makers, kiln-bake all their greenware at 2400 degrees for seven days, it just does not break or chip, and all Winfield fine china is guaranteed for one hundred years from the day you buy it." Then I would take from the large bag I carried, a section of railroad tie, and pound large steel nails into the hardwood with a Winfield China coffee cup. Believe me, I sold an awful lot of Winfield China. I even sold myself and purchased a beautiful Willow set for Elaine. I paid for it on time, of course. As I write this in 2007 that set is still used for all the fancy holiday dinners.

But, not every experience was a good one. I appeared one evening in Milwaukee for a scheduled music school appointment at a garden apartment, a fancy name for housing that's down below the frostline. I came down the three steps to the front door, rang the bell, and as a swarthy man covered with tattoos opened the screen door a bit I grabbed it and started for the living room all the while pleasantly introducing myself and telling the man how pleased his wife had seemed when I talked to her earlier in the day, when all of a sudden with one hand he grabbed the collar of my coat and his other hand clamped down on my belt at my lower back and he ran me straight through the living room, the dining room and the kitchen. Then with an amazing display of power he chucked me out through the back screen door....all of this occurring much faster than it just took me to type it. I had also dropped my bag somewhere during the wild heave-ho, but I didn't have to search long for it, because a moment later it too sailed through the screen door and almost knocked me cold as it bounced off my head. I decided to not try to go back in and sell them accordion lessons.

I only sold products or services I knew were legitimate. I always checked them out with the local Better Business Bureau, and/or the chamber of commerce. When one did not get a good review from them I went on to the next ad. And I always made more money in sales than I ever made in radio-TV, but when a station offered me a job I took it. Only those in broadcasting know why!!

One cold wintry Thursday night I had seven appointments, and I sold them all. Dean Gill told me before the next morning's songfest that I had set a record for sales in one day, and for me they came at just the right time. Elaine's parents were spending a few days with us at our small apartment at 5171 N. Teutonia, and I made big points when they picked me up after 11PM after my final sale. I had my father-in-law stop at a National Food store. Years later I would be National's radio and TV spokesman, but that never entered my mind as I bought two huge steaks, which Elaine broiled for us shortly after midnight as we celebrated the biggest money day I'd ever had. It was more than I'd ever made in a week on radio. That was a nice warm feeling on a very cold Wisconsin night.

Another below zero night found me on a dark farm road outside historic Galena, Illinois, the former hometown of Civil War General, later President, Ulysses Simpson Grant. I had just left a remotely located farm where I had failed to convince the farmer's daughter's father, who was exhausted from a day in his frigid fields, that Mary Ann would be far better off and much happier working for an airline. And though I could not legally guarantee her a job after she studied with us, our rate of success employing our graduates was the highest in the airline training school field.

Poor Mary Ann had been slobbering into her hankie for well over an hour, and who knows what other orifices were also leaking with emotion. She wanted more than anything else, like so many other young people whom I'd interviewed, to leave farm life forever behind her, and to live in a big, noisy, swinging city. And her mom just wanted Mary Ann to be happy. Farmer Brown was our problem here. He wanted his daughter to marry some big ole farm boy, and spend her life toiling on a farm as her poor mom had done. And I wanted Mary Ann to just stop her terrible bawling. Farming is a very tough life. I know from experience from my one summer living in the Hartsings' bunkhouse, and staggering blindly around in the middle of the night trying to console a cow with painfully swollen teats.

And now we had a new member of the family appearing at absolutely the worst possible time. It was my time to close the sale. I had given the complete presentation, when who should appear, but Uncle Louie, bombed to the gills. I knew this was it. Uncle Louie would blast the school, and probably throw me out. But he didn't. He said, in a slurring manner that if this was what Mary Ann wanted HE would pay for the entire course. And he wrote a check to the school for the full amount of the course. WOW!!! Usually I got a small down payment, which up to twenty dollars was my commission. This was a first for me. A coup, WOW!!!!

Ten days later the school called and left a message with my answering service, "Sorry Art, Uncle Louie's check bounced. Please run out to Galena and see what you can do about it." I had appointments scheduled in Dubuque, Iowa within the week, so I stopped at Mary Ann's farmhouse which was somewhat on the way. After I knocked on the door, I could hear movement inside the house, but no one came to the door. And as I drove down the long drive, I looked back and saw the final clue every door-to-door salesperson has seen many times. The curtain in the front room was pulled back and someone was peeking out, probably that damn Uncle Louie.

Yet another frigid winter's night found me in Elkhart, Indiana, the home of Alka-Seltzer and most of the trailer manufacturers in the United States. I was frustrated, having met only dark houses earlier in the evening, as people huddled in their homes hiding from the dreaded door-to-door salesman pounding at their latch. It is hard to find that your final appointment of the evening awaits you in a ramshackle, tar-papered-roof hovel, perched on the banks of the St. Joseph River, with the front door facing a slushy, snow-filled alley. There was no doubt I was calling on an indigent family, who in all probability wouldn't have one thin dime for Mary Ann's schooling. This fact was proven to me as her very nice parents offered me their "best chair" in which to sit and a spring or two jabbed me in my gluteus maximus during my presentation. When I took my leave of this desperately poor family, I walked out the door into a full-blown, base-of-Lake Michigan, Northern Indiana lake-effect BLIZZARD. Suddenly my attaché case popped open, spilling all my papers into the slushy alley's dirty waters. I badly needed an Alka-Seltzer, but with the nearby factory closed for the night, and not having a fizzing, sizzling tablet on my person, I, in complete frustration with the horrible weather and an evening of rejection, decided to end it all.

No, I did not throw *myself into the churning waters,* screaming "I love you, Elaine and my wonderful family," but I did fling my attaché case and all its soggy contents, into the roiling fury of the St. Joe River, and I shouted for all the world to hear that this was the end of my association with the airline training school. I went back to my room at the South Bend Holiday Inn, in the very shadow of Notre Dame's famed "Touchdown Jesus," and the following morning I phoned the wonderful man who was vice-president in charge of calming Art Hellyer down, Mr. Jack Davis, and I tendered my resignation.

Not only did Mr. Davis not accept it, he named me regional supervisor of all sales persons in Illinois, Indiana, and Wisconsin with an overwrite on their sales. I was in no position to turn that down. In fact, when I accepted a new lower paying radio offer, I stayed with the airline school part time in my new position for more than three years, when the double load just became too much for me to handle. It's been years since I last talked to Mr. Jack Davis, but I shall never forget this kindly man.

I just listened to a panel of automotive experts discussing electric cars on a network TV program. Remember I am writing this essay in 2007, and what I am going to relate concerning me, took place in the mid-nineteen-sixties. The "automotive experts" are talking about the possibility of electric cars in the next ten years, possibly 2015, and not one of the "automotive experts" as much as mentioned the electric-powered Chevrolet Corvairs that regularly were being test-driven between Detroit and Chicago forty years ago.

I became aware of them one cold winter night "not fit for

man nor beast," as W. C. Fields once said, as I pulled into the parking lot at the Holiday Inn at Kalamazoo, Michigan. Every parking spot on all sides of the building was occupied. As I was just going to head back to the interstate, I noticed a small shed I could slip my Volkswagen Beetle into, so I parked it, locked up and headed for a good nights sleep. Around 3 AM a voice from the front desk phoned me, and informed me I must vacate my cozy parking spot. I asked why and was politely told I was parked in a General Motors battery charging station for the electric cars they were testing. Fortunately, a number of spots were empty at that hour and I was able to quickly repark, and head back to my room. But I learned something that night that GM was keeping as hush-hush as they could. So, of course, the next time I was on the air I blabbed the whole story.

Another period between radio television jobs I was on the road selling for I.C.S., the highly reputable, "International Correspondence School" with their headquarters in Scranton, Pennsylvania, for over one hundred years. One would think selling "schooling at home" would be easy, studying in the quiet of the evening, in one's own domicile. What better way to learn how to be an accountant or librarian, or most anything except a brain surgeon? This job also offered the most important thing a door-to-door salesperson wants—real Qualified Leads!! The people we called on for ICS clipped an ad out of a highly reputable magazine or newspaper, filled in their name and requested information.

"Requested Information" was actually the big problem. No one expected a live human-being to knock at their door. They expected the information to arrive in their mailboxes, and when I came to the door they would let me know this BIGTIME. Selling for ICS was extremely difficult. As with each of the firms I repped, one hundred percent of the people I called on were astounded. The first words out of their mouths were, "I thought I'd get this information in the mail." And you know what? I would think that too.

Some of the doors I got in, some of those whose privacy I had disrupted would actually purchase the product, and the products I represented were good ones. Other people would politely get rid of me, others would rudely rid themselves of my presence, and some actually threw me out. Then others would politely listen to me, smile at me and issue a check to the company. The next day many would promptly at 9 AM phone their bank and stop payment on the check.

It all combines to verify the old saying, "If you can sell door-to-door, you can sell anything."

THE SATELLITE MUSIC NETWORK

* Essay 14 *

I asked Ralph Sherman, "What the heck is the *Satellite Music Network*?"
He replied. "Come to my office in Mokena tomorrow, and I'll tell you about it."

I had worked for WJJD, Chicago for three years in the early nineteen-eighties, and for the fourth time in my career I'd attained the Number One rating in my time slot. This time it was Saturday and Sunday from 6PM to Midnight. The major reason I took the job when WJJD went to the "Music of Your Life" format in 1982 was because I would NOT be required to drive into the city of Chicago again. Instead I would drive from my home in Naperville, Illinois to the WJJD studios in their transmitter building on the country-like western outskirts of Des Plaines, Illinois, adjacent to the I-294 toll road.

I drove to and from the Chicago loop for over thirty years, and I just would not go through that hell-on-earth again. When WJJD General Manager George Dubinetz offered me the job it also meant I would be playing my favorite music, the wonderful songs from the Forties, Fifties, Sixties, and Seventies with great vocalists singing every word so you could understand them. This way I could play everything good that was recorded in that period, from Glenn Miller, Benny

Goodman, Peggy Lee, Tommy and Jimmy Dorsey, Harry James, Dick Haymes and Helen Forrest, Artie Shaw, Dick Jurgens and Eddy Howard, Frank Sinatra, Perry Como, Doris Day, Tony Bennett, Frankie Laine, Dinah Shore to Elvis Presley, the Beatles, James Taylor, Bette Midler, Carly Simon and all the other great ones.

And I had a parking space of my own right near the station's back door. That too was of the utmost importance. Except for that one person every radio or television station has on staff who makes life miserable for his fellow broadcasters, everything was great UNTIL—until Plough Incorporated, makers of corn plasters and jock-itch powder, the unlikely owners of WJJD, decided the station needed a better image. I have never understood why a radio station should require an expensive Michigan Avenue studios facility when it is the image you project over the airwaves that determines your audience. The listeners couldn't care less if I were broadcasting from a cave deep in the bowels of the earth.

But WJJD did indeed move into fancy new and very expensive digs on Le Boul Mich, and after a few months of fighting major traffic again, and driving around and around searching for parking, and after being held up by gunpoint for the third time in my career, in the Grant Park underground parking facility and having the lot manager, sitting with his feet up on a desk as he watched TV, tell me when I reported the last one I would put up with, "Those things happen...there ain't nothing I can do about it." THAT WAS IT! I HAD HAD ENOUGH!!!!!!!!!!

So, on a Sunday Night in September of 1984 I opened the WJJD microphone for the last time, and I spoke the last words I would ever speak over a downtown radio station, "Folks I have a sad announcement to make to you and Mr. George Dubinetz, WJJD's vice president and general manager. Mr. Dubinetz and I have been friends for many, many years, and

The Satellite Music Network

we respect highly each others talents and abilities. I, in no way wish to harm that relationship. My problems are not with people, but rather with streets and highways, and automobile pollution and traffic, and finding a place to park my car in this people-infested and traffic-ingested mess they call Chicago.

Two years ago I resigned a near lifetime job at WLS-TV and the ABC Television Network that started in the fall of 1950. I also gave up my 15 years teaching position at Columbia College because I no longer would put up with the daily agony of driving 80 miles to and from the loop against the second hand on the clock, only to, at the end of the drive, start that nerve-wracking, anxiety-attack causing, search for a parking spot for my car.

Why didn't I ride the train? Everyone knows I love trains, whether model ones or the real pufferbellies, but the trains run only during commuters' hours. They did not run my hours. When I got off a radio-TV shift at 4:06 AM, or started a radio or TV shift at 4:58AM, the commuter trains were not running. I had no choice but to drive, and after the painful back injuries I suffered performing my duties on ABC-TV New Year's Eve 1965, driving a car was, and still is, exceedingly difficult. When I head my car west on the Eisenhower Expressway tonight, it will be for the last time, EVER. Tonight I am taking this vow, I will never come to the loop area again."

The next day I had two of my regular classes at St. Francis University in Joliet, Illinois, where I taught Broadcast One and Broadcast Two courses twice weekly. Before my classes I had dropped the Lovely Elaine at one of her favorite shopping centers, Louis Joliet Mall, and when the school bell rang and classes were over, I picked her up, and we had dinner at Al's Steakhouse in Joliet.

After a quiet drive home, we came in the door to a sound I detest as much as rock'n'roll...the telephone ringing. I answered it in a smart-ass way..."Art Hellyer, Former star of radio and TV." Mr. George Dubinetz's voice then said, "You are not a former star…you are still working for me. Come in tomorrow morning at eleven and we'll get this straightened out. Eric Zorn (*Chicago Tribune* Radio-TV editor) heard you last night and has been on the phone with me today. Eric is a big booster of yours and would like to sit in on our meeting? Is that all right with you?" I told him I would be there.

Less than forty-eight hours after I'd made my vow, I broke it for the only time. It was the least I could do for George Dubinetz. Tuesday morning I sat down at the table in the WJJD conference room, and before Mr. Dubinetz, could speak, I said, "George I meant what I said Sunday night. I came in today because I felt I owed it to you to say it to you in person." And that was, and will be my last ever time in the City of Chicago.

I have found that old saying to be, most of the time, true, "when one door closes, another one opens." Before the week was over Ralph Sherman called me and asked if I'd be interested in working for the Satellite Music Network. I remember asking him, "What the heck is The Satellite Music Network?" Ralph invited me to come to his office in rural Mokena, Illinois and talk about it. I was about to be given the opportunity to once again be a pioneer, as I had been in television broadcasting. Twenty five years before satellite broadcasting would become a "new innovation in broadcasting," it seemed I was about to enter its doors.

2PM the following day I was sitting with Ralph Sherman in a building like a small Pentagon. In the middle were two rooms where Dave Marsett, the network news director and his staff prepared and delivered the on-the-hour five-minute newscasts that were aired on all the Satellite Music Network stations in six time zones. Surrounding the news department were eight small broadcast studios….four of them were live 24/7, broadcasting musical programs from the Mokena studios. More formats were broadcast from the Satellite Music Network headquarters in Dallas, Texas. Ralph Sherman was operations manager of the "Stardust" division which played middle-of-the-road music by Sinatra, Doris Day, Dinah Shore, Ella Fitzgerald, The Kingston Trio, Glenn Miller, Frankie Laine, Rosemary Clooney, Benny Goodman, Tony Bennett, Peggy Lee, Perry Como, The Mills Brothers, The Ink Spots, Englebert Humperdinck, etc.

Back to back with each of the four broadcast studios were production studios used for recording material for the hundreds of stations on each network division. Stay tuned for more information about this phase of the Satellite operation.

The Satellite Music Network broadcasters lived by a generic 60-minute clock, with no hour hand. When a broadcaster gave the time he/she would say, for example, "it is 49 minutes past the hour," because often the Satellite Music Network programming was carried by stations in five or six time zones at the same time.

On Ralph Sherman's "Stardust" division, listeners were tuned in from ZBM, Hamilton, Bermuda, to KIXI, Seattle, Washington, and from Boston to Honolulu. I, having for many years suffered anxiety attacks caused by all the years I'd lived by the second hand of the clock, did not know if I wanted to tackle yet another "everything must be timed to the thousandth of a second" job. But I would, by my choice, never work in a big city again. From my house to Mokena was mostly back roads driving, although there would be a seven mile run on congested Illinois Route 53, and in the wintertime, as I would find out, there would be many white-outs to blindly pick my way through. But I'd done that many, many times before on my way to and from the loop to the radio and television stations, and on the pitch black of night farm roads of Illinois, Iowa, Indiana, Ohio, Wisconsin and Michigan when I was selling door to door. The real deciding factor though was

Ralph Sherman. Ralph had served with the Marine Corps in Korea and became a drill sergeant of such repute he was transferred to our nation's capitol to head up President Eisenhower's Marine Corps Drill Team. Ralph was the most unusual man I'd ever met. He was Marine Corps tough, and he was a softie, a nice guy; a hardworking, hard-driving if need be, no nonsense boss, but with a compassionate, understanding side. Ralph Sherman is two different people, but he is not a schizophrenic. He is the all-business man you see at the office during the day, and come evening he can step on a stage as a fine standup comedian and have you rolling in the aisles with laughter. He is one of a kind. Ralph was the deciding factor. I wanted to work for him and with him.

When I joined Satellite I had been on radio thirty-seven years, but this was something really new. In the production studio adjacent to the "Stardust" format studio, I trained for two solid weeks. Oh, before I further describe this operation I must tell you that every day I worked at Satellite I was in a constant state of concern. Why? Because one of the studio's walls had an "exotic" pet store on the other side. Why would this concern me? Because the slimy cobras and pythons could be heard slithering back and forth slamming into the wall immediately behind my chair 24/7. My extremely vivid imagination turned me into a basket case, a cobra in a basket case. Ralph was totally unaware of my fears as he showed me the ropes. After my two week training period I did two off-the-air 4-hour shows daily living by the minute hand. I also memorized the different colored buttons that must be used flawlessly to assure that all stations will cut in and out "to the thousandth of a second" at the very same times each hour: :05, :08, :20, :32, :40, :50, :59:50, ON THE NOSE!!!!!!!

Our music logs would indicate which type of song we were to play in the segments, and the music cartridges would each have a colored sticker. Following the twenty-past-the-hour segment, for example, we would play 4 songs: Green sticker (male vocal), Red sticker (Standard), Silver sticker (Big-band with vocal), Black sticker (Instrumental) and so on through the hour. Each break would contain commercials, but only eight minutes past the hour would carry commercials we would feed to the affiliated stations. Those were spots sold by Satellite and they were required to be aired on all "Stardust" stations. The rest of the breaks would be filled by the local stations with commercials, hopefully for them; or local promos, local weather and/or local traffic. The thirty-two minutes past the hour break was one where we would read the latest production information to all stations, or feed them commercials off the air, of course (30 seconds, to the thousandth of a second) to be played in their city, while they were each doing their local business. Each hour was extremely busy, and we had to sound cool, casual and collected no matter how hectic things might be. Every hour, except for the music, news, talk, commercials, etc., was identical to the last hour.

The only difference between my practice studio, which was primarily the studio we announcers recorded station liners in, and the real thing, was that I was not contacting the Hughes Galaxy 2 Satellite, twenty-three thousand miles in space, each time I pressed the buttons, which would then, in a nanosecond seek out all the stations "Stardust" was broadcasting on, trip their computers and in each community bring on the air the liners we had prerecorded for each and every station. To the listeners we seemed to be right there in their city. It truly boggles the mind. Remember this was twenty-five years before satellite radio became the "exciting" must thing for everyone.

After I passed the two weeks in confinement, in the off the air studio training, the third week I sat next to Ralph in the on-the-air "Stardust" format studio, and worked with him to get the feeling of the live studio. And the fourth week I started doing it all by myself.

Smooth-voiced, laid back Ralph did the 9AM to noon show daily, following the cleverest morning man I'd ever heard, Ron Baxley. He was a great talent. Too bad we must grow older and be forced, against our wills, into retirement. Ron Baxley should still be entertaining millions each morning. He looked and sounded so cool, so at ease. I must ask him if he is a mess as I am, inside my apparently calm exterior. I have never asked Ralph Sherman if he has to be pushed out onto the stage, with his knees sounding like a marimba band playing "Baba-Loo."

Not many people know this....I am not the cool-sounding cat people hear oozing through their speaker systems. Inside my skin, my skeletal system is shaking from head to toe. I've been told by station people and listeners, "Art, you are so placid, nothing ruffles you on the air. You calmly, gently speak to just one person. You are amazing." The late, Bob Platt my wonderful program director at my first Chicago station WCFL, was the first to say to me…"Art, I wish I could be like you…you have ice water in your veins." Well I don't…inside, I am a quivering bowl of jelly, but at the same time, I am my most relaxed when the microphone opens. Watch Woody Allen in "Hannah and Her Sisters." Woody is ME!!! Watch Jack Nicholson in "About Schmidt." You are watching ME!!! The Lovely Elaine knew me, and so does my beautiful lady friend, Jane Peterson, who has, along with my wonderful family, helped see me through the hideous loss of Elaine. Jane not only knows me, she does a perfect imitation of me, whether it be visiting the doctors office or sitting around berating myself for my many failures. Jane has me down to a "T." Many times I've told her she could have been a great actress. I believe the medical profession would never recover if Woody Allen and I were to appear TOGETHER in the same doctor's office.

The Satellite Music Network

I think the thing that most worried me was the fear of fouling up the entire network by pushing one WRONG button. The chief engineer at Satellite was a genius named Art Reis. Now, I don't know if he really was a genius, but he had me believing he was. I've known his type in many stations. When something breaks down these engineers will fully explain the problem and how they will solve it: "Art, you see this mazizer-flammer-jammer here, well the heat in it rose to 1254 degrees which is of course too high, and that caused the Heiser rod to expand and lockup the Rootzenhauser assembly. I'll just remove this breadboard from the IBM computer model number 349675-cc-38732945, and slip this latest titanium-alloy fladget in. Boy are we lucky I picked this up at Radio Shack yesterday or all 4000 of our stations could have been off the air for 43 days. There we go. I'll just plug that in and that's it. Art, when you see Ralph, please tell him I have restored the network to full capacity. You just have to know what to do. OK tell the announcers to start talking... I've fixed it." And he indeed had fixed it...Spooky, huh?

When we finished our four hour air shifts, we'd go into the adjacent studio, the one I trained in, to see if we had "liners" to record for the stations we were on. Ralph would receive thirty to fifty, five-second liners each day from stations we were on all over the country. Then he'd place, in our file boxes the ones we each were to record.

For example, when I finished my Saturday 6 to noon full network show, I would make a quick stop in the men's room, then I would go to the recording studio and check my file. I'd get out the copy for the various stations, open the mic and start recording. "Here are 35 liners from Station WKMC, Roaring Spring, Pennsylvania.....Each is to be done in five seconds, and will be played in Roaring Spring each time I activate the green button....Well let's see.....I'll cue up the tape reel....ok....now I'll sit down at the microphone and just start the tape and let it run...hey gang if I fluff a spot I'll just do a 'take two'.....Hi Roaring Spring—this is Art Hellyer...the tape is rolling....I have your 35 liners dated September to November 1985 here all set to go...number one...The Sun's shining...and you're with me, Art Hellyer on AM Stereo WKMC...Number Two....Art Hellyer on WKMC AM Stereo 1370...Temperatures in the fifties today....Number three... Temperatures in the seventies today....I'm Art Hellyer with the music on AM Stereo WKMC....Number four...sorry Bob I can't be there, here we go.....Enjoy the Keystone County Fair. WKMC will be there...AM Stereo 1370....number five Happy Thanksgiving from me, Art Hellyer and the staff at WKMC AM stereo 1370," and so on through liner number 35. These spots will flow right in as I push the green button, or whatever color button is scheduled for that particular break time on the network spots log, continuing the smooth flow of programming. It was all done so smoothly millions of listeners in thousands of cities and towns believed we were there in their community.

Split-Second-Timing was of the essence, of course. On July 27, 1984, Art Reis sent this message very much concerned with timing.

"To: All Announcers
From: Art Reis
Re: The clocks

I've seen several discrep reports lately regarding 'the clocks are one-half to one second slow.'

To get to the point: IT CAN'T HAPPEN, KIDS.

The way the clock system is designed, it can be off ONLY in increments of TWO SECONDS. That is, it can be off two seconds or GOD FORBID four seconds, or six seconds, etc. If the clock is off by one second, then it's the telephone time service that is off.....they still have not programmed in the extra leap-second which was added by the National Bureau of Standards on June 30."

I've asked this question of my gentle readers elsewhere in this book, "How would you like to live your entire working life in thousandths of a second?" One must really love radio-TV to live so strictly by the second hand.

A wonderful stage, radio, movies and television actor named James Gregory came into my life because of the Satellite Music Network. Jim Gregory played on Broadway as Biff, in "Death of a Salesman," just to name one of his starring roles. You have all seen him in scores of television shows and movies (The senator in "The Manchurian Candidate," the mean ornery rancher in "The Sons of Katie Elder," etc.) and TV shows (he was Sgt. Luger on "The Barney Miller Show," the lawyer on "Bonanza," etc.), yet we fooled him on The Satellite Music Network. He thought we were right there in Sedona, Arizona, his home the last years of his 91-year life.

I received my first of many, many notes from Jim Gregory, in 1986. He wrote the following from his home in Sedona on a "Get Well" card he had "recycled" himself. Remember, he started working as an actor in the nineteen-thirties, during the Depression, and all his life he, as did millions of people who barely existed during those terrible years, saved and recycled everything he could.

"8 February 1986
Dear Art:
In my innocence I dropped in at KVRD, Sedona, Arizona one afternoon, thinking I'd exchange a few pleasantries with you and the other announcers, etc., get a touch of "show biz" in this remote area of Arizona, also volunteer a few albums of my favorite recordings for your people to record and add to the stations musical library.

Well, I was soon put straight....all I saw was a young lady shuffling papers and answering phones. She informed me of the "satellite function," and I asked myself, "have I been away from the biz that long?" I thought you and Ralph Sherman, and Joe Lacina, and Ron Baxley, and Eddie Hubbard, and VLJ were right here in Sedona.

I came to Sedona last July, having had two strokes in Los Angeles, hoping to recover more quickly, but Art, it's questionable.

Trust things are going well for you. We enjoy your program.

> Yours truly,
> Jim
> James Gregory"

The girl at the station could have been fired for giving Jim my address at the Satellite Network in Mokena, Illinois, but that was a long time ago, and Jim, I am sorry to say, is gone now.

This short note on a postal card will give you an idea of why I looked forward to hearing from him:

"25 February 1986

Dear Art:

Thanks for the Glenn Miller cassette. Very thoughtful of you.

Next time you plan to peek at the Canyon, please stop by & I'll spring for a bottle of Ripple.

Yours for grand ole music. Sure were great songs!

Most cordially,
  Jim"

"7 January 1993

Dear Art:

Thanks for the dandy Christmas card. Great picture of

your model railroad locomotive.

My Pop was a "Hogger" (engineer) in steam, electric & diesel. I rode with him in the cab on many occasions. Don't squeal on me!!!

Holiday & best wishes to you.

Truly,

Jim

Card recycled, not the sentiments."

Jim Gregory had "recycled" a Christmas card, not mine to him, for this message.

I have a beautiful, autographed 8x10 of Jim Gregory on which he wrote this message:

"Dear Art For Pleasant Memories, Truly,"....then his signature. I love it because my shows on the Satellite Music Network were all built around memories. I had some wonderful telephone conversations with James Gregory over the years, and had him as a phone guest on my radio shows. He even sang songs he had written, and barbershop harmonies for my listeners and me. I'm proud of the stack of postcards and letters I have from this wonderful man whom we lost in September of 2002, and I smile wistfully in remembrance each time I see him in a late night movie or television show he appeared in from the Fifties into the Nineties. James Gregory was one of our finest actors and he was a colorful character and a nice man. I never would have known him if Ralph Sherman hadn't hired me to perform on that wondrous satellite network.

For many years I've enjoyed the "Steve King–Johnnie Putman All-Night Show" on WGN-AM radio. Well, when I was broadcasting on the first Satellite Network in the eighties, among the letters I would receive weekly were very nice ones from Steve King's dad, who was the mayor of Panama City,

Fla., and he indeed could have been my PR rep. I quote from one of his missives: "Art you sure are bright and sunny and full of fun and great information. And you play the GREAT music, Our Music. There is only one show on radio I enjoy more than yours. You can probably guess which one."

And speaking of Steve and Johnnie, this would be a good time for me to thank them for having my 1935 12th birthday gift from my mom and dad, a beautiful Dobro guitar, restored for me by the artisans at The Guitar Works in Evanston, Il. Thank you from the bottom of my heart Steve and Johnnie.

Next in my file is a letter from ZBM Hamilton, Bermuda. April 11th, 1985: "Dear Ralph!! Here are the new liners. They are all generic this time….also included are generic time announce liners. I hope it is possible to use Art's voice on these. Also please send picture of Art for our Bermuda billboards. Just a reminder we are "ZED" not "ZEE," although I think you all know that by now. Also…Bermuda Day is a National holiday on May 24th. The big Cricket games are a two day holiday in August. Our best to all at SMN *Mike Bishop,* Mgr., Bermuda Broadcasting Co., Ltd.." I recorded the 50 liners for ZBM remembering to say…"This is ZEDBM" not "This is ZEEBM." Okay!

"To Art Hellyer September 11, 1985 50 liners for WHYT Jackson, Mississippi Thank you Art."
"Here we go Jackson, Mississippi…tape is running…..Liner number one…..Good morning Jackson. It's 6AM. I'm Art Hellyer ..Time for NBC News ……..Liner number two….A chilly Sunday morning in the Capital City. 38 degrees at WHYT….Liner number three...This is Art Hellyer…Sunday Morning in Jackson, Mississippi....44 degrees as WHYT moves aside for the Baptist Bible hour" and so on until I've completed the 50 liners for Jackson.

The Satellite Music Network

Seattle, Washington   50,000 Watts KIXI-AM   Music you Remember   KIXI LINERS FOR ART HELLYER   May 20, 1985...   Ok everything is rolling nicely now.....“HI KIXI, this is Art Hellyer and I have your 35 liners dated May 20, 1985.....Tape is rolling and here we go......Liner number one.....Vacation in Kixieland a visit to Mount ‘Rain-eer’ is a great way to start.......Liner number two....I’m Art Hellyer— Welcome to Kixiland where Seattle residents are the top purchasers of sunglasses in the United States, I didn’t know that.....Liner number three...Here’s a special place to visit in Kixiland—The Hiram Chittenden locks in Ballard... ...Liner number four.....Art Hellyer welcoming you to the Emerald city....and KIXI. Be sure to ride across our two floating bridges on Lake Washington.”

I have many more liners to record this day....for cities like Eagle River, Wisconsin; West Palm Beach, Florida; Boston, Massachusetts; Corona, California; St.Croix, United States, Virgin Islands; Lewiston, Maine; Yuma, Arizona; and there are letters from Satellite Music Network stations:

“WTHI Terre Haute, Indiana:
Dear Art...You generate more mail, and more phone calls than all the other announcers combined. I had many people call for copies of the poem you recited on Wednesday 6-28-85, and darn the luck nobody caught the name of it. Here’s what I heard when I was in the newsroom...‘Love’s sweet refrain, Dreams....Need to hold you’.....Any help at all?

Once again I would be honored to mail out the copies of the poem for you, if you’d be kind enough to send me the poem.
Respectfully, Sally Hartz”

“KDEF Albuquerque, New Mexico   August 5, 1985
Dear Art:

The fan mail keeps rolling in. Here's your latest batch. Thank you so much for answering your mail...Nice touch....Most of the jocks don't. Had calls from some of the people whose letters you answered. They were surprised to find out you weren't broadcasting from here in Albuquerque. We must be doing something right. Most requests to the station include Eddy Howard, Fats Waller, Glenn Miller and Kay Starr...and song requests include 'More,' 'Tennessee Waltz,' 'Cold, Cold Heart,' 'Pretend,' 'April in Portugal.'

"BY THE WAY!! We got a 3.7 in the Arbitron rating. Tied for second overall for AM stations in the region. WE ARE EXCITED ABOUT IT!!!!! Much Thanks to you.
"Keep up the good work!!
Kindest regards,
Amy McGrane
 Executive Secretary"

"WBZW 1040-AM Knoxville, Tennessee November 1, 1985
Dear Art:
I am forwarding a letter and some information sent to the station by a gentleman who listens to you all the time and thinks you are here in Knoxville.
We have lots of people calling daily to speak to you, and they are really disappointed when they learn you are in Illinois. Dick and I really are pleased we went with Satellite Music Network. We think all of you do a great job, and you are all real pros. Keep up the good work.
Sincerely,
Huckaba Broadcasting, Inc.,
Kate Huckaba"

 "January 6, 1986 WXAM-AM 910 AM, Baton Rouge, Louisiana
 Dear Art: Perhaps it would interest you to know that you

get more mail, more phone calls, and your show receives more comments than anyone else.

You're very popular with the folks here in Baton Rouge.

Keep up the good work, and if you're ever in our neck of the woods, please be sure to stop by.

All the best,
Sandy Drake
Program Director"

And my favorite letter from my days as an air-personality on the world's first satellite radio network is this one that came up with a 78rpm record I'd been searching for, for many years. It came in the form of a billing invoice....

"WASR 1420-AM Wolfeboro, New Hampshire 03894
STATEMENT

One record requested on air by Art Hellyer, Sunday January 20, 1986,

And delivered to the studio within 15 minutes.

Mr, Hellyer promised first person who "hand-delivered Ozzie Nelson's 78rpm recording of 'It's Dark Upon Observatory Hill'—AN ARM AND A LEG.'"

PLEASE SUBMIT PAYMENT BY RETURN MAIL

Thank You!

I had this unusual message in my mail box one day.....

"URGENT telephone message for Art Hellyer from Dave Williams, WBAX-AM, Wilkes-Barre, Pa. 3:45PM 6-26-85: Please Call...Phone #717-555-5555 (not the real #) URGENT

"Before your show or earlier—re: The postcard you read last night, a listener thinks it was from her husband." I phoned this information to the Wilkes-Barre police department, and never heard another word about it. Very mysterious. Like from a John Grisham novel.

THE HELLYER SAY

My stay at the Satellite Music Network lasted a bit more than three years when the owners decided to move the entire operation to their headquarters at Dallas, Texas. Eddie Hubbard, Ron Baxley, and Joe Lacina moved to Dallas. My longtime friend and buddy VLJ took off for the warmer clime of Las Vegas, but most Chicagoland natives chose not to uproot their families, and found other jobs locally. Ralph Sherman lived in Joliet, Illinois, and quickly moved into the manager's chair at WJOL.

While broadcasting on Satellite I had a letter from Nancy McGowan, the owner of our affiliate at Madison, Wisconsin, asking me to give some thought to coming to work at her station…WMAD. I had always liked Madison, Wisconsin, is my favorite state, and I was nearing retirement age. Elaine and I talked it over. I told her I'd very much like to move to Madison, and work there the rest of my natural life. My dad worked right up until he died at 83, and I do not believe in retirement either. I abhor the thought of not working the rest of my life, so I took off for Madison for what was a good and a bad situation.

The money was more than Madison usually pays and that was good, and my show ran Monday through Friday, Noon until 4PM. That was good. Housing was bad, and carrying my LPs and 45s to and from the station was very rough because of the serious back injuries I had suffered on New Year's Eve 1965 on ABC-TV when a reveler beat the hell out of me. It was seen coast to coast and ABC-TV Network News ran it twice on New Years Day to show the perils of a broadcaster working on New Years Eve, and an estimated 40 million eyes viewed it, but that was part of my job. And yes, I could have sued ABC-TV for not providing me with protection, but I don't believe in law suits, nor could I sue the people who had kept food on my family's table and helped pay my mortgage over the years, not directly of course, but they did provide me with a weekly stipend through my paychecks. NO I could not ethically sue ABC-TV. So I've lived with these serious back injuries and much pain for a goodly part of my life.

And now the pain was really bugging me in Madison. Darn shame, because Madison's lakes are enchanting, and there are very few views in America as beautiful as the one from the Admiralty Room of The Edgewater Hotel right on the south shore of Lake Mendota, with a panorama of the entire lake, and the University of Wisconsin's campus. Driving into Madison on John Nolan Drive with lakes on either side and the magnificent State of Wisconsin Capitol building just ahead is something one can never forget. Son Jeffrey was driving just ahead of me one lovely evening in 1987, and he concurs.

I'm not a fisherperson. I can't stand those sadly pathetic little eyes pleadingly looking up at me, silently begging me to spare the poor little creature's life. Madison is a fisherperson's heaven, and I found it interesting to see businessmen returning to their homes after their days work in downtown Madison, with their cars pulled off the road, so they could fish for ten or fifteen minutes before continuing their drive.

Every Friday night I would drive the 129 miles to my home and then back to Madison on Sunday night, but my back just could not take it, and with great reluctance I ended my dream of Madison, Wisconsin working-retirement.

Once again, Ralph Sherman saved me. He asked me to do Saturdays from 1PM until 6PM and Sundays 2PM until 6PM at WJOL in Joliet, Illinois, and this was fine, because I had been teaching Radio One and Two since 1972 at The University of St. Francis just a few blocks away, and WJOL was heard throughout Chicagoland.

It was February of 1988 and I would stay at WJOL until December 18, 2001, when I was fired by the fifth WJOL owners group for whom I'd toiled. It was mostly a wonderful period for me. My shows were sold-out at the highest rates ever paid by sponsors on the station. In addition there was always a waiting list to get on the shows, and the sales-manager, sports-director, Don Ladas was not only a fine gentleman, he also was a superb professional.

Why did they fire me? "We are sick and tired of your wheelchair music, and your patriotic shows, and your reading of poems and song lyrics." This time, Ralph Sherman, who was responsible for every radio paycheck I received from 1984 through 2001, couldn't save me. Ralph Sherman, the best person for whom I ever worked, was, believe it or not, fired prior to my getting the axe.

There is a bit of additional irony here too. On June 21, 1988 Ralph Sherman wrote me the following note:

"Dear Art:

Just finished listening to tapes of some of your WBBM shows. They were great! It just reinforces my strong feelings about how nice it is to have you on our station. You're a real class act and a definite plus for our station and Saturday and Sunday listening. Major market stations made a real mistake, but a lucky one for us.

By the way, we will not carry any football games on Saturday. We do plan to have a sports assistant on your show to provide scores. We can discuss how this can best be worked into your program.

Best,
Ralph"

The "sports assistant" Ralph Sherman hired in June 1988 to do sports on my show was a new to radio, young person, named Scott Slocum who broke in on my Saturday show. On December 18, 2001, now WJOL program director, Scott

Slocum fired me, but I would bet the family jewels, the orders came from gutless higher-up management people. That is standard operating procedure for radio-TV front offices.

SPORTS OVER THE YEARS

* Essay 15 *

Art to Yogi Berra, *"Hey Yogi, you just broke my stopwatch."*
Yogi to Art. *"That's tough, I ain't buyin' you a new one."*

Bob Elson is in the Broadcast wing of the Baseball Hall of Fame at Cooperstown, New York, but he was always at his best as an interviewer. For many years during the off-season he hosted "The Bob Elson Show" from the Pump Room of The Ambassador East Hotel in Chicago. Everyone who was anyone appeared on Bob Elson's talk radio shows. He was doing in the early fifties on WCFL radio what is being done today on television, and he was better than, smoother than and classier than, and years ahead of, Larry King.

I was doing dozens of voice tracks daily on my shows in the early fifties, and am credited by radio historians with being the first broadcaster to do so. Nationally recognized "Old-Time Radio Guru," Chuck Schaden has said so in his writings. Today Jay Leno and Dave Letterman are doing film clip inserts on television, but it all started with Dr. K throwing voices at me back in the very early fifties. It's fun being a pioneer and seeing things I did in the Forties and Fifties being done today visually on television.

In 1953-1956 Downtown Nash, the people for whom I did over 200 quarter hours weekly on 7 radio stations, sponsored The Dugout Show on WCFL, the flagship station of The

Chicago White Sox radio network.

When I was a student at Radio Institute of Chicago in 1946, one of my classmates, Jimmy Fitzgerald and I decided late one afternoon between classes, we'd stand in the hallway at WJJD, on the second floor of the Carbide and Carbon Building, and try to meet Bob Elson as he came in for his 6PM sportscast.

And we pulled it off. We were standing in front of the hallowed doors of WJJD, when Mr. Elson, as we called him, got off the elevator. He was, as always, the picture of sartorial splendor in an expensive Brooks Brothers suit.

Our conversation was short because we knew the great man was in a hurry to get to the Associated Press and United Press International news machines to check and edit the latest sports news for his impending program.

We quickly told him we were students at Radio Institute of Chicago just four blocks north on Michigan Avenue. He told us he had spoken to a graduating class there, and our conversation was over as he said, "Good luck, boys," and walked through the doors we dared not enter.

Well, in our classes the next day Jimmy and I told our awe-struck fellow would-be broadcasters of our meeting, and we fibbed a bit about the length of our "interview." I never in my wildest dreams thought I'd ever actually work with Bob Elson, or for that matter, I never dreamed I'd be on radio in what was then the nation's number two market.

It was thus, to my astonishment, I found myself working a daily show with Bob Elson. And I found myself working my all-time dream job. I would call the middle-three innings of some of the White Sox home games, which would give Bob Elson a break during which he could go to a phone booth across the street from the park on 35th street and phone his bookie, Tommy O'Leary, and bet on the ponies at Rockingham, Hialeah and Arlington Park among others. I couldn't go on the road with the team because I had the morning show on WCFL Monday through Saturday. Downtown Nash was my major sponsor, much as White Owl Cigars sponsored Elson. So we shared the interview duties, something Bob, with whom I got along just fine, wasn't too happy about. It was interesting though that as time went by I frequently ended up doing the show by myself while Bob would visit before the game with baseball or political bigshots. So I found myself interviewing my idols: Joe DiMaggio, Ted Williams, Luke Appling, Hank Greenberg, Willie Mays, Stan Musial, Yogi Berra, and so many others.

One day I will never forget, Yogi knew he was coming on with me in just a few minutes, but he continued to warm up Whitey Ford. Two minutes before airtime I came out of, what else? The Sox "DUGOUT" to remind Yogi it was almost airtime, then I went across the infield to the Yankees dugout. Yogi was strolling toward me as I took my cue from engineer Ernie Nottger well above the field, back of home plate, in the play-by-play broadcast booth. I clicked my stopwatch and placed it next to me on the rickety old wooden bench. Then the red light came on and I introduced the show, "Good afternoon Ladies and Gentlemen, this is Art Hellyer bringing you the Dugout show, sponsored by Downtown Nash, the working mans friend. Our guest today will be the great New York Yankees catcher, raconteur and philosopher, Mr. Lawrence Berra." During my introduction, Yogi threw his big catcher's mitt on the bench knocking my stopwatch to the rough concrete floor, and, as I soon found, breaking it. So my first words to Berra were, "Hey Yogi, you just broke my stopwatch." To which Yogi fired back, "That's tough. I ain't buyin' you a new one." Things got worse when after a few minutes of baseball talk about his youth "on the hill" in St. Louis and growing up just a few doors removed from another future major league catcher, Joe Garagiola, I said, "If Yogi Berra doesn't mind I'm going to pause now and talk about my fine sponsor, Downtown Nash," at which point Yogi chimed in with, "I wouldn't drive one of them junkers. I only drive Cadillacs." I've told this story for years privately and at sports banquets I've emceed and/or attended and people love it. Why? Because everyone loves Yogi Berra. You just can't help but love him.

Another car story involved Yogi's manager of the New York Yankees, Casey Stengel. I had purchased from my sponsor Downtown Nash, a restored 1917 Jeffrey, the forerunner by one year of the Nash. It was a huge phaeton model with new leather seating, a new black canvas roof, the standard color of those earlier days, fresh black paint, and they sold it to me for four hundred dollars. The pistons must have been five inches in circumference, and the four-cylinder block was a monster.

In addition it stood very, very high above the ground. I must have had arms like hamhocks, because somehow I was able to steer the beast. And shifting it through the "H" pattern with the very long stick in the middle of the floor was certainly not for the weak-kneed.

One summer I drove my "new" car to Comiskey Park for every White Sox home game, and as I would turn off Lake Shore Drive into 31st street on my way to my parking spot, strangers would hop aboard for a free ride. One gentleman who was a regular passenger of mine would plop himself deep in the backseat, take a big puff on his cigar, and always say, "Driver, take me to the ball park."

At one period of time in the early fifties, the White Sox would drive the relief pitchers for both teams from the bullpen beyond the 440-foot sign in center field, to the mound. Chuck Comiskey, the son of the original White Sox owner, "The Old Roman," and in the nineteen-fifties, himself, the owner of the Sox asked me if I, as a publicity stunt, would drive the pitchers to the mound in my 1917 Jeffrey (Nash) for a Sunday doubleheader with the New York Yankees. I told him I would love to. So, on a hot August Sunday afternoon, after I did the dugout show on WCFL, I drove the car around the perimeter of the grass to the bullpen. The Rambler convertible that usually drove the pitchers to the mound was nowhere to be seen.

Bob Finnigan, the public address announcer informed the crowd that the car they could see in the bullpen would be bringing relief pitchers, if needed, to the mound. I was seated at the wheel as the announcement was made, and I saw 440 feet away, Casey Stengel running out of the Yankees dugout, wildly waving his arms, and shouting at the home plate umpire. No way could I hear him, of course, but I sure could hear the public address system crackle to life and Bob Finnigan's announcement, as he said, "Yankees manager Casey Stengel has just informed the umpiring crew for today's games, his pitchers will not ride, to quote Mr. Stengel, in that junker." He used the very same word Yogi had used. I guess if you were a New York Yankee you only rode in Cadillac's.

Then classy Sox pitcher Billy Pierce came running over to me, and hopped into my ancient monstrosity and asked me to take him for a ride around the field. I did so, and the crowd gave us a standing "O." As Bob Elson always said, "You can't beat fun at the old ballpark."

Connie Mack owned and managed for fifty years the Philadelphia Athletics. Longer than anyone ever in baseball history. Mr. Mack, real name Cornelius McGillicuddy, retired in 1950 but stayed on, for many years, as owner-advisor to the Athletics. So it was in 1953 that I was interviewing him before a Sox-Athletics game. He was dressed as always in a dark suit, white shirt and tie, and a straw hat...the picture of 1910's male splendor.

I brought with me that day a letter he had written me, in answer to a request I had sent him in 1941, asking for a tryout with the Philadelphia Athletics. As I told him during the only interview I would ever be privileged to have with this baseball legend, "Mr. Mack, when I received this letter from you, I could not believe you would take the time to personally answer a sixteen-year-old's letter." He then told he me he answered all young ball players who wrote him because he felt obliged to do so, and he always hoped he could help young players. I then told him I'd like to read the letter he had sent me, right there on the dugout show. He was a bit embarrassed but gave his permission...

I first pointed out that he had hand-written it on Chase Hotel stationery. And he said, "Yes, when we're in St. Louis for a series with the Browns we always stay at The Chase... it's a comfortable old hotel and all the players like it." I then read the letter on the air, "June First, 1941. My Dear Mr. Hellyer: Am going to advise you to try to get some club, near your home town to give you the trial you desire. You are pretty young to start and though you seem to have the height and weight that is necessary it would not be a bad idea to play semi-pro ball this year. Please excuse my delay in answering. Sincerely yours, Connie Mack."

When I concluded reading the letter I said, "Another thing that impressed me Mr. Mack was you writing, 'Please excuse my delay in answering.' That was a very, very nice thing to say to a sixteen-year old." And he replied, "Mr. Hellyer, I always carry with me every letter I get, and I answer them when I can. Baseball has been very good to me, and that is the least I can do."

I have never forgotten that interview I had with Connie Mack, and I still proudly display the original copy of his fine letter to a sixteen-year old American Legion baseball player in a small town on the Illinois prairie.

We always concluded the Dugout Show with a presentation to the guest, of "a $39.95 Benrus wrist watch." In the early fifties most Americans couldn't afford to buy a watch that expensive, so it was a nice gift. And my friend Bob Elson, who would qualify as Webster's Dictionary definition of the word "frugal," appreciated the $39.95 Benrus watch also. Bob wore a Rolex, but he appreciated the Benrus greatly.

We were standing at the pitchers mound when Bob suggested we interview each other one fine summers day, and skip the player interview. He went on to tell me he'd like me to write on my agency information daily report sheet the name of a White Sox player who had been traded that very morning. And then after we'd interviewed each other, and after the Dugout Show was off the air, I was to give Bob the watch. Why? Because he owed a close relative a birthday gift. I didn't do it. And, I know the very words Bob used under his breath when I told him, "You &@!^%#!" Bob would be introduced to a person, have a nice chat with him, give him a big smile and a warm handshake, and as he'd walk away, under his breath I'd hear him say. "You &@!^%#!"

There was a long-standing unwritten law in baseball, "No women are allowed on the playing field, or in the dugout or the clubhouse." I was well aware of this unspoken rule, and didn't realize I had violated it until Bob Elson came running the length of the dugout breathlessly shouting at me, "What in God's name are you doing? Get that woman OFF THE FIELD!" I was carrying in my arms my seven-month-old daughter, Debbie.

Bob Elson was ALWAYS the picture of sartorial splendor and as he strode toward me in his five hundred dollar Brooks Brothers suit I could see he was anxious about something.

"Art, I just saw a red Nash Rambler convertible. My daughter is graduating from high school in three weeks and I want to get one for her gift." I told him that would be a beautiful gift. I wouldn't mind getting one myself, but I certainly could not afford it. I said to Bob, trying to be helpful,

"I'll talk to Jack and Babe Metnick (owners of my sponsor Downtown Nash), and see what their dealer's cost is. I just bought a new Rambler station wagon from them, and I paid $1695.00 dealers cost. So the convertible will probably cost you a little more." Bob looked at me aghast, "Art...I don't BUY cars....they are given me....I'm Bob Elson. Cadillac gives me a new car every year."

I told the Metnick brothers about Bob's request and they laughed at me. Obviously the Pope himself would not get a free car from them.

It was at this time I found myself "Sports Editor" of "Chicago....Your Host" Magazine.

When one finds himself in a prominent position on radio and/or television many outside opportunities present themselves. I also know first-hand, that when one is not in a position of prominence, one can't even get through the door of a broadcast facility. So it was, because I had the number one rated radio show in Chicago, I was now a sports columnist. I wrote this column for the November 1953 issue...Volume 1 Number 1...:

"A SPORTY WORD

Art Hellyer

"Well, football season is here once again, and the 1953 baseball season is just a memory. The New York Yankees and the Brooklyn Dodgers have completed the annual pilgrimage to each other's bailiwicks, and the hot stove league will now go into session and continue until next season gets underway. And then next year at this same time another hot stove league gets underway and the talk will again be of the Yanks and the Dodgers. And thus I presume shall it ever be.

"This was an interesting baseball season. One club to stimulate interest gave a case of beer to each lady attending the game. By the seventh inning, the bags were loaded.

"It was rumored that the reason for the slump in a certain well-known player's hitting was caused by the fact that he went after too many high balls.

"Lord Jaguar attended his first baseball game and found it extremely dangerous. They're still explaining to him that Minnie Minoso didn't really die on second when he was attempting to steal the base. His Lordship also thought Lou Kretlow was the best pitcher on the White Sox because he hit every players bat.

"And then there was my friend Bob Ryan who could have been a great baseball player, but he was so honest, he wouldn't steal a base.

"J. Worthington Metnick, the big business tycoon refused to ever again enter a baseball park because he just can't stand to hear an umpire call a strike.

"From the above you can see this was quite a baseball season. The Cubs got hot at the end of the term and managed to avoid the National League basement, and though the White Sox didn't win the junior loop bunting they did help to make it an interesting season."

I interviewed Casey Stengel twice, once on the field at Comiskey Park, and then on "The Bill Veeck Show," on which I was the announcer for State Farm Insurance, the sponsor of the show. I sat with Mr. Veeck in the three rows of bleachers, with cheering fans painted on the TV studio wall in back of us. It was a crummy set, but Bill Veeck made up for it. He was an extremely colorful man, who always told interesting stories.

A veteran of WWII, he lost a leg in action with the Marine Corps in the South Pacific, and had been fitted with a wooden leg, with a special hole in it. Mr. Veeck was a heavy smoker and as he'd puff away he would tap the ashes into the hole in the prosthesis. When he would finish a coffin nail, he would drop it into the special compartment in his leg. I never saw him catch fire from this practice, nor have I ever heard he did. If he did so at home I'm sure his lovely wife Mary Frances had a pitcher of water standing by at all times ready to be poured down the walking cuspidor.

I would sit one row behind and to the left of Bill Veeck in the make-believe stands. My sister-in-law Carol Miller, who was Chicago's first live TV prompter, would be standing next to the one black and white camera, holding upright the cue cards I had printed earlier in the day while I was toiling in the Channel 7 local announce booth. The stage manager Jerry Kupcinet, Irv's son, would be, holding his stopwatch in his left hand, watching the clock on the wall, listening in his headphones to the words from our director Richie Victor, while the make-up artist would be making last minute adjustments to Bill Veeck and me. The Max Factor Number Nine face powder, always started me sneezing, and most of the time you saw me on your television screen, my nose was running. There are all sorts of hazards in this medium.

The clock was 5 seconds from 9PM and Jerry Kupcinet, listening to Richie Victor in his headphones, was counting those final five seconds on the clock, one finger at a time. 9PM straight up, Jerry pointed his right index finger at me, the red light on the single black-and-white camera flashed on, and I spoke:

"Good Evening baseball fans...I'm Art Hellyer and this is THE BILL VEECK SHOW, brought to you by...STATE FARM INSURANCE COMPANIES, and now here is the owner of The Chicago White Sox...BILL VEECK."

Thunderous crowd noise. Are the painted fans on the wall cheering? Nope...Lenny Kaye (Dr. K), my daily morning show wizard of the turntables is plying his trade. From his case of special audio-effects he has produced crowd noise.

Bill Veeck talks for a certain number of minutes....I deliver a 60 seconds commercial, and Casey Stengel wanders onto the bleachers carrying a huge bag of popcorn. One of baseball's greatest figures of The Twentieth Century had joined us on our not-very-good reproduction of a major league baseball stadium. Mr. Veeck chatted with him for awhile, then I asked Mr. Stengel if he'd tell us the "Bird in the Cap" story.

Casey Stengel then delivered one of his very special stories: "You know Art, I've been with a lot of teams in the minor leagues and then in the major leagues, the Dodgers, the Braves, the Giants, and some others I don't even remember, and I've played a lotta baseball games, and I've managed the New York Yankees baseball club, some of 'em even won pennants and world serious, some even say I went for a ball one time when I was playing outfield, and they say I made a great catch, and then a great throw to throw a runner out, and the crowd cheered and I ran over to the stands and bowed and took my cap off and a bird flew out, and I don't know if I did that....maybe I did, but if I did, where did I get the bird, and I don't remember ever seein' a bird near me when I was in the outfield, and if there was a bird in the outfield, I would've felt it landing on my head, and how did I stuff the bird under my cap, and how did it stay there?....I don't think it cudda set up under my cap and stayed on my head while I was running around that outfield and then catching that ball and then throwing that runner out and then running over and taking the cap off my head and the bird flying out...I don't think that ever happened. If it did and someone remembers it I want him to call me and tell me about it, or stop me on my way into the ballpark and tell me about it or yell to me on the field and I will walk over to the stands and he can tell me about it and I will give him an autographed American League baseball with Mr. Harridge's name on it."

The "Bill Veeck Show" aired one baseball season and of all the people who sat in our grandstand, Ted Williams, Joe

DiMaggio, Stan Musial, Nellie Fox, Bob Feller, Roger Maris, and others, the one I remember most is "The Ole Perfesser, Casey Stengel."

I was also the announcer on "The Bobby Hull Show" on WBBM radio, when he and Gordy Howe were the talk of the National Hockey League. Bobby had a one hundred mile per hour slap-shot that terrorized every goalie in the league. Yet, off the ice, Bobby was a very quiet-spoken man who was always dressed in a fine suit, white shirt and tie.

One evening, Elaine and the family met me at WBBM, so after the show, I, of course, introduced them to Bobby who had done the program in his white shirt and tie. When I asked Bobby if it would be okay if I took a few pictures of him with the kids, he said it would be fine, but I must wait until he put on his suit coat, and straightened his tie.

Later that evening at the Chicago Stadium, where we were watching the Blackhawks play the Montreal Canadiens, it was hard for us to believe we were watching that very same man as he came roaring in on Montreal's great goalie, Jacques Plante, and fired a one hundred mile an hour whistler past him.

It was a Sunday and I was in my second year working in Milwaukee radio. I had completed my 6AM to 2PM shift at WISN and had taken the two streetcars and a bus to get me to 5171 North Teutonia Avenue, where Elaine, baby Larry and I, occupied a small one-bedroom apartment. Television was just starting to make itself known, and only a few people had sets. We were not among them, because on my salary of seventeen dollars and ninety five cents a week, it was all we could do to pay the rent and put food on the table. The least expensive TV sets, Hallicrafters, Dumont and a few others had seven inch screens, and retailed for close to two hundred dollars. The "GIANT SCREEN," ten-inchers, and that's the way they were advertised, sets by RCA Victor, GE, Magnavox, Philco, and a few others sold for better than two hundred fifty dollars, and all were out of our reach. And television still was local. The few stations on the air would broadcast from 6PM until Midnight, then run test patterns during the night. Network cable had only recently been strung from New York to Chicago.

So I would bring segments of the radio station's Sunday Milwaukee Journal and Milwaukee Sentinel home, and Elaine and I would read until suppertime. It was while reading one Sunday afternoon, I looked up and glanced out the front window, and stammered, "Elaine!!! Bill Osmanski is walking up our front sidewalk." Elaine quite naturally said no way could that be my football idol, the great Bears fullback, Bill Osmanski. We heard the apartment house outer door open, then our next-door neighbors interior door opened and closed, and of the millions of buildings in the world, the Osmanskis were within the very bowels of our apartment house. Amazing!!!!!!

On December 8th, 1940, the Chicago Bears were playing the Washington Redskins in the National Football League title game at Griffith Stadium in our nation's capital. On the second play from scrimmage, Bill Osmanski took the handoff from Bears quarterback Sid Luckman, galloped to the left, off guard and down the football field 68 yards with one of the officials, future *Sun-Times* writer and television personality Irv Kupcinet,(one of the game officials) who had been a star quarterback at the University of North Dakota, and on the 1935 College All-Star football team, trailing him all the way to make sure Osmanski didn't step out of bounds on his way to the first touchdown of the game. The Chicago Bears would win the game by the unlikely score of 73-0. I was a high school senior doing my homework while listening to the broadcast. And now, here in Milwaukee, I had just seen Bill Osmanski walking into our apartment building. I wanted so much to go next door and ask our neighbor, Choc Quilling and his wife if they'd introduce me, but I was too nervous to do so, and Elaine didn't think I should because "Art, there's a good chance it's just someone who looks like Bill Osmanski." The next day I asked Choc about it and he assured me that was indeed Bill Osmanski and his wife Mary I had seen, and he said they would have welcomed me.

Life is strange, isn't it? My first week at WCFL in 1950, Alice, the switchboard operator came running excitedly into the studio to tell me Bill Osmanski was on the phone, and he wanted to talk to me. Well, folks in radio-land, I had just come up through the radio minors, and I couldn't believe my ears, when I heard the great Bill Osmanski telling me how much he enjoyed my shows, and how he'd like to have me as his luncheon guest at the Chiselers' Club, a private club for dentists only, in the basement of the Pittsfield Building at 55 E. Washington Street.

Bill Osmanski and his brother Joe, also a Bears fullback became my close friends, and Bill became my dentist until one day in February, 1984, I was in the chair "expectorating" as he always called it, when Bill suddenly left the dental chair, and I could hear him asking his nurse, "Judy, who is that in the chair?" My beloved Dr. Bill Osmanski was in the early stages of Alzheimer's disease.

Bill and Joe Osmanski shared the fullback position at Holy Cross University and they loved to tell of the game against Harvard when their mom, in the stands, suffered a mild seizure and had to be rushed to the hospital. Bill asked for permission to go with her, and when he returned the game was in the 4th quarter with Harvard leading 13-0. The final score was Holy Cross 14, Harvard 13 with Bill scoring both Holy Cross touchdowns in the closing minutes of the game.

Elaine and I occasionally sat in the Osmanski box, as Bill's guests, in the upper deck at Wrigley Field, at Bears games. Bill explained the reason he preferred sitting there was because one could see the plays unfolding, and the holes opening for the running backs. They were indeed great seats. One year, the Osmanski brothers invited me to the United States College Football Awards luncheon in the Knicker-bocker Hotel. Seated at our table with the Osmanskis and me, were three great stars of the Chicago football Cardinals, Paul Christman, Charlie Trippi, and Marshall Goldberg, two of the all-time great Green Bay Packers, Cecil Isbell and Don Hutson, and super quarterbacks, Otto Graham, Bobby Laine and Johnny Lujack. The twelfth seat was empty, and we were all wondering who would occupy it. Suddenly, the football greats at my table were breathless and excited, and two or three could be heard saying, "Oh my God!! COACH IS AT OUR TABLE." Slowly making his way to our table, on crutches from a recent hip surgery was George Halas, one of the founders of the National Football League, and arguably the greatest coach in NFL history.

Recently, my friend Pat Carson and I had mid-afternoon lunch at Walter Payton's excellent restaurant in Aurora, Illinois. While Pat was munching on her delicious pork sandwich, and I on my Milwaukee bratwurst, we played a rousing game of Scrabble, which Pat won, on my portable board. It's a friendly place and even our server, Terrie, leaned over the playing field and suggested a few words.

Sitting there where Walter himself would often hold court, and answer questions about his magnificent National Football league career, brought back a poignant memory of a day when I sat with him in George Halas's private office in downtown Chicago.

I had phoned Mr. Halas and told him I'd like to do an in-depth interview with Walter Payton. He told me he'd have Rudy Custer, the Chicago Bears' front-office man, who wore many hats in the Bears organization arrange it, and Rudy would call me with the information.

A few days later I found myself seated in the office immediately adjacent to Mr. Halas's, when one of the five greatest running backs in the history of the National Football League casually strolled in and we talked for over an hour, as though we had always known each other. Walter Payton, a terror on the gridiron, did indeed live up to his nickname, "Sweetness." Walter Payton died much too young, and I am one of the lucky ones who will always remember how great a football player he was, and how gracious a human being he was.

My dad was chairman of the board at St. Joseph's College in Rensselaer, Indiana, for many years, during the halcyon years when the Chicago Bears trained there, and Mr. Halas was on the board that asked my dad to assume that august position. My dad always had a smooth way of putting the bite on people, and he asked George Halas to finance a new campus building. He said, "Sure, why not?" or something like that, I suppose. So Halas Hall proudly stands among the other ivy-covered multi-million dollar buildings on the campus where so many great professional football players have trained, and where Gil Hodges was a college-student baseball player on his trip to major-league-stardom.

Through my dad I had met Mr. Halas a number of times, and he also listened to my shows in the fifties when I was on WCFL, which was the Chicago football Cardinals' flagship station, and George Halas had more than once called me, either to my face or in letters to me at the station, a traitor for working there. It was all good clean fun, I think. For three years in the early fifties I did the Pre-game and Post-games shows on "The Chicago Cardinals Football Network."

My back was in terrible shape and I had a once-in-a-lifetime, dream assignment from ABC Radio Sports. I was to cover everything I could in conjunction with the 50th Anniversary All-Star Baseball Game at Comiskey Park. The festivities covered three full days, July 4, 5, 6, 1983. There was no way I could drive myself in, and my five offspring were all working. Then daughter Victoria said she would take a day off, so I decided to skip the 4th of July short program, and there was no way I could sit through the entire 7:30PM All-Star game, in addition to a full day starting with a breakfast and concluding with a "post game until 2AM" party at the Hyatt Regency, so I decided to cover the middle day as well as I could. Vickie picked me up at 9AM, and drove me directly to our reserved parking place at Comiskey Park.

We skipped the Media Brunch and conference, and went straight to the Old Timers workout, where all the living greats were available for short interviews. With Vickie as my Photographer, I carefully chose the players I would put on my tape recorder in the short period of time we were allotted….All great Major Leaguers.

Number One. In my opinion, the greatest of them all, a man who knew exactly the right time, at age 37, to leave the arena, so we would remember him at his peak, rather than a player whose great skills were diminishing, the "Yankee Clipper," the incomparable Joe DiMaggio. The epitome of class, in center field for the New York Yankees he was baseball's equivalent of Nureyev, Baryshnikov, and Nijinsky. In 1941 Joe DiMaggio struck a baseball for a hit at least once per game in 56 straight contests, making Les Brown and vocalist Betty Bonney, the biggest names in the recording industry that year. If you are too young to remember, their Columbia 78rpm recording, "Joltin' Joe DiMaggio" sold over a million copies.

Only the great Pete Rose has come within shouting distance of that record. Pete hit in 44 straight games, and the record stands as the most difficult of all sports records to surpass. And did you know scientists have researched and found hitting a baseball to be the most difficult endeavor in all the sports world?

Number Two. Ted Williams...the incomparable hitter...a man who could see the ball precisely, from its ejection from the pitchers hand until the moment his Louisville Slugger contacted the nine-inch sphere and sent it to some remote part of the ballpark. To this day he is the last major leaguer to bat .400 in a baseball season. And his last ever at bat was, of course, a home run. Ted Williams, arguably the greatest baseball player of all time served his country with honor in World War Two AND the Korean War. Imagine the records 'The Splendid Splinter" would have set if he had played baseball those seasons?

Number Three. Hank Greenberg, who left so many record-breaking chances behind because he felt it was his duty to enlist and he went off to World War Two for four years. Greenberg played only nine and a half seasons, but was the American League Most Valuable Player twice, and he led the major leagues in home runs four times. He came home from the United States Air Corps in 1945 just in time to win the American League pennant for the Detroit Tigers with a Grand Slam on the last day of the season. He then helped beat the Chicago Cubs in the World Series with two home runs and seven runs batted in. Had he not returned from the war when he did, the Chicago Cubs would have, in all probability won their first, and only World Series since 1908. It was not the Billy goat curse that whipped the Cubs. It was Greenberg.

Hank Greenberg was traded to the Pittsburgh Pirates in 1947, becoming the National League's first one-hundred-thousand-dollar player.

Number Four. Earl Averill, a terribly bitter man who just five weeks after I interviewed him at the 50th annual All-Star game, passed away. His wife wrote me a beautiful letter thanking me for sending her a tape of the interview. She said it was so wonderful to hear her husband speaking of his career, something he hadn't done in years. She also wrote, "Thanks to you Mr. Hellyer for making Earl laugh again. I hadn't heard him laugh in years. I will treasure the tape you sent me and play it often, for the rest of my life. God bless you Mr. Hellyer."

Earl Averill hit a home run in his first major league at bat, and batted .332 his rookie season with Cleveland in 1929. He was the only American League outfielder to be named to each of the first six All-Star games.

Number Five. Bob Feller. The fire-balling Van Meter, Iowa farm boy, at age 17 was throwing 100 mile an hour fast balls past major-leaguers. He pitched three no-hitters and a major-league record-sharing 12 one-hitters. He missed four years in his prime serving in World War Two, for which he was decorated with five campaign ribbons studded with eight battle stars.

Number Six. Luke Appling played shortstop for the Chicago White Sox for twenty years. Twice he led the American league in hitting, once with a .388 average. "Old Aches and Pains" played for the Sox his entire career from 1930 to 1950, yet never played on a pennant winning team. His bad back forced him to retire, after probably setting a major league record for foul balls, and his uncanny ability to select just the right pitch resulted in "Luscious Luke" Appling topping the .300 mark 14 times. Luke Appling, Jimmy Dykes, Nelson Fox, Ted Lyons and lefty-pitcher Billy Pierce are my all-time favorite "pale-hose."

Number Seven. Cincinnati Reds pitcher Johnny Vander Meer tossed TWO consecutive no-hitters. Will anyone ever again do that again? I don't think so. In the second one, against the Brooklyn Dodgers, he walked the bases full in the ninth inning with one out, and got out of it. After his amazing accomplishment, a Cincinnati sports writer started a campaign to have a granite statue of Vander Meer carved and placed in Fountain Square in downtown Cincinnati. I asked Johnny if he had posed for it, and he replied, "First I've heard about it." Fleeting fame!!

Number Eight. Warren Spahn. Baseball's all-time winningest left-handed pitcher with 363 victories. Spahn won twenty games, thirteen times, led the National League in wins eight times, had two no-hitters, and won the Cy Young award in 1957. He also holds the National League pitcher's home run record with thirty-five. It boggles my mind to think what he, and so many others would have done if they hadn't served our country in World War Two.

Number Nine. At the 50th Anniversary All-Star game festivities at Comiskey Park, Willie Mays left me feeling I was a lousy interviewer. Each question I asked him was either followed by a grunt, or just a vacant stare. It wasn't until I read revered and respected Jerome Holtzman's column about Mays two years later, on July 24, 1985 in the *Chicago Tribune* I knew otherwise. I will give you a short quote from Mr. Holtzman's column, "Say Hey, Willie Mays…Still a classic pain, and has been for years." So I guess I wasn't the only one who found him extremely difficult to speak with.

Number Ten. Carl Hubbell …in the 1934 All-Star game the great lefty struck-out FIVE of the greatest baseball players of all time, in a row. Babe Ruth, Lou Gehrig, Jimmy Foxx, Al Simmons and Joe Cronin each went down swinging at Hubbell's baffling pitches. Carl Hubbell was the National League's Most Valuable Player in 1933 and 1936.

After the interview session, we were invited to the Babe Ruth stamp First Day issuance ceremony. I have been a United States stamp collector since the nineteen-thirties, and this ranked for me as tied with the interviews of the Hall-of-Famers as the two most important, non-playing, events of the three days of festivities. Postmaster General William Bolger formally dedicated a U.S. Postal Service Commemorative stamp in honor of Babe Ruth in an on the field ceremony following the Old Timers' Game. First day of the sale would begin the next day during the All-Star game and cancellations were made by the U. S. POSTAL SERVICE. I have three special Babe Ruth cards that were issued at the ballpark only that day. My envelope is stamped FIRST DAY OF ISSUE Chicago, July 6 1983, 60607, and the wonderful Babe Ruth USA 20 CENT stamp is affixed. A great collector's item I treasure.

The following day, Wednesday July 6, 1983, I attended only one event, the Commissioner's BY INVITATION ONLY luncheon at the grand ballroom of The Hyatt Regency hotel. At my table, the guest to my immediate right was Danny Kaye and to my left Leo Durocher. I was sandwiched between two of the most outspoken characters ever that day, and I was in stitches with laughter. Also at our table were Ralph Kiner, Stan Musial, Bill Dickey, Lefty Gomez, Hank Greenberg, Lou Boudreau and Buck Leonard. And no one was allowed to ask for an autograph.

Buddy Rich, whom Gene Krupa himself proclaimed the greatest drummer in the world, provided our music that day. And I felt as if I'd died and gone to heaven. Who says baseball is not sentimental?

And speaking of sentimental, I'd like to talk for a moment about the "Iron Horse of the New York Yankees," the great Lou Gehrig. My dad was one of the three founders of the Catholic Youth Organization, the others being Bishop Bernard Sheil, who baptized me, and well-known boxer, Packy McFarland. I even recall dad suffered a serious head injury when the boxing stands were under construction, prior to the first CYO tournament, and one of them fell on him. Somewhere in my collection of memorabilia I have dad's CYO "Medal of Champions," number THREE.

Through his association with the CYO, dad was often interviewed by the sportswriters of the day, and when Arch

Ward of the *Chicago Tribune* became the founding father of the Baseball All-Star Game in 1933, he sent dad two tickets. Mom declined dad's invitation, so I, as the eldest of their progeny, had next refusal. I, of course jumped at the opportunity, and because of that stroke of good fortune I got to very shakily, at nine years of age, shake the hands of Babe Ruth and Lou Gehrig. Knowing me, I was paralyzed and probably barely mumbled a word, but they did proffer their hands, and my icy one trembled in their monstrous grasps. I had actually touched these two, arguably, greatest baseball players of all time on the very instruments that held the Louisville Sluggers that propelled hundreds of American League spheres into the rarefied ozone.

Lou Gehrig was so strong, so muscular, how just six years later, almost to the date I shook his hand, could I accept what was printed in The Sporting News? I have kept this copy all of these years:

"CLINIC REPORT ON GEHRIG   New York, N.Y.— Amyotrophic lateral sclerosis is the term applied to Lou Gehrig's condition in the official Mayo Clinic report, signed by Dr. Harold C. Habien. The report made public by the Yankees on June 21, states: This is to certify that Mr. Lou Gehrig has been under examination at the Mayo Clinic from June 13 to June 19, 1939, inclusive.

"To whom it may concern:
After a careful and complete examination, it was found that he is suffering from amyotrophic lateral sclerosis. This type of illness involves the motor pathways and cells of the central nervous system and in lay terms is known as a form of chronic poliomyelitis (infantile paralysis). The nature of this trouble makes it such that Mr. Gehrig will be unable to continue his active participation as a baseball player, inasmuch as it is advisable that he conserve his muscular energy. He could, however, continue in some executive capacity."

THE HELLYER SAY

On the Fourth of July, 1939 at Lou Gehrig Appreciation Day, the "Iron Horse" stepped to the microphone at Yankee Stadium and spoke these words, "For the past two weeks you have been reading about the bad break I got. Yet today, I consider myself the luckiest man on earth." Sixteen years to the day he replaced Wally Pipp at first base, Lou Gehrig died in his home. The date was June 2, 1941. The "Pride of The Yankees" was just 37 years old. Despite terrible back spasms over the years, and many broken bones, including seventeen different healed fractures that showed in Xrays late in his career, he played in every game for over thirteen seasons.

Today, were he and Babe Ruth playing, they each would have won multiple Most Valuable Player awards, but in the years they played, one could win the MVP only once in his career. That rule was changed in 1932, and Gehrig who had won the award in 1927, won it again in 1936. The MVP was awarded Babe Ruth in 1923. Imagine how many MVP awards the most-feared back-to-back sluggers in baseball history, Gehrig and Ruth, would have won had the MVP rule been changed ten years earlier, in 1922. And they both shook my hand. I should never again have washed it.

The two things I remember most vividly and warmly from my 55-year radio-TV career, are my Supper Club shows on WBBM, and announcing baseball on WCFL from Comiskey Park.

On the Supper Club I worked with LIVE musicians, mostly from World War Two big bands, who each day would share with me the warm bond of friendship musicians have as part of their love of their art form and their love of those who share that art form with them. They were the joy of my broadcast life, so much fun to work with. Our air shows were a love fest...for the music and each other. Oh! How I miss them and those shows!!!!! It is cruel how rapidly time fugits!

Elaine was browsing in Anderson's Bookstore one day in

the summer of 1990 when she discovered a new baseball book on the shelves, "Prophet of the Sandlots" by Mark Winegardner, so she purchased it for my August 7th birthday. It is the story of Tony Lucadello, the baseball scout who signed more future major leaguers than any scout in baseball history, his lovely wife Virginia, "The Girl from Edison's Drugstore," and the young sandlot baseball players Tony signed, including Mike Schmidt, Fergie Jenkins, and Jim Brosnan. In all Tony Lucadello scouted and signed forty-nine young men who made it to the major leagues. No one, to this day knows why he took his own life at age 76 on May 8, 1989.

I sent Virginia Lucadello a letter telling her how impressed I was with the book about her husband and this was the first of five letters I would receive from her: "Sept 11, 1990   Dear Mr. Hellyer: Thank you so much for your kind letter. It really lifted my spirits. I have received many phone calls and letters from all over the country from strangers who still care about baseball and the basic things in life that matter a great deal to a lot of us—like character and integrity and the simple pleasures of life. Your music is a perfect example of that way of life. Tony loved it and often told me of listening to you as he traveled. You did indeed brighten many hours for him. I hope your music will brighten lives for years to come. I'm sure it has helped many, many travelers overcome the loneliness they feel for home and loved ones. In fact you have been, in a way, family for them. Again, thanks for your kind and caring letter. It has helped me more than you know. God Bless! Warmest regards, Virginia Lucadello from Edison's Drugstore."

In early December 1990 I had recommended the book as a Christmas gift for baseball fans, and I received this lovely letter from her: "Dec 30, 1990 Dear Art: I can't begin to thank you for the tape you sent to me. Your gracious comments were really appreciated. It is people like you who help others through a difficult time. With my family on

Christmas we listened to your kind words and it was a comfort to us all. I know you have touched many lives through your programs, and helped them feel better about themselves. I wish you a happy and healthy New Year and may God Bless you and yours. Warm regards, Virginia."

May 12, 1993, Virginia sent me this note: "Dear Art... Thank you again. I so much enjoy listening to the tapes you send me, and I appreciate you remembering me. On May 15, I will have the honor of throwing out the first ball in the annual 'Tony Lucadello Baseball Tournament.' Wish me well, as my arm isn't what it used to be. The girl from Edison's Drugstore is sliding down toward 80, but good friends like you keep me thinking young. I hope Tony's last signed ball player, Mickey Morandini does you proud in your Fantasy Baseball. It was really nice hearing from you. Love, Virginia." Tony surely married a true baseball fan. On her 1994 Christmas card, among many warm lines she wrote, "I hope they settle the Baseball Strike soon....I really felt cheated by missing the playoffs and the World Series."

"May 17, 1998

Dear Art and Family:

Thank you for the tape of your Valentine's Day show. I have listened to it several times and really enjoy it. So many of the songs bring back memories of when Tony and I danced to them. Although I recently suffered a small stroke, I was still able to throw out the first ball in the recent annual Tony Lucadello tournament.

Your family has really had a siege of cancer problems. Hope things are better by now. (Writer's note...The Lovely Elaine died of breast cancer five days before Virginia wrote this letter to me.)

I am so sorry the station won't be taping anymore of your shows. Over the years they have helped me through some very rough times. Also, through your shows I feel I have come to know you and yours as friends.

Take care Art, and may God Bless you and your family always.

Love,

Virginia

"The Girl from Edison's Drugstore" joined her beloved husband Tony Lucadello on August 12, 1999. She was 82. Everyone who came in contact with this lovely lady will never forget her.

Each summer's day, in the early to mid-1950s I was lucky enough to work major league baseball, AND without a parking hassle. I had my very own parking spot with my name painted on it. And I had my own Comiskey Park–American League pass. I could walk through the press gates at Comiskey Park AND Wrigley Field where Whitey, the Andy Frain chief-usher, would greet me daily like a long-lost friend.

Before going on the hallowed field for the pre-game "Dugout Show," and later, high up to the announce booths on the top roof at Comiskey Park, I would always stand at the lower middle level and gaze out at the warm green playing field where grown men would each day play a little boy's game, and often I'd have myself a good emotional cry. There is a beauty and a tranquility that only a baseball field has two hours before game time.

And there is a beauty to this little boy's game that no other sport has. It often is a ballet, and as Bob Elson frequently pointed out on his broadcasts, "Baseball is a game of inches." I often think about that phrase as I am falling to sleep at night. Inches, or fractions of inches are involved in almost every pitch and play. Baseball is indeed a game of inches, and it is, I believe, the only major sport that is played without some kind of timing device.

I really love baseball. Owners and players, Please, Please do not ruin this most beautiful of all sports with greed. No one needs ten million dollars or more per year to live comfortably.

Please play the wonderful game of baseball as we did when we were little boys, and as I played it with our five children when we were all so young........FOR THE LOVE OF THE GAME.

WE GET LETTERS

* Essay 16 *

**"I'd never heard of Art Hellyer as I listened to the
mellow baritone voice of an obvious professional.
I sat back and let the tide of radio's glory years wash over me.
Here was an announcer who made you feel like you were
the only one he was speaking to."**
*—Feature Columnist Rev. Greg Asimakoupoulos,
Daily Herald, May 11, 2002*

"Art Hellyer   June 14, 1948
WMAW Radio
Milwaukee, Wisconsin

"Dear Mr. Hellyer:
"I am in the throes of getting started myself on my television
program, and the preparation work is more than I bargained
for. Until I find my way around WPIX, I cannot be of any
help to anyone else, but I will keep you in mind and submit
your name to the proper person—one never knows. Have you
any ideas for television other than just radio news? They have
so many regular news commentators from their own papers
here in New York, that it occurred to me if you have some
new angle on this, it might be an easier introduction. I promise
you however, I shall be on the alert.

THE HELLYER SAY

"With my kindest regards to you, your wife and the little one, I am,

Sincerely,

Gloria Swanson"

To this day I find it remarkable that The Queen of The Movies, Gloria Swanson, even remembered me. I was a twenty-four-year-old nobody, with less than two years experience in small city radio, and just one of so very many to whom she spoke on her 1948 PR tour. I also find it hard to believe, Gloria Swanson, who two years later would again star in a movie of the ages, "Sunset Boulevard," was my very first celebrity interview. The Lovely Elaine and I had talked about it the night before in our very, very tiny apartment less than a mile from WMAW's studios in the Towne Hotel at Third Street and Wisconsin Avenue in downtown Milwaukee. Elaine said she'd like to walk baby Larry in his blue StorkLine buggy to the station, so she could see, in person, her female movie idol.

So it was on a delightful early spring day in 1948 Elaine was sitting in WMAW's neo-deco outer lobby with infant Larry hunkered down in the StorkLine, while in Studio A I was interviewing the great lady. I am looking this moment at a picture taken as we were talking on the air. A gloriously beaming smile is lighting Miss Swanson's classic face, and her bejeweled left fingers are wrapped around the base of the latest post-war RCA Victor microphone stand. Her left arm is dripping with tons of silver bracelets, and her body is wrapped in a colorful sari-like floor-length gown. The tiniest tuft of hair is visible peaking from beneath the semi-turban, and her eyebrows are perfect slivers highlighting her big flashing brown eyes looking at me as though I were William Holden. I am clad in my first and only suit, a symphony in gray by Robert Hall, and the tie I am wearing is a silk one purchased on September Second, 1945, at Neiman-Marcus in San Antonio, Texas, where I was proudly stationed at Randolph Field, The West Point of the Air, on the the historic day when the Japs signed the surrender, bringing an end to World War Two, which they visited on the world. The civilian tie was my way of celebrating that joyous event, and Miss Swanson's eyes seem to be scorching my eyeballs. I have a big fluffy head of hair I wish I still had, and people who have seen this picture say that I look like I am about to take a bite out of the beautiful screen star. Elaine was holding Larry in her arms as Miss Swanson and I, having finished our on-air chat, exited the studio. Everyone who toiled at the station was in the small lobby excitedly waiting to get a glimpse of the great lady. I then introduced Elaine to Miss Swanson, whose first words to my very young wife were, "Oh! I just love babies. May I KISS his bottom?" Gasps could be heard throughout the assemblage. Holy smoke!!! Did we hear her correctly? Well, to make a long story short, Gloria Swanson NEVER kissed Larry's bottom, and the interview in Studio A went, I was told by our station manager Jack Bundy and program director Woody Dreyfus, "very well, indeed."

"The Towers of the Waldorf   New York   June 15, 1950. Dear Art: I wish to thank you for your extreme thoughtfulness. Your musical salute was positively a most enjoyable birthday gift. Thank you again.
Sincerely,
Cole Porter"

"Art Hellyer   WCFL Chicago, Il. July 20, 1952
Bob Hope and Jane Russell invite you to a private screening of 'Son of Paleface,' Monday evening July 21, 11:00PM. Esquire Theatre   Regards, Paramount Pictures."

The Lovely Elaine and I had some beautiful pictures taken that night with Bob Hope and Jane Russell, and on another famous July Night…July 12, 1957, after I'd been fired by Marty Hogan, WCFL GM at 5PM, we had over ten thousand dollars damage in our basement from the most torrential rainstorm in Chicago's history, and those very pictures were part of the rubble.

"Art Hellyer WCFL Chicago, Il.
Dear Art: From our Toast of The Town stage this Sunday night November Seventh, 1953, as Eddie Fisher, Kitty Kallen and The Mills Brothers sing ten of the songs you've helped make famous, I am proposing a long overdue toast to you top disc jockeys of the country. I'd be deeply appreciative Art, if you'd direct the attention of your audience to this unusual triple booking of great recording names on our Sunday stanza. Thank you   Sincerely
ED SULLIVAN"

The next letter thrilled my dad. "My Buddy," was written by Gus Kahn, and was my dad's favorite song. While growing up I must have heard dad singing it hundreds of times:

"HAMPSHIRE HOUSE
NEW YORK CITY   Nov. 18, 1953

Mr. Art Hellyer
WGN
Chicago, Illinois
Dear Mr. Hellyer,
I want you to know how much I appreciate your help in making Gus' birthday such a memorable one. It was certainly nice of you to play 'My Buddy' twice. Thank you.

Sincerely,
Grace Kahn
Grace Kahn"

Telegram from Harry James and Betty Grable:

"Dear Art: We cordially invite you to join us at Linn Burton's Steakhouse on Tuesday, November 24, 1953 to help us celebrate our opening at the Chicago Theater. Art we hope to see you there. Sincerely, Harry James and Betty Grable."

The following letter in 1954 could not have come at a better time. The National Safety Council and the AAA had gone to court seeking cease and desist orders to stop me from talking on radio and TV about the desperate need for safety belts in automobiles:

"Dear Mr. Hellyer: I've listened to you campaigning for safety belts in automobiles for many years, and I'm convinced you are right. Therefore, as of July 1, 1954, I have ordered all automobiles and trucks operated by our company to be fully equipped with them. I believe you have made a major contribution to automobile safety, and the saving of lives. We, here at Northern Illinois Gas Company thank you. Sincerely, *Marvin Chandler*, President"

In the very early nineteen-fifties I interviewed couples getting their certificates on "The Marriage License Show" daily on first WGN Radio, then in the mid-fifties on WCFL. These shows emanated from Cook County Clerk Richard J. Daley's offices, and I never thought it strange that he was the only guest on the show each Saturday morning for years. He would answer questions sent to his office each week, and weeks when no questions arrived, we would make up questions, all pertaining of course, to the duties of his office. What he was doing was keeping his name before the people on powerhouse fifty thousand watt radio stations. It was very shrewd because in 1955 County Clerk Daley ran for Mayor, and the rest is history. I was called every four years to be his announcer on his campaign radio and television commercials. I got to know Mr. Daley very well over that twenty plus year period and I found him to be a warmhearted human being, in addition to being a superb servant of the people.

The following letter is just one example of what a fine, down to earth person he was:

"Mr. and Mrs. Art Hellyer   November 10, 1954
Skokie, Illinois
Dear Elaine and Art:
     Many thanks for your beautiful flowers. I am most appreciative of your thoughtfulness and good wishes. Believe it or not they are still in full bloom. And as pretty as the day they arrived. Thank you both again.
Sincerely,
Dick Daley
Cook County Clerk"

"Art Hellyer   WMAQ-NBC, Chicago, Il. May 7 1955 Dear Art: Thank you for hosting my tribute at The Ambassador East Hotel, and for playing "Sweet Thing" on every show for a month. You're a Sweet Thing. RCA Victor and I can't thank you enough. With love, *Dinah Shore*."

I believe a bit of information is called for before you read the next letter. The day before Gale Storm appeared on my morning show, Dr. K, my fantastic turntable technician interspersed a new recording by my guest, "Her Nibs Miss Georgia Gibbs" with his usual embellishments, including burps and raucous belches. "Her Nibs" had been forewarned by song-plugger Barney Fields, but she blew her top, told us off in three languages, grabbed her mink coat and stormed out of my life forever.

"Mr. Art Hellyer   October 5, 1955
WCFL
666 N. Lake Shore Drive
Chicago, Illinois

"Dear Art:
You won't believe me, but I consider my visit with you an outstanding highlight in a kaleidoscopic montage of faces. I might have been pretty sleepy when I walked into your hornet's nest, but it didn't take long for me to perk up after some of those fantastic goings-on. I don't know when I'll be ready for it, but I hope to see you again some day.

                              Sincerely,
                              Gale Storm

P.S. Dear Georgia Gibbs sends you a fond embrace (Half-Nelson)."

The saddest letter I received in my entire fifty-five year radio-television career came to me in the mid-nineteen-fifties, shortly after Richard Adler and Jerry Ross had guested on our show. Richard and Jerry wrote "Pajama Game," "Damn Yankees" and other great Broadway hits and Jerry died at age 29 on November 11, 1955, after, already having composed over 250 songs. His death, at such a young age, was a terrible shocker to all of us.

THE HELLYER SAY

"Richard Adler-Jerry Ross
18 West 55th Street
New York 19, N.Y.

Circle 5-5030   December 3, 1955

Dear Art,

What can I say except that this is a mighty hard one to write principally because it has to be the last time I'll have occasion to use the above letterhead. That I guess is my whole trouble in life now. But life must go on and I must go with it. I wish I knew exactly what my future plans would be, but as yet I am too shaken to make a definite choice as to the nature of the project. I must, however, start writing soon, and as soon as I know what it will be I shall inform you.

I would like to take this opportunity to wind up a series of thank you's for the contingency of Adler and Ross. It made Jerry a very happy boy to know he had a good friend like you plugging away at his songs and helping to make some of them hits. What else is there to say except thanks, and let's, for God's sake, stay friends throughout the years. How about a letter? Just a little one.

L and K,
R"

For many years in the nineteen-fifties I did the pre-game show and the football scoreboard on the Chicago Football Cardinals games on WCFL, and I would vociferously let it be known on the shows that I was a rabid Bears fan. I received much heat for this from the station management, sponsors and even from Paul Christman and Charlie Trippi and other Cardinal star players. How I lasted seven years I still don't know but it was fun, and George Halas, co-founder of the NFL and Owner-Coach of the Chicago Bears became a close friend of the Hellyer family, I am proud to say.

We Get Letters

"CHICAGO BEARS FOOTBALL CLUB
233 WEST MADISON STREET
CHICAGO 6, ILLINOIS   DE2-5400
FEBRUARY 17, 1957

Mr. Art Hellyer
Station WCFL
666 Lake Shore Drive,
Chicago 11, Illinois

Dear Art:

Thank you for your letter, which you sent me after the Bears-Detroit Lions game. I am sorry I didn't reply before today, but as you can well imagine, we were knee-deep in everything at that time.

I was quite amused to note that you wrote your note in the color red ink that carries the connotation of the south-side team. While I don't have an opportunity to hear your shows on the Chicago Cardinal Football Network, I have heard several people remark about your comments, and it is a real pleasure to have a rabid Bear fan in the enemy camp. I am so glad to have your loyal support.

Many thanks for your letter, and here's hoping we can keep you a proud Bear fan.

Sincerely yours,

George Halas"

On one of my radio shows early in April of 1960, I had a phone caller-in who insisted the Salk vaccine was "very dangerous," and that Dr. Jonas Salk and President Eisenhower refused to permit their children and/or grandchildren to be inoculated against the polio-virus.

This shocked Elaine and me, so to put the record straight, I wrote the President and Dr. Salk and I soon received these answers:

"THE WHITE HOUSE
WASHINGTON

April 14, 1960

Dear Mr. Hellyer:

Your April eighth letter to the President, received in his absence, has been referred to me.

The Eisenhower grandchildren have received Salk vaccine as part of their usual conformance to school group programs, both when residing in Alexandria, Virginia, and now in Gettysburg. The eldest, David, received his injection first—in April 1955.

Sincerely,
Mrs. Anne Wheaton
Associate Press Secretary
to the President"

"University of Pittsburgh
School of Medicine

April 18, 1960

Dear Mr. Hellyer:

Dr. Salk is out of the city and will not be back for some time, so I think I will answer your question by saying that you must know the answer.

Sincerely,
Lorraine Friedman
Secretary to Jonas E. Salk, M.D."

We Get Letters

"Dave Garroway   48 east 63rd Street, New York 21, NY....
October 2, 1961
Art Hellyer WBBM CBS RADIO Chicago, Illinois 60610
Dear Art: Your column is pasted on my bathroom door, where I can see it while I am sitting on the john. I will read it and re-read it because it's just exactly what I should have sense enough to do, and, generally, don't. Thank you for a strong stimulus and an exceedingly wise idea beautifully crystallized. Peace. Dave"
(A personal note, Dave Garroway sponsored me for membership in the Sports Car Club of America)

"To Larry, Mike and Jeff...   APRIL 8, 1962
Future success & pull for the N.Y. Mets.
CASEY STENGEL"

"November 1st, 1963
My son Art:
   I consider you my son, husband of my daughter Elaine, and brother of my daughter Carol. Take good care of both of them.
   I am sure Carol will ask for advice once in awhile. You being the only brother she has, she will come to you, which is quite natural.
   Be good, hold your temper. Be a good hubby and father.
   You have been a wonderful son-in-law. I still say, I wouldn't change you for any other one.
                                        Love,
                                        Lydia Miller"

I had read in *Broadcasting Magazine*, that Gene Autry, whom I had interviewed twice over the years, and for whom I had won the audition to be his "Melody Ranch" announcer from Milwaukee in 1948, was looking for new talent for his Hollywood stations.

So I wrote him personally and received this warm answer from him:

> "GENE AUTRY
> RIVERSIDE DRIVE
> NORTH HOLLYWOOD, CAL.

December 3, 1963

Art Hellyer
American Broadcasting Company
360 N. Michigan Avenue
Chicago 1, Illinois

Dear Art:

Thank you for you letter of November 13th together with the brochure. I am forwarding them to Mr. Lloyd Sigmon who is in charge of all personnel of our broadcasting and television properties. I am sure you will be hearing from him.
Kindest personal regards, and it was good to hear from you again.

> Most sincerely,
> **Gene**
> GENE AUTRY"

A sidebar: Did you know Gene Autry was the only serviceman in World War Two allowed to wear cowboy boots while on active duty? Also, Mr. Sigmon phoned me and after we talked it over, Elaine and I decided—once again—we'd stay in Chicago.

As I look back over the years, I certainly had my chances to go to Hollywood and New York, but when it came to nitty-gritty time we always decided to stay where our families were. I recall many people I worked with over the years telling me they liked the way I always put my family first. I've always been a homebody, and now writing this book in my dotage I know why Irving Berlin was a recluse, because I am indeed a member of his club.

"TO: All Ch.7 Employees   Date   2-10-1964
FROM: Red Quinlan, GM
SUBJECT: Employees in The Fire.
The performance of all employees in Sunday's fire in our building was commendable indeed. The quick thinking of everyone, the calmness in the face of severe dense smoke, the the spirit of cooperation, the tenacity and steadfastness in the face of danger, were qualities common to you all during that emergency. It would be unfair to single out certain individuals because all of you were so great, But I'm sure you won't mind a special nod to Jim Grinnell who kept us on the air, the boys in Tape, Telecine, and the control rooms, Art Hellyer who choked his way through a station break, Frank Genereux and Jim McPharlin who lost a battle with a glass door, and Hazel Ludes who swallowed a lifetime supply of smoke before she had to close up her switchboard and escape.

No one is asked to jeopardize his or her life in such an emergency, yet many did. I can only salute you and call your magnificent efforts to the attention of everyone.

Red Quinlan"

May 16, 1964
Art Hellyer
WBBM-CBS
Chicago, Illinois
To My Pal ART, Thanks For The Spins. Liberace.   Then

THE HELLYER SAY

under his signature he has drawn a grand piano with a candelabra on top. Quite a production by arguably THE entertainer of the 20th century.

"UNITED STATES SENATE
EVERETT McKINLEY DIRKSEN
MINORITY LEADER, ILLINOIS
MARCH 29, 1965

Mr. Art Hellyer
American Broadcasting Company
190 N. State Street
Chicago. Illinois
Dear Art:

I am glad you are bringing the family to Washington for a sojourn between April 11 and 14. Insofar as I know I shall be here and will be happy to see you, your lovely wife and the youngsters.

With every good wish,

Everett McKinley Dirksen"

We spent the better part of the day watching the United States Senate in action, and twice riding the open-car subway trains under their august, hallowed chambers. On one of our trips, Senators Wayne Morse of Oregon and Peter Dominic of Colorado were fellow passengers in the little open conveyance.

I have wonderful pictures of Senator Dirksen down on the floor of his office crawling around and playing with Jeffrey and Victoria, the two youngest of our five children. When the good senator struggled getting back up on his feet, I could see the outline of a back brace protruding through his white shirt, and I offered to assist him. When his two feet were once again safely attached to the floor, he leaned over toward me and said softly, in that great rumbling stentorian voice we all remember so well: "Art, promise me, you'll never mention on your fine radio and TV programs, my bad back and the brace I wear. I don't want our fine constituents back home in Illinois thinking perhaps I can't perform my duties here." I promised him I would never mention it on the air and I never have. This, in fact is the first time I've done so, and it doesn't matter now.

Senator Dirksen made another statement to me I found most interesting, "You know, Art, I'm a Republican and Senator Douglas is a Democrat. We sit across the aisle from each other, and most people think we are not friends. The truth is all of us lucky enough to serve in the House and Senate are good friends. We respect each other's opinions, and well, Art, frankly—we all are members of the greatest country club in the world. Yes sir, Art, as the old saying goes, we all thank God we live in the greatest country in the world."

Ask any of my family about the Senator from Pekin, Illinois, and they will, in unison, agree he was one wonderful man.

> "UNITED STATES SENATE
> COMMITTEE ON
> THE DISTRICT OF COLUMBIA
> ROBERT F. KENNEDY, N.Y.
> September 9, 1965

Mr. Art Hellyer
American Broadcasting Company
WLS-TV
190 N. State Street
Chicago 1, Illinois

Dear Mr. Hellyer:
Thank you for your letter of July 11, letting me know of the action taken by General Motors. I am sorry there has been a

delay in responding to your nice note.

I appreciate your apprising me on this matter, as it may prove useful in future Senate hearings on the subject of auto safety. Your comments were most welcome and informative.

For President Johnson and myself, I want to also commend you and thank you for all you've done on your radio shows over the years to further the manufacture of safer automobiles. Our mutual friend Ed Guthman is no longer here in Washington, but is out in California where he is national news editor of the Los Angeles Times. The next time I see him however, I will relay your thanks to him.

Sincerely,

Robert F. Kennedy

On our trip to Washington, D.C., in April 1965, we visited Senator Robert Kennedy in his Senate offices and found him to be a very gracious gentleman. He showed us the three walls in one of his offices where he had tacked up homework done by his children. He also had his assassinated brother's presidential desk across from his own. It was a very touching, humbling visit. I received his permission to take a picture of Elaine with him, and my hands were shaking so much I almost dropped the camera. I find it impossible to believe as I look at that picture today proudly hanging on the wall of my Studio H, that my beloved wife left us over nine years ago and her partner in the picture has not walked the face of this earth for forty years. Each of them died too young, with so much more good to do.

The following was probably a big mistake on my part:

"Mr. Robert Hyland   12-24-66
VP/General Manager
KMOX RADIO, CBS,

We Get Letters

St. Louis, Missouri
Dear Mr. Hyland:

Remember the family in "Meet Me In St. Louis?" Papa was offered a job in New York, and the family was most reluctant to leave St. Louis. Well, I have the same situation here, in reverse. I have polled Elaine and our five youngsters, and they all voted to stay in Chicago. Our roots are deep here so I shall honor their wishes.

Your offer was most flattering because it is not every broadcaster who is offered the 6PM and 10PM news on KMOX. I also am aware I would be doing the most-listened-to news on the number-one station in the Midwest, and as you have said, 'the greatest station in the country.'

I regret, that at this time, I must say 'no,' but perhaps we can get together sometime in the future.

Thank you for the offer, and Happy New Year to you all.
Cordially,
Art Hellyer
Art Hellyer"

"OFFICE OF THE MAYOR
CITY OF *CHICAGO*
RICHARD J. DALEY
September 26, 1968

Mr. Art Hellyer
American Broadcasting Company
360 N. Michigan Avenue
Chicago, Illinois 60601
Dear Art:

Thanks for the support you have given me

on your daily show relative to the recent events
during the National Democratic Convention.
I am grateful for your help and assistance.

Kind personal regards,

Richard J. Daley
Mayor"

"CHICAGO TRIBUNE
The World's Greatest Newspaper

Art Hellyer   June 6, 1969
WLS-FM
360 N. Michigan Avenue
Chicago, Il 60611

"Art:
Hope you and Elaine had a pleasant trip to the Ozarks. Did
you buy more property at Branson? Very wise investment.
Alleine and I are going to the Smokies with the same idea.
I bought a new radio for the office, because the other one
had too much interference in it. Now the BEST radio show
I've ever heard, yours, comes in fine. Keep up the good work.
Best Wishes,
Ed Holland
Chief Cartoonist, *Chicago Tribune*"

Ed Holland would call in to my shows and we became
close friends. We still exchange Christmas cards and notes
throughout the year, and we enjoyed many lunches together at
the Press Club, or in his fabulous office on the topmost level
of Tribune Tower. I found it interesting viewing a number of
his cartoons in various stages on his separate drawing boards.

We Get Letters

Chester Gould, the founder of and the original cartoonist who created Dick Tracy, occupied the only other office in that sky-scraping tower, and it was fun to watch him creating the latest menace to Dick Tracy's continued existence. On the circular outer walls of his cubicle Mr. Gould had many of his characters, including my two favorites, "Prune Face" and "Flat Top."

Watching these two great cartoonists was something else. Their fertile, imaginative minds were something to behold. Ed Holland drew a new "Zodiac Calendar" for the *Tribune* front page every month, and for years I was pictured in his August drawing. I am a Leo and my favorite Ed Holland "Zodiac" is in front of me as I write this. It is the front page August 1, 1970, and Ed Holland has me standing in front of an igloo, and I am presenting an Eskimo with an electrical appliance. I am saying, "I have your air conditioner for your igloo," and the printed copy next to me reads, "Leo people are excellent salesmen." Ed Holland and his beautiful wife Alleine retired to eastern Tennessee some years ago, and Ed has been commissioned by many private individuals and business corporations to render paintings for them.

I am the proud owner of an original Ed presented me with. It is an oil painting of a gorgeous redheaded nude strolling a tropical beach in the South Pacific.

"Holiday Inns Inc., 3742 Lamar Avenue, Memphis, Tennessee 38118....December 7, 1971.

Dear Mr. Hellyer Thanks for your nice letter. I appreciate your comments. I am enclosing a Complimentary Holiday Inn pass you might enjoy using. I am also enclosing an autographed picture.
Sincerely yours, Kemmons Wilson....Chairman of the Board....Holiday Inns, INC."

I am so sorry I lost the pass. It had a beautifully engraved front side indicating it was a free pass. On the backside it said, "Not good at this Holiday Inn. Not good at that Holiday Inn, in fact, NOT GOOD AT ANY HOLIDAY INN."

"Prof. Art Hellyer
Columbia College   Broadcast Communications
600 South Michigan Avenue
Chicago, Illinois 60605   March 24, 1980
Dear Art:

I want to thank you for taking the time to write such a thoughtful and considerate letter. It was VERY thoughtful of you. Your name and Chicago radio go hand in hand. We had a very good season and being ranked Number One for seven weeks was a great honor. We believe we gave the fans of Chicago something to be proud of.

Thank you for your continued support. Please keep rooting for us. With best wishes and kindest personal regards, I am yours,

Ray Meyer, Basketball Coach, DePaul University"

Letter from Edgar Award Mystery writer Stuart Kaminsky...
          "Northwestern University
          School of Speech
          Evanston, Il. 60201   November 25, 1980
Dear Art Hellyer:
I'm glad you enjoyed my Toby Peters novel. There are now five Toby Peters books in print. Another, *High Midnight*, which deals with Gary Cooper and Ernest Hemingway, will be out next spring. I'm working on one beyond that which will have a circus background, and Emmett Kelly as Toby's client.
I remember you well from your radio mornings in the 1950s and 1960s. Many was the morning you helped me rise with a smile instead of dry mouth and a frown.

With all my good wishes, I am,
  Stuart
    Stuart M. Kaminsky, Ph.D.
    Professor and Head of the Division of Film"

(Note...From page 90 of Stuart Kaminsky's 1995 mystery classic *Lieberman's Thief*, I proudly quote, "There were no parking spaces on the street in front of his house, not even the one by the fire hydrant. A van with a clergy sign on the pulled-down visor was illegally parked there.

"Art Hellyer was joyfully announcing the next string of oldies on the radio as Lieberman turned the corner on Birchwood and drove around the back into the alley."

Thank you, Stuart.....I am thrilled to know that my favorite Chicago detective listened to my shows. Thank you.

"Art Hellyer   Satellite Music Network....1982
My love and thanks, Art, for your warm thoughts.
    PEGGY LEE"

"COLUMBIA COLLEGE CHICAGO   600 S. MICHIGAN
    CHICAGO, ILLINOIS 60605   312 663 1600
Dean of the College
June 14, 1984

To: Mr. Arthur Hellyer

Dear Art:
Your record of accomplishments at the College is impressive. I am even more impressed when I realize the extent of your physical disabilities and the way in which they affected your teaching. You handled these difficulties with grace.
We are grateful to you for the many services you performed

for the College in the many years you taught here. None of those services is more important than what you did for our students. It is for the sake of educating students, after all, that the College exists. Providing for that goal through the services of active professionals like you is, at times, treacherous. Not everyone can teach what he does, though he may do his professional job very effectively. In your case, the College found an able teacher coupled with a highly regarded professional. That is the combination upon which the College depends for its success, and the students for theirs.

Thank you for the many dedicated years you gave the College. I wish it were possible to say that every teacher at Columbia could claim as much pride as you do, and could do so with equal validity. That is a worthy goal for the College to pursue.

My best regards to you, Art.

Sincerely,

LYA

Lya Dym Rosenblum
Dean of the College"

And this Memo from:

"College Of St. Francis 500 Wilcox St Joliet, Il 60435

To: Art Hellyer

From: Sr. Rita Travis, Chair

Date: March 11, 1986

Re: 1986-87 Schedule

"I want to thank you for the great job you have been doing with the radio courses and the radio students. The students sing your praises continually, and I am thrilled that you are part of the faculty. I have prepared the fall 1986 schedule and have set up Radio 1 in its usual time. I presume (and hope) that you are planning to teach it again this fall.

Again, thanks for all you do for the department!!"

We Get Letters

"CHRYSLER CORPORATION

Lee A. Iacocca
Chairman of the Board
Chief Executive Officer   October 31, 1985

Mr. Art Hellyer
Satellite Music Network
P.O.Box 877
Mokena, Illinois 60448

"Dear Mr. Hellyer:
Thank you for your letter and for your kind words.
I appreciate your support concerning the use of safety belts. You certainly have done your part to publicize the importance of their use in saving lives. I'm also heartened to hear that you agree with me concerning fuel standards, and I hope that you will continue to make your voice heard on this issue as well. I only hope some constructive action is taken in the near future.
    Best Wishes.

                     Sincerely,
                     Lee Iacocca"

Sydney Johnson lived in San Antonio, Texas, after she retired from her long career as music-librarian with Paul Whiteman's great orchestra and later with my all-time favorite chorale, Fred Waring and the Pennsylvanians. She wrote me many letters over the years I was heard on the world's first Satellite Music Network. With one of her lettters in 1985 she included her personal original copy of Paul Whiteman's payroll for their appearance the week of Jan.20-28, 1928, at the Mosque Theatre in Newark, New Jersey. It gives the name of each band member, his position with the band, his pay for the week and each bandmembers signature. I won't give you all thirty-six names, but will list some of the prominent performers:

Harry Barris Piano 175.00, Bix Beiderbecke Trumpet 200.00, Henry Busse Trumpet 350.00, Bing Crosby Vocal 150.00, Jimmy Dorsey Sax 200.00, Matty Malneck Violin 150.00, Mike Pingatore Banjo 300.00, Al Rinker Piano 150.00, Ferde Grofe Arranger 375.00, Frank Trumbauer Sax, 200.00. Paul Whiteman's salary was not revealed. I find this most interesting, and thank Sydney for sending it to me.

The original Satellite Network moved from Mokena, Illinois, to Dallas, Texas, in 1987, and I took a job with one of our affiliates, WMAD in Madison, Wisconsin. Please see my Satellite Music Network essay elsewhere in this book for all the details. One of my loyal listeners over the years was a lovely lady, Ethel Linnane, who lived in Corpus Christi, Texas, and wrote me frequently. The first time I introduced Sammy Kaye's gorgeous song "The Old Lamplighter" on the Satellite Network, Ethel caught me in a terrible error and never let me forget it. I described the lighting of the lamplight this way...."The Old Lamplighter would reach up to the gas-light's diffuser with a long pole with a flaming torch at the top. He would then touch the flame to the gas-filled jars wick, and a beautiful soft light would light the street." Ethel informed me that would result in a terrible explosion, so when she heard I was going to work at WMAD, she quickly sent me the following Western Union Mailgram:

"Dear Art: All good wishes as you join WMAD. Remember to play 'The Old Lamplighter' record, though per-haps best you avoid explanation of lamp lighting procedure. Vaya Con Dios. Ethel."

Over the many years of my Radio-TV career a few listeners sent me checks as a thank-you for "entertaining" them or for playing their favorite song, and I returned every last one of them. The years I worked for the Satellite Music Network I seemed to receive more than ever.

A lady in Arkansas, a man and wife in Nashville, a lady in Santa Barbara, California, one in Seattle, Washington, and others. I would sit in "Stardust Division" program director Ralph Sherman's office and as I returned each check I would do so in his presence. Usually that was it, but one lady refused to take no for an answer. Her name was Jenny Goodwin and in her eighties she was still working fulltime for the Sanford, Maine, water company. Two or three times a year she would write me an interesting 4–6 page letter and enclose the largest listener checks ever proffered me....one thousand dollars, and of course I would return every one of them.

On March 1, 1987, she wrote her usual long letter and she made out for the first time the envelope, the salutation, and the one thousand dollar check to "Art & Elaine Hellyer." In the final paragraph she wrote, "Please accept this check with my pleasure. Better than giving it to the government or nursing homes. So please, please do not send this check back because if I could not afford it, I would not do it. Will close with my best wishes always. Love, Jenny Goodwin"

Of course I returned the check again. Sadly too, I never heard from Jenny again.

Letter from Mrs. Bill Osmanski, wife of the former great Chicago Bears fullback who led the NFL in ground-gaining and on December 8, 1940 scored the Bears first touchdown in the 73-0 NFL Championship game with the Washington Redskins, and now was suffering from Alzheimer's disease...

"3-12-89

Dear Art, The Eddy Howard-Glenn Miller tape is well worn already. I wish you could see the joy on Bill's face— especially with your personal remarks on your show. Thank you so much for all the time and trouble you have gone to.

I hope some day soon that you and Joe and Bill can meet for lunch. Bill does enjoy getting out. He has a lot of energy to spend. Again...many, many thanks Mary O."

As I look back at almost sixty years of mostly low pay, no job security at all, working every Saturday, Sunday and every Thanksgiving, Christmas and New Year's Eve day and hundreds of seven days/nights weeks, I wonder now how I did it, but not WHY I did it. I can't think of any other field where one meets and gets to know people like Irving Berlin, Joe DiMaggio, Ted Williams, Willie Mays, Jackie Gleason, Bess and Harry Truman, Doris Day, Robert Kennedy, Richard Nixon, Gloria Swanson, Andy Griffith, Merv Griffin, Liberace, Spike Jones, Ernie Banks, Ray Meyer, George Halas, Patti Page, Peggy Lee, Mel Dormer, Rosemary Clooney, Margaret Whiting, Ed Holland, Heinrich Strorigl, Perry Como, Bing Crosby and Anton Myrer, the man I, and others, consider to be the greatest American novelist of the Twentieth Century.

Tony Myrer's first letter to me was dated April 20, 1982. It is a two full pages typed letter and I excerpt it:

"I am pleased you liked 'The Last Convertible.' The book had its origin that turbulent spring of 1969, my college 25th reunion. I knew I wanted to write a book about our generation, but I couldn't find the kind of dramatic symbol that would tie it all together. Then in 1976 Cadillac made that announcement about producing the last convertibles, and I saw how a car, exactly the right kind of car—OUR kind of car—could catch it all up; the big bands and dance pavilions, the car trips and double dates, and then the war, with its haste and fears and misunderstandings, and then coming home, and the slow parade of years, with their rivalries and loyalties and betrayals, and the whole plan for the novel fell into place in a day and a night.

"It's funny Art—so many harsh things have been said about our generation (conformist, materialistic, apathetic, acquisitive—all those long unkind adjectives!) and they weren't true of us at all. Actually we were intensely romantic and committed, and fantastically innocent too; and we CARED: we did care, terribly—about so many things. I guess I wanted to say that about us more than anything else. And I wish I'd gotten your letter a touch earlier—I was in Chicago three weeks ago in connection with the new novel; I would have liked to contact you, even if only briefly. And isn't it great the way the big bands are coming back? New bands echoing the great ones we knew, and radio stations playing more and more of the old classics? And so many vocalists of our hey-day issuing new releases of the old tunes! Again, thanks for taking the trouble to write. Next time I'm in Chicago I'll take the liberty of getting in touch with you. It will be fun to reminisce a little about those lost, golden days before the whole world changed so irrevocably for us all.

"As to my autograph—I can do a lot better than that! Am sending you an inscribed copy of 'The Last Convertible' under separate cover.

"All warm best wishes, TONY MYRER"

My personally inscribed copy of "The Last Convertible" arrived shortly thereafter and Mr. Myrer wrote on the flyleaf, "To Art Hellyer—Who loves those golden evenings with the big bands, and who has brought them all back again.
Tony Myrer
Saugerties, N.Y. 12477"

January 11, 1983

"Dear Art:

"Glad to get your note, and Eric Zorn's piece in the *Trib*:

really overjoyed that you've rocketed back on top again with the big band format. All power to W(onderful) J(umpin') J(ive) D(ancebands)!!! (writer's note...reference is to radio station WJJD, Chicago on whose megacycles I was staging my latest comeback).

"George Spink sent me a sheaf of fabulous clips about Mayor Jane Byrne's Great Summer Festival Bash—including the Basie roof-raising (which MUST have happened during the sock chorus of WOODSIDE)...

"As I imagine you know, back here in the Second Big Band City, WNEW has turned its November "Month of Remember" into a delightful annual habit, featuring a big band and/or vocalist each day of the month, and resurrecting some of the out-of-the-way recordings of "forgotten" classics from those golden evenings. It has been an enormous hit throughout the listening area—nostalgic letters and memorabilia have poured in by the tens of thousands....

"Let me off uptown,

Tony"

On their 1987 Christmas card, Tony wrote:

"So pleased to get your rousing communiqué, and know that you are still swingin' down the lane. The Artie Shaw band came through last spring; and we've had some big band bashes up at Hunter Mountain around Labor Day.

"Your 'Hiawatha' exhortation gave me a laugh—at one point a few years ago I did play with the idea of setting a novelette (or novella or whatever) on the 'Wolverine", which was the great Chicago-Boston choo-choo of my palmy days; maybe I'll get out my sheaf of notes and take another look!

"Pat & I hope you and Elaine are in good health and spirits this tumultuous & catalytic year. Tony"

In their annual Christmas card to me, this one in 1994,

Tony Myrer wrote, "A melancholy roll call in the obit columns this year: velvet-voiced Dinah (Shore), underrated Max Kaminsky, Toots Mondello and the irrepressible Cab Calloway.....but life, Art goes on, happily and we caught the Glenn Miller band last week. Pat and I hope you and Elaine are in good health and spirits, this tumultuous and catalytic year."

January 2, 1995, Tony wrote, "Dear Art. Wish I could have been there New Year's Eve for your 49th Anniversary clambake. This year—half a century to the day when we crawled around on Guam getting ready for the Iwo operation—has been full of swingband memories: there was a wonderfully kooky guy on the jungle network who used to play out-of-the-beaten-path numbers, like Krupa's 'The Sergeant Was Shy,' Parrish's 'After Hours,' Shaw's 'Comin' On,' Basie's 'Blame It On My Last Affair' (with the underrated Helen Humes), Calloway's 'Foolin' With You,' and other such esoterica. His intro ran something like: 'And now my beloved sack rats, coming straight at you with the big band music you can't live without, emanating from the very heart of downtown Agana...' Etc. I'm ashamed to say I've forgotten his name. A very personal vice of mine; I never forget a face, never remember a name. Listening to Ray Smith's 'The Jazz Decades' over WAMC last Saturday night. He played Coleman Hawkin's 'Body And Soul,' which brought back such a perfect flood of memories my eyes filled with tears...I must be getting dotty in my fumbling old age.

And so here comes 1995. Let's hope it's a better platter than crazed, violence-laden, vindictive old flip-side '94. Remember that wild line in the Hines record: 'Play it till nineteen-fifty-one!' Immensely pleased you're still playing the real thing. Have you noticed that when the big-time hucksters REALLY want to move a product, they fall back on Goodman or Miller or Shaw or Dorsey for background music? They know, they know....

All good fortune to you for the New Year.... TONY "

And then from Tony's wife.....February 20, 1996, "Dear Art....I wanted to let you know my beloved husband ANTON MYRER, died on January 19, 1996 of acute leukemia from which he had suffered for 9 months. It has been so unfair and terrible, but what isn't? That is why he hasn't written you about your wonderful last two tapes. He ENJOYED them so much and played them on a little recorder in hospital where he'd been in isolation for these last months. Tony fought gallantly all the way. We heard your Benny Goodman songs even toward the end. I held hands one last time during Bohème on the little radio. He died in my arms.

"Your marvelous enthusiasm and support of 'our' music meant a great deal to him and I wanted you to hear. Keep the faith.

With thanks,
Patricia Myrer
(Mrs. Patricia Myrer)
Saugerties, NY"

After I received the above letter I dedicated a complete four hour show to Tony Myrer. Each chapter in "The Last Convertible" is named after a Big Band Classic song, and the book is my all-time favorite novel because it truly is the story of our lives, the people of my generation. I spoke of his being wounded in action in World War Two following his graduation from Harvard University in 1941. And I talked about his remarkable war novel of three wars "Once An Eagle," of which the Armed Forces Journal of the National War College wrote:

"'Once An Eagle' deserves to rank with, or perhaps above any one of these three great pieces of military fiction—

Stephen Crane's 'The Red Badge of Courage,' 'Fix Bayonets' by Col. John W. Thomason, USMC, and 'What Price Glory' by Capt. Lawrence Stallings, USMC." "Once An Eagle" is required reading at the Army War College and West Point.

I sent the tape of the show to Patricia Myrer and on March 31, 1996, she wrote me:

"Dear, dear Art Hellyer,

I can never ever thank you enough. Your beautiful, moving and true tribute to my darling Tony has sustained me through a terrible week. This is a tape that will be played again and again. How very generous and kind of you. Benny's 'Stardust' just about finished me—in the best possible way.

"I was glad too, of your reminder of dear Fran Allison and the old Don McNeill Breakfast Club. They are strong in my memory. And what a beautiful speaking voice you have! Tony and I were talking about it in the case of the other tape you sent shortly before he died.

You will be glad to know that I have heard from several people who listened to your show about Tony. He always loved Chicago and its open-hearted people, and he admired you.

"Thank you again from Tony and from me. They say matter is never destroyed, only altered and the Comet so recently in the sky has reminded me of him and you and OUR time, the BEST.

Love, Pat Myrer"

I have tried many times to contact Patricia Myrer in recent years at their home address. And I have written The National War College, but I've heard nothing. I am very worried.

I am a packrat, and I have kept everything I ever felt I should keep since I was a little boy. So as I have been final-editing, I have been going through scores of drawers and boxes in my broadcast studio, the attic and basement and garage and even my bedroom dresser. And I have been finding articles, letters and all sorts of written and printed items dating as far back as the nineteen-twenties.

Just this moment on October 18, 2007, I found this letter from Patricia Myrer behind my dresser:

4   23   2003
"Dear Art,

"You must forgive my long silence—heart failure & then radiation treatments. One shouldn't live over 70 without grandchildren! Your kind Christmas card was received in hospital and especially appreciated.

"I still play your wonderful tape, dear Art. It sustains me.

"Tony's work is having a splendid revival. If you were in a bookstore last December you saw 'Eagle' in a new Harper hardcover, as well as Harper Perennial soft-cover classics of our beloved 'Convertible' & other Myrer titles. 'Convertible' is also a play in the Czech Republic, where all Tony's titles are in print. I tease his ghost that he must've had a Czech lover.

"Take care of your dear self. All love, Pat Myrer"

On February 7, 2008, I received this most welcome letter:

"To Art Hellyer   3 February 2008
    Dear Art:

The New York Society Library kindly forwarded your letter trying to locate me. I am still at the old address, but entirely unavailable either in person or by phone. I am quite ill and almost stone deaf! Lord, what a bore. I hope you are better. I was happy to learn of your book. And I thank you for including Tony's and my letters to you.

"Sorry I am not able to be more communicative, but I send

you good wishes & love, Pat Myrer"

My heartfelt thanks to the New York Society Library for forwarding my plea for information to Patricia Myrer. And thank you dear Pat for writing me the above letter. I consider it a most important addition to *The Hellyer Say*.

March 28, 1994
"Dear Art:
"I've recorded a variety of your shows since WCFL 1957, WBBM 1965, WOPA between 1966 and 1968, and WLS-FM 1969-1972. Oh, how I wish I had recorded many, many more hours. And now I am so happy to share these tapes with you. It was splendid meeting you while you were doing your show last Saturday at Bailey's Carpet One. And it was so meaningful because I got a chance to say thank you for all the great memories over the years.

"Again thank you.
"Easter is a time
For celebrating the new.
But it's also a time
  For lovely traditions
  And warm memories,
  Like those shared on the radio
  with Art Hellyer.
Happy Easter to you and your family,
Cathy and Jack Hackenbrock
50-year Art Hellyer listeners."

As I write this essay in 2007, one of the finest newsmen and gentlemen I've ever known personally, ABC-TV's John Drury, lies dreadfully ill with ALS...Lou Gehrig's Disease. I find that additionally hard to believe as I look at his extremely bold handwritten letter to me dated:

October 19, 1995
"Dear Art.

"I'm listening to your 50th Anniversary of VJ DAY broadcast in my car as I drive home from work.

"What a joy it is to listen to a real radio broadcast done by some one who knows what radio is all about.

"I love the integration of WWII music with the interviews. On a plane, I once sat next to a survivor of Wake Island and learned for the first time the men on that island were captured and used as slave labor in Japan. And now I am hearing you actually interviewing Marine Corps Sgt. Howard Chittendon who was captured the first day of the war and was forced to work until the last day of the war in Japanese war factories.

"WHAT A STORY....WHAT A BROADCAST....WHAT A BROADCASTER!!!

"Thanks for the tape, Art. It is greatly appreciated.
Sincerely,
JOHN DRURY"

May 12, 1998, my wonderful family and I lost the Lovely Elaine to the horrors of breast cancer. *Chicago Tribune* features writer Eric Zorn wrote me this touching letter, which though I am terribly lonely, I strive to live up to:

May 21, 1998
"Dear Art: What terrible news—cancer is such an unfair enemy. I hope that Elaine can give YOU the strength you'll need to carry on alone, as I know she would want you to do. All the best......Eric Zorn"

And this note from my next door neighbor Jeff Leston's mom, Elaine Leston, after my Elaine died still breaks me up....

"Dear Art....I just wanted to tell you this. Your wife was outside emptying water from a garbage can and I said to her, 'Elaine, are you supposed to be doing that?' She laughed and said, 'No, but don't tell Art, because he takes such good care of me.' I'll always remember that—the special way she said it. Elaine Leston"

January 15, 2003
"Dear Art:
    "When you bring so much enjoyment to millions of listeners around the world on the internet, it would be unconscionable for you to retire. You have the BEST SHOW on both sides of the Mississippi.
    "Remember Art....DO NOT RETIRE!!!!!!!
Millie and I send our love.
Chic Cicchelli
President.....The California Art Hellyer Fan Club"

My answer to this wonderful man is, I have no intention of retiring. I hate the thought, but if radio stations continue to discriminate against performers because they are "too old," where do we find employment? WalMart?
    My voice is the very same voice I had fifty years ago, and I have a vast knowledge of the world I didn't have fifty years ago. It breaks my heart to not be entertaining people and making them happy. It is my life, but tell that to a thirty-year-old station manager. He/She/It couldn't care less about people of maturity.
    My e-mail address is ART_HELLYER@YAHOO.COM and I am always available.

"Four Beers Joe   October 8, 2004
"Mr. Art Hellyer:

341

"My friend and undergraduate roommate at Aurora University, 1953-57, Dr. (University of Maine) Kent Smith sent me information about you he took from the internet. He also told me he had emailed you and you would get back to him on cassettes of your morning show on WCFL in the 53-57 period. I am hopeful you will find some. We would be delighted. 'Four beers Joe,' 'I am throwing this case to you,' 'Get a nickel back on every bottle Jim'—all are phrases I remember from your great shows, and they have been a part of our conversation all these years since.

"WE have been fans from afar for years not knowing what happened to you. You were and you continue to be OUR HERO.

Dr. Don Carver   University of Georgia, Athens, Ga."

10/5/04

"Mr. Hellyer:

I first heard you on the radio in 1953-54 as a freshman at Aurora University. I had come to Aurora from a small town in Iowa, and my roommate came from Florida. We were both pretty homesick for a while, but you helped us get over it as we became regular listeners to your program and delighted in your great sense of humor. Eventually I ended up teaching at the University of Maine, and my roommate, Don Carver is at the University of Georgia. We've kept in close touch over the years, in fact my wife's college roommate became Don's wife. It never fails in our phone conversations, emails, or whenever we'd get together that you don't eventually become one of the subjects of our discussions—one of us will say something like 'There's no light in the mensroom,' 'Get a nickel back on every bottle Jim,' 'No Tickee, No Shirtee' etc., and that gets us started in 'Hellyer Humor,' bringing back many wonderful memories of your broadcasts.

"As has unfortunately been your sad experience as well,

Don lost his beloved wife two years ago from breast cancer, so I know it will lift his spirits to learn of the book you are writing, and the possibility of getting audiocassettes of your broadcasts.

"Best wishes and I'll look forward to hearing from you.
Sincerely,
Dr. Kent Smith
University of Maine,
Orono, ME 04473"

Elsewhere in this book I have mentioned a number of lovely people I would have never known had I not been on the radio. Among them are three 50 plus year listeners, Virginia Gora and Mel Dormer. Each can tell you the birthdates of our 5 wonderful children, and all the dates and call letters of the stations that hired me and fired me. Here are recent notes from them:

"July 2, 2007
Dear Art: Please allow me to introduce myself. First my occupation. I manufacture women's wear for inclement weather. I specialize in insulated bras. My name is Hugo Winterhalter.

"I remember you first saying that over forty years ago. We've been friends a long time Art thanks to the radio. And thank you for brightening thousands of hours for me and so many other people. Your friend, Mel Dormer"

"August 7, 2007
HAPPY BIRTHDAY, GREAT ONE!!
Dear Art...It's so nice remembering you on your birthday, and recalling all the pleasant times I've listened to you on the radio. Your quick wit and your fab sense of humor have been so appreciated by me. Not to mention, your great taste in music. God Bless you for all of the above. I'm sure your

343

millions of fans feel the same way about you. Virginia Gora."

"Dear Art....Best wishes from one of your oldest fans...1953-1957 St. Joseph's College." Ron Knaus, Middleton, Wi., Dec. 10, 2007."

I have received thousands of letters from listeners over the years, in fact forty-five years ago when we moved from Skokie, Illinois, to the house I still live in, in Naperville, Illinois, I stored in our new attic at least a dozen large cartons of listeners mail. At some point Elaine asked me to "Please chuck out all those boxes in the attic before they catch fire from spontaneous combustion." I complied, but only after re-reading all of them and saving one last all-time favorite. Webster's Dictionary definition of the word "crony" is "an old friend," and here is THE STANDOUT LETTER OF MY CAREER. Actually it was a Penny postal card I received at WISN-CBS, Milwaukee, Wisconsin.

Among my around the clock assignments was the daily 8:25AM Newscast for S.O.S. On Wednesday November 10, 1948, I had read an item this gentlemen had a problem with: *"This is a note for the smart Alex who announced the news at 8:25am-November-10th. I just want to remind you that the man you called Old Cronie is our great honest President!! We'd like you to show him more respect from now on. You evidently were on the Dewey bandwagon AND CAN'T TAKE IT!!!! Mr. Harrison."*

A final, personal note—I proudly cast my first presidential vote ever, on election day 1948, for Harry Truman.

ON BEING 80 YEARS OF AGE

* Essay 17 *

MY FRIEND ART

Art, says the dictionary,
Is a certain knack
But regarding my friend
What a woeful lack
Of describing what he's about
Or defining him in a single word
It just can't be done,
It really is absurd.
Art, my friend, is quicksilver
Ever changing, ever new
A chameleon presence
A personality stew.
Flashing his talent
In ways sometimes bizarre
He leaves no doubt
That he's always a star.
Quick to anger
Then equally contrite
Like the old saying,
His bark's worse than his bite.

THE HELLYER SAY

Living to 100
Is probably his aim
But knowing Art,
At 200, he'll still be the same!

—Wayne Atkinson, American Broadcasting
Company/ABC network announcer,
American painter and poet

My first thoughts each morning as I pinch myself and find I am alive for another glorious day are, Why ME?

Why was my close friend Richie Sanders struck and killed instantly by a Chicago and Northwestern Railroad Streamliner at the York Street crossing in our hometown of Elmhurst, Illinois, when he was only twelve years old? Richie whose big old two-story house was so much like the one I lived in, just four blocks away, with the Chicago and Northwestern, and the Union Pacific Railroad tracks the central divider between our family's homes. So many, many times Richie had safely crossed those same tracks, and so many times I had been with him.

Paul Hackert, Jimmy Kehoe, Hank and Tony Kindl, Jack Huntsha, Ralph Hartsing, Paul Albert, Frank Sturges, George Berg, Jack Grussell, Bill Shattuck, Billy Brazelton, Jim Roorda, Jack Hackert, Mel Cruger, Orville McKinley, and so many others with whom I shared those innocent boyhood days....All of us crossed those same tracks thousands of times, always the gates, and the bells and flashing red warning lights were operating, but somehow our friend and buddy Richie Sanders didn't make it.

Why not me? Or one of the others? Why did we always make it, and bright, always alert Richie did not?

I can remember walking over to Richie's house on a moonlit, crisp winter night, crossing the railroad tracks, and saying a frosty "Hi" to others as they too were arriving for a Boys Scout meeting at Richie's toasty warm family home.

And warm April and May nights, long before any of us heard the words "air-conditioning," three or four of us would sit in Richie's second floor bedroom, doing our homework projects, with the windows wide open and the tantalizing smell of springs lovely fragrances, gently delighting our olfactory nerves.

As we looked out on the quiet street, a Ford, and then maybe twenty minutes later a sleek Auburn Speedster, would slip through the lovely spring evening. And sometime later we'd hear voices and laughter for a moment as a Buick convertible, with its top down, headed south toward the tracks where it probably would make a right turn on Park Avenue and find a parking spot at York Street, adjacent to Max Borger's Rexall drugstore, where a summer-cooler delicacy awaited the lucky occupants: a five-cent ice cream cone filled with their favorite flavor, just so it was chocolate, vanilla or strawberry.

Places to park were easy to find on those nights when most people were home listening to their Philco "No Stoop, No Squint, No Squat" radios or enjoying the magic music coming from their 78 revolutions-per-minute RCA Victrolas. It didn't bother them that after each record ceased playing its two-minute-plus song, someone would rise, walk over to the Victrola, turn it off, remove the magic black disc, and put another one on the turntable and go through the entire procedure again.

It was the same thing with the radio. When Fred Allen's show, or Jack Benny, or Fibber McGee and Molly, or Mister District Attorney, or The Quiz Kids, or any of hundreds of shows we'd listen to weekly, ended, one of us would get up, walk to the radio and manually adjust the dial to the frequency that would bring in the next program we wanted to hear.

On my eighteenth birthday, August 7, 1941, I qualified for a drivers license. Did I rush over to the only place one could procure a driver's license in our area, the DuPage County courthouse at Wheaton, Illinois, to take the test? No I did not. I still have my first license. It is dated November 7, 1941, one month before the Japanese sneak attack on our giant naval base at Pearl Harbor changed every American's life forever.

Why did Richie Sanders die at age twelve, and why am I still here at age eighty?

Why did the most handsome graduate of our class of 1941 at York Community High School, Billy Caldwell, die at the hands of a Jap fighter pilot, thousands of miles from the quiet streets and the lovely manicured lawns of our Norman Rockwellian hometown?

Why did fellow friends and Loyola University classmates of mine, who enlisted the same day I did, die at Normandy and the Battle of the Bulge, yet I am still here at age 80?

On October 11, 1959, fellow ABC-TV announcer Randy Kent and I were on duty in the twelfth-floor announce-booth at WBKB (now WLS) TV. Randy had a very bad back problem, and as we sat side-by-side in Studio C, the local booth, I held an electric heating pad on the sore area. We did all the usual things that night, network-local announcers do. But I took all the ABC-TV network announcements, so Randy would not have to make those wild runs between studios. I've described that requirement of our job elsewhere in this book.

Randy's shift ended at 12:15AM, when I concluded the on-camera Midnight News, and he headed to his home in Highland Park. I finished my shift with sign-off at 4:03 AM, and headed to my home in Skokie.

The very next day, October 12, 1959, Columbus Day and my dad's 61st birthday, Randy Kent was scheduled for back surgery at Highland Park Hospital. When he left for home at the end of his shift the night before, he said it was "routine, nothing to worry about."

I called the hospital later that day to check on Randy's "routine surgery." The nurse said, "I'm so sorry to have to tell you this, Mr. Hellyer. Mr. Kent has passed away." Randy Kent was 39 years old and left a widow, and four young children.

Why did he die at 39 and I am still here at age 80?

Leonard Kratoska, my brilliant AFM record-turner and partner on the Art Hellyer Show...the man I dubbed Dr. K...TT (Turntable Technician), of whom I've written in great detail elsewhere in this book, had a tube sticking out of his chest for cancer chemo-therapy. We were sitting in the front-room of the home he had been born in 64 years earlier. I had just driven him back the few short blocks he could no longer walk from his favorite Bohemian restaurant.

I would take him there two or three times weekly in an attempt to get some food into his now very frail body. The Gulbransen concert organ he had entertained us on so many many times sat silently. Never again would Elaine, our children and I sit here enchanted as Lenny, a truly great musician, would challenge the mighty instrument to keep up with his flying fingers.

We talked of all the radio shows we did together, and of so many of the off-the-tops-of-our-heads, ad-libbed skits we had presented. He talked fondly of the many happy hours my family spent with him and his late dear mom, "Mother K" as I called her on the radio. He told me how much he loved and admired "Elainy." That was his own nickname for, my bride, The Lovely Elaine. I recall Elaine saying to him one time, "Lenny, you're the only one who has ever called me that." He was very special. Our five wonderful children loved Lenny, as did I. We all had such great times with him and his mom. Swimming in his beautiful pool, always followed by a lavish cookout, and to wind up the evening, a Lenny Kaye organ concert.

Quick story about the swimming pool. One morning on "Swim-World's" commercial I said "Dr. K...How would you like 'Swim-World' to put one of their fine pools right in your backyard?" Two weeks later, and for years after, we enjoyed that pool so much. We were all average swimmers, but the best we ever saw up close was Bob Ryan's gorgeous wife, Olive. She was poetry in motion in the water, and could have been a professional. Even dear sweet Ollie is gone now.

Lenny in a very soft voice was reading from a few of hundreds of "get-well" cards he had received, when he looked right at me, with tears in his eyes and said, "Art, I look like a cadaver. Please remember me as I was when we did our show together." I have no idea what I said in reply. I know I was crying, as I am as I write this, and I held him in my arms, and I could feel that terrible tube in his chest. The date was May 1, 1989. I did the usual as I left to drive the fifteen miles to Naperville to pick Elaine up at work at 5 PM. The "usual" was to point to the left-over half-sandwich from lunch I had placed in Lenny's refrigerator, and remind him to eat it for dinner.

Later that evening I phoned Lenny to make sure he'd eaten. There was no answer, and there should have been. So, with fear and trepidation, I phoned McNeil Hospital. Lenny was there. I spoke to him briefly. He sounded very bad. In a very faint voice he told he loved me, and to say "Hi to Elainy." 9AM, May 2, 1989, I phoned the hospital. Dr. K had died.

Why did Lenny Kaye die at 64, and I am still here at 80?

Richie Victor, Johnny Harkins, Carl Tubbs, Herbie Cunniff, Johnny Kern, Grover Allen, George Paul (who even today is still directing in New York The Barbara Walters Shows on ABC-TV) were all directors of my on-camera news shows at WLS-TV, and my ABC-TV network news stories. Each became a very close friend and between shows, or when I was working the WLS-TV local announce booth they would come in sit down and chat about everything from current news to music to sports to the best restaurants. I learned so much from these very knowledgeable gentlemen. Television directors are exceedingly intellectual people, if only because of the nature of their work. In one nine-hour shift they can direct shows that run from an interview with a president of the United States or a CEO of a top 400 company, to a movie star, to a group of drug addicts. They must be versed on everything from baseball stars to movie stars to rock stars. So each time they would sit and chat with me, I was adding to my education.

To single one out is perhaps unfair. They are all great men with great minds. But I wish to talk about Carl Tubbs because Carl has been gone a long, long time. And I still miss him. Carl directed my newscasts, and stories from the field, and he did so with the precision of a brain surgeon. Carl did it with a rare precision, and I especially enjoyed it when he would stop into the booth, and discuss our most recent venture.

Carl would refer to specific shots and tell me why I could have put a different spin on the story, just by a verbal inflection or a different eye contact. He was truly remarkable, and I looked forward to his critiques. He helped me put a polish on my deliveries.

Everyone was aware of a growth Carl Tubbs had on his forehead. We all assumed he was born with it, much as my sister Loretta has a birthmark on her left eye we always accepted, and never really noticed. This is why we were all shocked when Carl went to the hospital for surgery. And we were all shocked and devastated when this wonderful friend and superb director died from what was a malignant cancer. I never could adjust to not having those visits with Carl. I still think of him and his wife Jane often. Why did Carl Tubbs die in his forties and I am still here at 80?

Grover Allen was another fine director at ABC-TV who died much too early, in his forties. Forty-nine, if I remember correctly. On two of the occasions I was hospitalized for my serious back injuries, Grover drove a long way to visit me and cheer me.

Not long after one of those visits I was at Grover's funeral. I was on my aluminum crutches and could not sit down, so I stood in the nave of the church, and afterward as I slowly walked away from the building, the funeral cars passed within a few feet of me. I will never forget this: Grover's wife leaned toward the right rear window of the car she was seated in, and mouthed, "God Bless You" to me. I couldn't stop crying. This lovely, strong woman whose husband lay in the hearse just ahead of her, could say that to me. It stunned me, and proved what I've always believed—women are much stronger than men. They have to be just to put up with men. I want to live long enough to see a woman elected president of our country. Most women are so much more compassionate, understanding and empathetic than men. Again I ask: Why did Grover Allen die at 49, and I am still here at 80?

Years before Patti Page recorded her multiple-voiced songs for Mercury Records, a man named Fran Weigle had done the same thing on the Decca label. In the fifties and early sixties Fran Weigle was one of our WBKB ABC-TV Network announcers and we would work together on Saturday and Sunday. Saturday afternoons were not as busy as the weekdays with soap opera feeds going out all the time at different times, requiring network IDs at various and odd times from 7:59:47AM until 6:59:47PM. All we had on Saturdays was mostly sports, and the network IDs were far fewer than on weekdays. So it was one Saturday afternoon Fran Weigle and I were having a quiet day. In fact so quiet we would two-voice the local IDs, and just do the other more important part of our jobs, logging the commercials. When people would ask me what I did for a living I would say. "I am a glorified bookkeeper for ABC-TV."

It must have been about 1:40PM as Fran and I were

chatting, he turned toward me, gave me a blank stare, tried to stammer something, then fell flat on the floor. I could not believe what I had just seen. But I did have the presence to slip his tie down and open his shirt collar. He was breathing and he had a pulse, but we did not have 911 in those days, so I dialed our switchboard. Always reliable Hazel Ludes was the operator on duty and I told her what had happened and she said she'd call the fire department directly across the street from our studios in The State-Lake Building. I had read about mouth-to-mouth resuscitation, and I was just going to attempt it when two firemen stepped out of the elevator across from studio C, and thank God, took over.

They revived Fran, who was embarrassed and wanted to stay on the job, but they would not allow that. Fran was taken to Henrotin Hospital, and I phoned his wife who, of course, headed there too.

Announcers, at least in those days had only an "in-house" telephone line. We had no access to the outer world except through the operator. So Hazel stayed in touch with the hospital, and later that afternoon she reported to me that Fran Weigle had had a stroke. Fran Weigle collapsed working next to me, and never returned to work. He died, in his fifties, a few years later. I'm 80, and still here. Why?

When I was working in Milwaukee in the late forties I often tuned in to WGN late at night, where among their staff of superb announcers, one always stood out—a man named Bill O'Connor. He was really a great broadcaster.

In October of 1951 I was rushing down the hall on the nineteenth floor of the Chicago Furniture Mart at 666 N. Lake Shore Drive, having just concluded a radio show on WCFL. As I approached the elevator I almost bumped into a handsome Irishman who was speaking the same words I was speaking, "I've been wanting to meet you, I'm Bill O'Connor." Only I said, "I'm Art Hellyer." We had seen each other on the TV screen, and now we were meeting for the first time. From that moment on, Bill O'Connor became, and remained, my best friend for the rest of his life, which ended just eight months before his 80th birthday.

I don't know why I've survived this long in a business where the average age of death is 48, but in spite of all the slings and arrows, and sadness, and all the ups and downs, I am glad I am still here to see my children and grandchildren all happy and prospering.

THE LISTS

* Essay 18 *

**My heroes, my favorite foods, my favorite movies,
TV shows, music, sports teams, etc.**

My favorite foods? Up until I was told some nine years ago I am diabetic and must eat only 40 carbohydrates a meal, my favorite food was Chinese. Since then I've learned that nothing other than fast-food-fries is worse for us than Chinese foods and Chinese toys and Chinese paints, etc. So what is now my favorite food? OATMEAL!! I have 36 carbs of it every day for my breakfast, and some days I have it for all three meals. I love oatmeal. Before I became diabetic I had favorite candies: Winans' chocolate creams, Mounds bars, anything by Hershey's, and Mars Candy's Milky Ways and Three Musketeers. That love affair is over for sure.

I used to love baked potatoes slathered with farm-fresh butter, then at my first session with my diabetes dietitian I was told bread and potatoes would just plain kill me. Well, about two years ago Trader Joe's came out with a seven-grain sprouted bread that is only FOUR carbs per slice, so now I allow myself two slices of that delicious bread daily. Hopefully the Trader man will develop a four-carb Idaho spud.

THE HELLYER SAY

Over the first eighty years of my lifetime these have been my favorite movies.

All-Time Favorite Movie...*Erin Brockovich*, not only because Julia Roberts is gorgeous, and a national treasure who is the greatest actress of this time, but because this is the true story of one woman fighting a multi-billion-dollar, life-destroying business and bringing it to its knees. I love to see big-biz robber barons groveling. This flick is inspiring and gives little people like you and me, who are constant victims of unscrupulous big-biz, hope of a better world.

All the following are tied for second place...

Sleepless in Seattle, You've Got Mail, When Harry Met Sally...Romantic comedies are my favorite art form, and when they costar Tom Hanks and a beautiful little lady half my age, Meg Ryan, with whom I am in love, though she is not aware of it, they are the best.

My Cousin Vinny...My all-time favorite comedy. Fred Gwynn, in his last role ever, plays the fastidious, always correct judge, and Joe Pesci is equally hilarious as the defense attorney who after many attempts finally, but just barely, passes the bar exam.

Being Julia...My brother Dick says no actresses today are as good as Katherine Hepburn, Bette Davis, Olivia de Havilland, Rosalind Russell and many, many others of the thirties, forties and fifties. Well I beg to differ. In my opinion Annette Bening is certainly in their class. She received the National Board of Review's Best Actress Award, and she was nominated for, though did not win it, but should have, in my opinion, an Oscar, for playing Julia Lambert in this 2005 film. If you've not seen this movie, rent or buy the DVD and I believe you will agree with me. This beautiful lady is one of the all time greats.

Penny Serenade.....I cry with the best of them and this is a real tear-jerker. Starring two of the greatest actors of all-time, Irene Dunne and Cary Grant, and directed by George Stevens, it is the tragic story of newlyweds who adopt a child. This one requires three clean handkerchiefs each time I watch it.

My Man Godfrey...William Powell, suave, debonair, living in a depression era garbage dump, gets involved with another of the greatest of all time, Carole Lombard, in both a screwball comedy and a heartwarming story. This movie is one of the top ten classics of all time, in my humble, non-Roger Ebert opinion.

The Pelican Brief...This tautly tense adaptation of John Grisham's runaway best-seller is brilliant. Julia Roberts writes her speculative "Pelican Brief" about the "murders," then contacts Denzel Washington, a newspaper investigative reporter, and tells him her story. When they have finished, the girl, who is just another girl until she flashes her famous smile, is lucky to be alive for birthday number twenty-five. Between them they have shaken everyone in our nation's capital, to the president himself. Be prepared to chew off every last one of your fingernails. But it is worth it.

People Will Talk...A poignant film and at the same time a brilliant comedy. Cary Grant is the head of a medical clinic, and in the highlight of the film he lays out Lionel train O-gauge trackage across all the halls and into and out of the upstairs bedrooms of his home. He and Walter Slezak have an agreed-upon set of whistles they sound to keep the trains running smoothly, until Walter forgets his, and gives the wrong one, resulting in a massive three train pileup. Hume Cronyn, Sidney Blackmer and Jeanne Crain, an early screen love of mine, and Basil Ruysdael, who was a deep-voiced, superb NBC network announcer, and one of my first broadcast idols, round out a wonderful cast.

Dawn Patrol...Errol Flynn, Basil Rathbone and David Niven star in this 1938 classic about RAF pilots in World War One. Authentic planes from the teens and three superb actors make this a terrific flick.

The Thin Man...One would assume Dashiell Hammett had William Powell in mind for his "other" detective, Nick Charles, when he wrote "The Thin Man." And beautiful Myrna Loy played his wife, Nora Charles, magnificently. Their dog Asta even learned his lines perfectly. Hard to believe this great classic series was filmed over SEVENTY years ago.

The Quiet Man...Director John Ford's real name was Sean O'Feeney, and this Irish film was his greatest epic. John Wayne, Maureen O'Hara, Barry Fitzgerald, Victor McLaglen and Ward Bond must all share equal billing in this masterpiece.

Treasure of the Sierra Madre...The all-time classic movie-study of avarice and greed. Humphrey Bogart, Tim Holt and Walter Huston are prospectors hunting their fortunes in gold in the mountains in Mexico, and nothing, to say the least, goes right for them. I have seen this film by director John Huston at least a dozen times, and each time I am fascinated by the remarkable portrayals by the outstanding cast of characters.

The African Queen...Katharine Hepburn and Oscar-winner

Humphrey Bogart are just marvelous in this Belgian Congo World War One story film. The scene as they see the German battleship is one of the most heart-stopping in silver-screen history.

Citizen Kane...Orson Welles and John Houseman brought along their CBS Network "Mercury Theater on the Air" cast, that shocked the nation on Halloween 1938 with their startling portrayal of H. G. Wells' "War of the Worlds," for this masterpiece, considered by many critics to be the greatest movie ever produced.

Von Ryan's Express...Frank Sinatra could do no wrong in my personal opinion. "The Chairman of the Board" was America's greatest pop singer AND an Oscar-winning movie actor. This is a taut action film about an American combat pilot, Colonel Joseph Ryan (Sinatra) in World War Two, who is shot down by the Nazis and sentenced to a Nazi prison camp. He earns the name "Von" Ryan, because early on he does his best to schmooze his German captors, just to survive. Realizing this is no way to exist under these madmen he lays out a plan for a daring escape. As soon as he and his fellow prisoners are free, he commandeers a German freight train, and then takes off on a spectacular trip through and over and under the Alps, with a large segment of the German army in full pursuit, across Italy to Switzerland, and freedom. It was so exciting I chewed my fingernails to the cuticles, and it took a valium the size of a hockey puck to calm me down.

Compulsion...In my opinion, Orson Welles tops his performance in "Citizen Kane" in this outstanding movie.

The Lavender Hill Mob...An early 1950s English film with hilarious scenes and Alec Guinness, a great actor who could play any type role from comedy to tragedy. Alec is a mild bank clerk who is melting down the bank's gold and pouring the precious hot liquid into molds of the Eiffel Tower for resale. As a child I did the same thing, but it was hot lead I was pouring into molds to make toy soldiers.

Elaine and I saw this film in the Glencoe (Illinois) Theatre on a frigid winter night over fifty years ago, and I still find myself laughing when I recall the scene where all the police cars came roaring together in the town square and wrapped their squawking police radio antennas around each other.

Bridge on the River Kwai...This great film about World War Two won SEVEN Oscars. Alec Guinness (Oscar) as a tough British colonel, proved he could play any type role. Guinness, Jack Hawkins, William Holden, and James Donald are just a few of the great actors who suffer terribly as captives at the hands of Japanese colonel, Sessue Hayakawa. British Director David Lean won his first Oscar for this brilliant film.

The Music Man...By Meredith Willson, a guest on my shows many times. A brilliant musician, writer, producer, he had an extremely imaginative mind. Academy Award-winner Shirley Jones, Robert Preston, who won the Tony for his Broadway performance in "The Music Man," and Buddy Hackett (who made many appearances on The Art Hellyer Show over the years, and could be just as funny at Six AM as he was on The Ed Sullivan Show at Eight PM), Hermione Gingold (also on my shows), Paul Ford, who told me he didn't start his acting career until he was 48 years old, and that was as the colonel on the Phil Silvers show "Sgt. Bilko," and 7-year-old Ron Howard were the leads in this, one of my two all-time musical favorites. One of the great musical scenes of all times takes place as Robert Preston cons the town folks, "Right here in River City," into buying band instruments for their children.

He moves back and forth among the citizenry shouting out the horrors of pool halls, to win them over. An absolute classic the likes of which we will probably never see again.

Love Affair...Charles Boyer and Irene Dunne are each engaged to someone else. The first time they see each other, it is love at first sight. To test their new-found love they agree to meet again in six months and, we all know the story. Two beautiful people in a beautiful movie. Another of the great classics of all time.

Desk Set...I love all the Tracy-Hepburn films, but this one is my favorite. It was 1956 and Katharine Hepburn heads a group of women who operate a question-answering service for a television network. Her sidekick, Joan Blondell, gets off some hilarious lines throughout the film. Then along comes Spencer Tracy with his wall-to-wall, room-filling computer, and life will never be the same.

Life with Father...Clarence Day Jr., writing of his boyhood days and growing up with a tyrant for a father. Nobody ever played a poignantly humorous role better than *(My Man Godfrey, The Thin Man)* William Powell, and the stellar cast includes Irene Dunne, his long-suffering wife; Elizabeth Taylor, Edmund Gwenn (Santa Claus in *Miracle on 34th Street*), ZaSu Pitts and Jimmy Lydon.

The Glenn Miller Story...My all-time favorite big-band leader, and my all-time favorite music should have made this flick perfect for me, but there is a glaring error in it. Glenn Miller recorded on Bluebird his million-selling "Little Brown Jug" in 1939. Charming June Allyson (as Mrs. Glenn Miller) spends a great deal of time prodding Glenn (Jimmy Stewart) to play it. Then, in the band's first broadcast from Paris, shortly after

Glenn disappeared on December 14, 1944, while flying over the English Channel, Mrs. Miller gets all weepy at the Miller ranch, in California, "Tuxedo Junction." Glenn's longtime pianist Chummy MacGregor is at her side, as Ray McIntyre fronting the band "introduces" "Little Brown Jug." I always strove for accuracy on my radio and television shows, and this flaw bothers me very much.

Broadway Melody of 1940... Fred Astaire and no, folks, not Ginger Rogers, but Eleanor Powell, an equally brilliant dancer, joined by the actor-dancer who, a few years later would be elected to the United States Senate, George Murphy. Loaded with superb Cole Porter songs, this is my all-time favorite dance film. I love a DVD feature that allows me to click to Astaire and Powell tap-dancing to Cole Porter's "Begin the Beguine." I can watch it all day.

*Philadelphia Story...*Very young superstars Cary Grant, Jimmy Stewart and Katharine Hepburn star in a modern adaptation of Shakespeare's "The Taming of the Shrew." This is great comedy at its very best. Nothing more need be said.

Duck Soup... I loved the Marx Brothers in everything they did, but this one is my favorite. Arguably the most hilarious scene in any movie in Hollywood's long and brilliant history finds Groucho at war, standing in a bunker with shells bigger than any ever fired by "Big Bertha," making gigantic holes in the walls, and sailing past the star who fills the air with Grouchoisms. Undoubtedly, Groucho Marx's greatest moment in a lifetime of great moments.

*Hannah and Her Sisters...*Academy Awards for Best Writer, Woody Allen; Best Supporting Actress, Dianne Wiest; and Best Supporting Actor, Michael Caine. Mia Farrow also does her usual fine job as Hannah. This is a superb motion picture. When you see Woody Allen in this flick you are seeing ME, especially the scenes with the doctors. I love it.

Bringing Up Baby...Katharine Hepburn and Cary Grant star in the greatest "screwball" comedy ever filmed.

Best In Show...I am a tremendous admirer of Fred Willard's "off the top of his head" acting ability, and it has never been better than in this film about the Mayflower Kennel Club's annual dog show. The entire story is very good, but Willard makes it a tour de barque.

Voice of the Turtle...Elaine and I were married March 14, 1947. This movie starring Hollywood's handsomest man, Ronald Reagan, and sweet Eleanor Parker was our first movie after we married.

Life Is Beautiful...This film had seven Academy Award nominations and won three Oscars. Roberto Benigni (Best Actor Oscar), in the Nazi concentration camp with his young son, is heart-breaking AND heart-warming

Autumn in New York...I was the only man in the 200 seat theater in the multiplex, and I counted twenty-two women. The photography was glorious, the acting by Richard Gere and Winona Ryder was superb, and the story was beautiful but tragic. As we got deeper into the sadness, all the ladies were crying. I was sobbing. By the time it ended I had soaked two handkerchiefs. Wonderful movie. The critics rapped this film. I loved it.

Pride of the Yankees...One of the best baseballs films ever made, it poignantly tells the story of the great Lou Gehrig.

THE HELLYER SAY

Gary Cooper's finest role.

The Trip to Bountiful...Geraldine Page won the 1985 Best Actress Oscar for this film that found her trapped in a small apartment, like a child, by her son and his crummy wife. What keeps her going is her dream of escaping and returning to her childhood home in Bountiful, one more time before she dies. This is a warm, at times funny, movie.

Love Actually...This is a superbly charming film, with Hugh Grant, Emma Thompson, Bill Nighy, Billy Bob Thornton, Rowan Atkinson, a delightful young lady named Martine McCutcheon, and many other English folks falling in love. I've seen it three times and I will watch it many more times. It leaves me feeling so good, and Hugh Grant was never better.

Grand Prix...The greatest motor racing movie of all time. No other automobile film comes within 1000 miles of this one.

Breakfast at Tiffany's...AUDREY HEPBURN. Another one of the movies I can watch over and over. We all fell in love with Audrey, and then she was suddenly gone forever.

The Emperor's Club...Son Michael brought this DVD to me saying, "You'll love this movie, Dad. It's your kind of film." He was so right. A Mr. Chips type story only, in my opinion, even more poignant. Robert Donat would be proud of Kevin Kline as the revered teacher, who forever changes his students lives. You must see this film.

Twelve Angry Men...Henry Fonda produced this dramatic courtroom masterpiece in 1957, and to keep the costs down he filmed it in black and white. But he didn't spare costs when it came to talent. Besides himself, he hired Martin Balsam, Lee

J. Cobb, E.G. Marshall, Jack Klugman, Ed Begley, Sr., Jack Warden, and Edward Binns. Sidney Lumet directed the film and it received tons of awards here and in Europe.

A Few Good Men...Another gripping courtroom drama. In my opinion, Jack Nicholson's and Tom Cruise's greatest movie performances. The rest of the cast including Demi Moore, Cuba Gooding, Jr., Kiefer Sutherland, and Kevin Bacon, with direction by Rob Reiner make this a four-star winner.

Seabiscuit...In my opinion, the surprise film of the very-early 21st century. The true story based on the magnificently researched best-seller by author Laura Hillenbrand. It is a truly inspiring story of three men and a lovely little horse who made all of us who were living in the days of the Great Depression forget our problems for a while. Just one of those daily problems being, would there be food on the table that day for the family? This was before air-conditioned houses, and cars with heaters, electric windows, power steering, or, or...Well, it wasn't until the late thirties that some options, like a heater or an AM radio, were available.

In the wintertime we drained the water out of the petcocks in the radiator and engine block every night so the block wouldn't crack, and then refilled the radiator and block the next morning. We shoveled coal into the Holland Furnace every night, and banked the fire hoping it would stay lighted until morning. Many mornings it did not, and we wakened to a twenty-degree house. And in the summer time, we opened the windows, and turned on the fan just to keep the oh-so-hot air in motion. "Air-conditioned" was a word the movie theaters used on their signs to describe a crude method of cooling...large blocks of ice in a small shed on the roof, with a large fan blowing across the top of the ice chunks. Twenty minutes into the first film of a double-feature, the ice was a pool of warm water. Not too effective. Certainly not perfected for use in the home. Movies, radio, FDR and a valiant little racehorse named Seabiscuit helped us through those dark days when most American families didn't know where their next dollar would come from.

FIVE MOVIES STARRING JACK NICHOLSON……

One Flew Over the Cuckoo's Nest…I was a member of the Academy of Motion Picture Arts and Sciences for many years and I voted for Nicholson as Best Actor, and for Best Actress-winner Louise Fletcher, who portrayed the tyrannical nurse in the mental hospital to which Nicholson had been sentenced. Both deservedly won the hardware.

As Good As It Gets…I have printed on the DVD cover "BEST MOVIE I'VE EVER SEEN." I often do that after viewing a Jack Nicholson film. Gorgeous, extremely talented Helen Hunt co-stars in this superb film.

About Schmidt…In this movie Nicholson portrays me….He really does….

Anger Management…You tell me if you have ever seen, even Cary Grant at his best, a better "screwball" comedy. When Dr. Buddy Rydell (Jack Nicholson) climbs into bed with Dave Buznik (Adam Sandler) I fall out of bed in a fit of hysterics. Ranks with *My Cousin Vinnie* and *Bringing up Baby* as the funniest movie of all time. Nicholson has anxiety attacks and heart attacks, and tons of other problems.

My favorite moment in a movie…TIE…Robert Redford's home run into the lights above the right-field upper deck in *The Natural*, and the final scene in *An Officer and a*

The Lists

Gentleman always leave me sobbing; Fred Astaire and Eleanor Powell dancing to Cole Porter's "Begin the Beguine," in *The Broadway Melody of 1940*; and Deborah Kerr and Yul Brynner dancing to "Shall We Dance" in *The King and I* is a another showstopper for me.

My favorite Christmas movies...in order:
The Bishop's Wife...David Niven, Loretta Young, Cary Grant.

Miracle on 34th Street...Maureen O'Hara, Edmund Gwenn, John Payne.

Jean Shepherd's "A Christmas Story"...Peter Billingsley, Darrin McGavin, Melinda Dillon.

Christmas in Connecticut... starring Dennis Morgan, Barbara Stanwyck and Sydney Greenstreet.

Alastair Sim's *"Scrooge."*

My all-time favorite actress—first place...TIE...Julia Roberts, Barbara Stanwyck, Diane Keaton, Eva Marie Saint, Maureen O'Hara, Annette Bening, Deborah Kerr, Olivia de Havilland, Eleanor Powell, Irene Dunne, Katherine Hepburn, Claudette Colbert, Joan Fontaine, Meg Ryan, Jean Arthur, Myrna Loy, and Audrey Hepburn.

My all-time favorite actor—first place...TIE...Cary Grant, Gregory Peck, Jimmy Stewart, Spencer Tracy, William Powell, Bing Crosby, James Garner, Robert De Niro and, of course, Jack Nicholson.

Second place...TIE..My all-time favorite movie actors and actresses...

THE HELLYER SAY

Rosalind Russell, Jack Lemmon, Grace Kelly, Sir Alec Guinness, Greer Garson, Dustin Hoffman, Loretta Young, Orson Welles, William H. Macy, Gene Hackman, Woody Allen, Tom Cruise, Paul Newman, Tom Hanks, Robert Preston, Robert Redford and John Wayne.

All-time favorite TV shows, not in order after the first five:

Rumpole of the Bailey

All Creatures Great and Small

The Jackie Gleason Show...He was, indeed, "The Great One."

The Tonight Show (Steve Allen, Jack Paar, Johnny Carson, Jay Leno) and the Late Show with David Letterman (TIE).

Seinfeld...A bunch of losers with a superb, winning TV show, and a perfect cast.

(TIE) The Voice of Firestone—Fred Waring and The Pennsylvanians...and The Bell Telephone Hour

The Odd Couple...Perfect casting on this show.

Newhart...I loved everything Bob Newhart ever did on TV and his wonderful "Button Down" comedy albums. I played his skits on my radio shows many, many years.

Maverick...(I was the ABC-TV Network announcer) No one but James Garner could have played the title role.

Mary Hartman, Mary Hartman

The Lists

Fernwood Tonight

Everybody Loves Raymond...Fantastic Cast!!!

Frasier...Great cast.

Gunsmoke...Listen to the radio version for the world's greatest use of sound effects.

The Carol Burnett Show...She just may go down in history as the greatest of all time.

The Lawrence Welk Show (I was the ABC-TV network announcer, the great Bob Warren was the on-location announcer)...This was not a "Mickey Mouse" band as so many would say. Welk had superb musicians and vocalists and dancers working for him. I still watch this show on PBS on Saturday nights. Probably the only good music show left on TV in this new century.

The Rifleman...I was the ABC-TV network announcer on this show, and the show must have been on at least one season when the star, Chuck Connors, came to visit us at the ABC-TV flagship station in Chicago. Well, I knew he was a former Chicago Cubs first baseman, and first basemen are generally lanky men so they can reach out and head off errant throws. But this long drink of water really surprised me. He was TALL, and I actually asked the stagehands, on-camera, for a ladder so I could climb up to his ears so he could hear me. He was a good sport and a very nice person. After recording some promos together, we sat down next to each other. His legs stretched so much further than mine, I at six feet felt like a midget.

THE HELLYER SAY

Cheers…Great cast.

Candid Camera…Alan Funt created the first show of this type, and it is still the best.

McHale's Navy (Back in the sixties this show was a "must see" for me)

I Love Lucy…no comments needed.

Barney Miller…Great cast.

The Jeffersons….No other actor could have played George.

The Rockford Files, Sanford and Son, The Honeymooners (great cast), All in the Family (great cast)

The Andy Griffith Show…Great cast. Opie was fantastic (see the *Dead Bird* episode), Mr. Peepers—Wally Cox, a wonderful performer all but forgotten as Robinson Peepers, the shy science teacher at Jefferson High School. Tony Randall was his best friend, Harvey Weskit. Patricia Benoit, the school nurse was his girlfriend, and Marion Lorne, in my opinion the true star among stars of this outstanding comedy of the early 1950s. Sadly, I don't believe there is any kinescope available of this fine show, and it went off the air just before two-inch black-and-white videotape appeared on the scene.

The Dick Van Dyke Show, The Mary Tyler Moore Show…Each show is proof that the best comedy is good clean comedy.

Are You Being Served?…Another of the great screwball

English sitcoms.

Bewitched…I was the ABC-TV network announcer, and in the early days of TV we frequently had breakdowns, so director Richie Victor would ask me to go to the studio N network booth and "Fill the time any way you like, guy." No matter who we were, we were always "GUY" to Richie. I would make spooky noises and then in a whispery, spooky voice I would reassure America, "REEEEEEEEEE-LLLLLLLLAAAAAAAAAX, it's not your expensive brand new TV SET—SAMANTHA DID IT." I have a letter of commendation from Steve Early, of ABC-TV's top brass in New York, congratulating me on my "Unique Announce-ments."

The Ernie Kovacs Show…A GENIUS!!!!!

The Steve Allen Show…Quite possibly the most talented person ever to work on television.

The Bob Cummings Show (I was the ABC-TV Network announcer)…I especially loved the bombing runs his "Grandpa" would make in the World War One fighter plane.

The Jack Benny Show, with Mary Livingston, Rochester, Dennis Day, Phil Harris and Don Wilson, made a fine transition from 1930's radio to 1960's TV. Always a superbly written show with an extremely talented cast.

The Perry Como Show….I especially looked forward to his glorious Christmas specials from everywhere from Hollywood to Salzburg.

The Dean Martin Show, The Nat "King" Cole Show, The

Dinah Shore Show, Your Hit Parade, The Andy Williams Show...All Real music, not the garbage they call "music" today.

Get Smart...I loved this spoof of spy shows with Don Adams.

Liberace, Al Jolson, Bob Hope, Frank Sinatra, Sammy Davis, Jr., and, sadly, the forgotten man, in my opinion, the greatest performer of the Twentieth Century, Bing Crosby. I guess it's a matter of personal preference, but I do know this, they were each great, and there is no one like them today.

My Three Sons (I was the ABC-TV Network announcer for Chevrolet)...A wonderfully warm-hearted show starring Fred MacMurray.

Red Skelton...a TRULY GREAT talent who could make you laugh, cry and pee, all at the same moment.

Burke's Law...Gene Barry and Regis Toomey were the stars of this ABC-TV Show, and it was my pleasure to handle the network announces involved. I really enjoyed this slick show where Chief Detective Burke was chauffeured in his Bentley to the scene of the crime.

Rocky and Bullwinkle...Adults loved this show. (I was the ABC-TV Network announcer on this daily 4:30-5:00PM funfest.)
Your Show of Shows...Sid Caesar, Imogene Coca, Carl Reiner, Howard Morris...FANTASTIC HUMOR in 1950 on black-and-white 7-, 10- and 12-inch screens.

Studs' Place...This show was telecasted live from NBC in Chicago from November 1949 to January 1952, and emanated from bartender Studs' "Place." For some reason "Studs' Place" was in New York City for a short time, when Studs (Terkel), in one of his philosophic chats, said "Hey...We're in Chicago...What's this New York Stuff?" So the joint became a Chicago BBQ restaurant with its various denizens....Chet Roble played down and dirty piano. The great folk singer Win Stracke became my friend and made many appearances on my radio shows. I was the new kid in town in 1950, and it wasn't until a few years later I had the good fortune to meet the stars. I admired this very early TV effort greatly. Studs Terkel is a great philosopher who, since those primitive days of TV, has written many best-selling books. I am indeed proud to have known this brilliant genius all these years. And it's comforting to know that even now in 2007, as I write this, Studs Terkel can be reached at the Chicago Historical Society

77 Sunset Strip...Remember the episode of this sixty-minute show, when no one but Ephraim Zimbalist, Jr. appeared? Remarkable.

Barnaby Jones, Person to Person, M*A*S*H, George Gobel Show, The Real McCoys.

You Bet Your Life!...How lucky we were. There will never, ever be another Groucho!

The Goldbergs...Gentle, kind Molly. We miss you.

The greatest athlete of all time, in my opinion...TIE...Jim Thorpe and Lance Armstrong.
Chicago's greatest all-time athlete...Michael Jordan.

The top major league baseball teams of my lifetime:
One...The Joe McCarthy Era and the Casey Stengel Era New

THE HELLYER SAY

York Yankees
Two...The 1930s' St. Louis Cardinals
Three...The Charlie Finley Oakland Athletics

My sentimental favorite baseball teams were the 1930s' White Sox clubs managed by Jimmy Dykes, who also played third base. With a small budget he managed depression-era teams that usually were in the pennant races. After his last game as a player, he had himself carried off the field on a stretcher.

My all-time favorite baseball players....Joe DiMaggio, Henry Aaron, Lou Gehrig, Luke Appling, Ted Williams, Bob Feller, Nolan Ryan, Ernie Banks, Stan Hack, Stan Musial, Roberto Clemente.

The top professional football teams of my lifetime:
One....The 1940 George Halas Chicago Bears
Two....Curly Lambeau's Green Bay Packers of the 1930's
Three...Vince Lombardi's Green Bay Packers
Four...The Sammy Baugh Washington Redskins
Five...(Tie) The George Blanda Oakland Raiders...the Johnny Unitas Baltimore Colts.

My all-time favorite professional quarterbacks:
Brett Favre, Sid Luckman, Baugh, Blanda, Unitas, Bart Starr, Joe Montana, Bobby Layne

The top professional basketball teams of my lifetime:
The Larry Byrd Boston Celtics
The Michael Jordan Chicago Bulls
The Magic Johnson Lakers

My favorite college basketball teams of all time:
My alma mater, Loyola University, Chicago, fielded a squad

of eight players for the 1963 NCAA "March Madness" and they won it all. And Coach Ray Meyer's Great DePaul Blue Demon teams.

Two of our five wonderful children, Victoria Elaine and Jeffrey Stephen are University of Illinois at Urbana-Champaign graduates, so the 2004-2005 team must rank as my other all-time favorite. Coach Bruce Weber collected ALL of the NCAA Coach of the Year awards and rightly so. This wonderful group of young men who played as one, finished the season 38-2. Their first loss was after twenty-nine consecutive wins, and it was in the final five seconds of the contest. Unfortunately, their second loss was in the last game of the NCAA finals. I will not, in my lifetime, see the likes of this truly great team again.

The top professional hockey teams of my lifetime:
One…The Maurice Richard Montreal Canadiens
Two…The Gordie Howe Detroit Red Wings
Three…The Wayne Gretzky Edmonton Oilers
Four….The Bobby Orr Boston Bruins
Five….The 1938 Chicago Blackhawks who won only 14 games in the entire regular season, yet won the Stanley Cup with the aid of a goalie named Alfie Moore whom they found in a Toronto saloon, after their regular goalie, Mike Karakas, was injured.

My all-time favorite golfers….Ben Hogan, Tiger Woods, "Slammin'" Sammy Snead, Arnold Palmer, Jack Nicklaus, Byron Nelson, Babe Didrikson Zaharias, Jimmy Demaret, Erv Miller.

My all-time favorite track star…Jesse Owens, who in the 1936 Berlin Olympics taught Adolph Hitler a lesson. Years later in the fifties it was my good fortune to often talk with Jesse

Owens as we recorded shows for our sponsors at Globe Transcription Service, Don Lavery's fine recording studios in the Carbide and Carbon Building on North Michigan Avenue in Chicago.

My all time favorite tennis star...Don Budge, Maureen Connolly.

Guttiest athletes of my lifetime...Lou Gehrig, Jackie Robinson, Maureen Connolly, Lance Armstrong.

Presidents I most admired in my lifetime...not in order, too difficult to do...Franklin Delano Roosevelt, Harry S Truman, Dwight Eisenhower, Ronald Reagan, George H. W. Bush, William Jefferson Clinton.

Much of my tens of thousands of hours on radio were devoted to music, so, of course, I must list my favorite songs. This will be extremely difficult to do, because, as my children have pointed out, thousands of times I have said, after playing a song on my shows: "That is my all-time favorite song," and each time I said it, they tell me, it was a different song...

For over fifteen years, I taught my *Broadcast One* and *Broadcast Two* and *Golden Age of Radio* students at Columbia College on Michigan Avenue in Chicago and my classes at the University of St. Francis in Joliet, Illinois, to always tell the story of each song they played. Listeners enjoy that information and most station managers hate it.

Station managers are mostly blithering idiots who really believe if you stop playing the music, the listeners will tune elsewhere. That's the reason for the lunacy of playing, as some stations do, "uninterrupted music for forty-five minutes," or "five in a row." These front office mental midgets who foist this on the listeners are depriving them of the joy of hearing about each song, and being told who the performer is.

I was fired by many of those blue-suited bird-brains because I believe the listener is not a sponge that just sits there and soaks up the music, but rather an intelligent, caring human being who enjoys hearing about the songs and the artists.

Three magnificent managers in my fifty-five chaotic years on the air agreed with me, and encouraged me to do it my way...The legendary Jules Herbeveaux at WMAQ-NBC, WLS-FM's Harvey Wittenberg, who eventually joined Mike Rapchak, Steve Hodges and me in being fired by ABC New York's top brass because we played good music, and Ralph Sherman for whom I worked for seventeen years at The Satellite Music Network, and WJOL in Joliet, Illinois. If all managers were like these three we'd still have quality radio to listen to.

My favorite singers...It is impossible for me to place them in "favorite" order. I loved to listen to all of them: Merle Haggard, Perry Como, Eddy Arnold, Dean Martin, Bing Crosby, Frankie Laine, Frank Sinatra, Johnny Cash, Jim Reeves, George Strait, Dick Haymes, Helen Forrest, Rosemary Clooney, Willie Nelson, Eddy Howard, Marvina, Roy Orbison, Nat Cole, Ella Fitzgerald, Jo Stafford, Doris Day, Ray Price, Lannie Garrett, Margaret Whiting, Sarah Vaughan, Johnny Hartman, Tammy Wynette, Patti Page, Waylon Jennings, George Jones, Dinah Shore, Peggy Lee, Sammy Davis, Jr., Ray Eberle and Bob Eberly, Ray Charles, Bea Wain, Englebert Humperdinck, Alison Krauss, Anne Murray, Roger Whittaker, Vic Damone, Jerry Vale, Gisele Mackenzie, The Mills Brothers, Keely Smith, Ed Ames, Andy Williams, John Gary, and so many, many more......

THE HELLYER SAY

From my fifty-five years on radio, these are my top twenty-six all-time favorite songs.....

Number one all-time favorite......Ray Charles singing *America The Beautiful.* Everytime I hear this rendition I get chills and goosebumps.

If I Loved You...Richard Rodgers and Oscar Hammerstein II wrote this glorious song of love for "Carousel." Billy Bigelow, played by John Raitt, and Jan Clayton, playing Julie Jordan, introduced it on Broadway. And a man who became a wonderful friend of mine, Perry Como, sold over two million copies for RCA Victor.

The Nearness of You...I loved to recite these gorgeous lyrics on my shows as I introduced this great love song, "It's not the pale moon that excites me, that thrills and delights me...Oh, no! It's just the nearness of you." The romance of the words by Ned Washington, and the beauty of the music by Hoagy Carmichael combine to make this one of the outstanding love songs of the ages.

Vaya con Dios...I would sing along with the chorus every time I played this wonderful song by Les Paul and Mary Ford.

Thanks for the Memory...No duo ever sang a song more beautifully than did Bob Hope and Shirley Ross in 1938. Bob made it his theme song.

To Each His Own...Dozens recorded this one, but it was Eddy Howard's song.

Blue Spanish Eyes...Either the vocal by Englebert Humperdinck or the instrumental by Billy Vaughn.

No Other Love...Notes stolen verbatim from Fredric Chopin with gorgeous lyrics penned by Oscar Hammerstein II.

Mood Indigo...The greatest big-band leader of all time, in my opinion, Duke Ellington, was responsible for the music, and Irving Mills and Barney Bigard wrote the lyrics.

In the Still of the Night...Nelson Eddy was in the studio with me just two months before he died, and when I asked him his favorite song of all the ones he sang on the silver screen, his reply was Cole Porter's "In the Still of the Night." He heard no argument from me.

Harbor Lights...Chicago's all-time favorite bandleader Dick Jurgens, who was born in California, recalled one morning on my WCFL show how much he enjoyed all the times he played "The Aragon Ballroom" on Catalina Island. Every evening in the late nineteen-thirties, at exactly 8:30PM, he would pick up his trumpet, wave to the band to follow him, and they'd walk to the end of the pier and invite everyone in the boats in the harbor to join them as they strolled under the sky back to the ballroom, as he and his band were playing "Harbor Lights." I can't think of anything more romantic. Life was so much nicer then, wasn't it?

Among My Souvenirs..."There's nothing left for me, of days that used to be, I've watched them fade and die, among my Souvenirs." This song was written in England in 1927 by Lawrence Wright and Edgar Leslie and introduced by Jack Hylton's English orchestra and almost simultaneously in the United States by Paul Whiteman. But when Connie Francis got hold of it thirty years later, it became a million-seller and landed on *Variety*'s "Fifty-Year Hit Parade."

The Lullaby of Broadway...I do truly believe this to be my all-time number one show-tune favorite. I first heard it in 1935 when I was twelve years old, and I saw the musical on stage in 1981 with Jerry Orbach, one of the stars of the excellent television show "Law and Order." His rendition of the song, along with the large chorus, brought down the house. People were literally standing and cheering, with tears running down their cheeks. Elaine, who loved classical music and Broadway show tunes, could not contain her emotions, and I, of course, was covered with goosebumps from head to toes. It was absolutely soul-stirring.

Stardust...Back in the nineteen-fifties a very shy man, named Hoagy Carmichael, came into the WCFL studio one morning with A&R rep Paul Gallis. This would be the only time I'd ever spend with this man who composed my all-time favorite song with lyrics, in 1928, when he returned for a reunion at his alma mater, the University of Indiana at Bloomington.

He sat down at the piano in the student lounge and started noodling at the keyboard. As he did so, Stu Gorrell, a classmate of his who would write the lyrics for Hoagie's "Georgia on My Mind" in 1930, walked into the room and said, "That sounds like dust drifting down from the stars," and that dear friends in radio-land was how the name of the song was conceived. It was born as an instrumental and stayed that way until the song's publisher, Irving Mills, asked a staff writer of his firm, Mitchell Parish, the same man who would write the lyrics for Glenn Miller's great theme song, "Moonlight Serenade," to compose lyrics for it in 1929.

More than one thousand artists have recorded "Stardust" in over fifty different languages, and today in the year two thousand and seven it remains one of the most popular songs of all time. If I had to pick one favorite arrangement of this classic of classics it would be the 1940 RCA recording by Artie Shaw.

Deep Purple...this song was written in 1935 by Peter De Rose as a piano solo, and *Variety* magazine named it one of the top songs of the year. Then in 1939, Mitchell Parish wrote lyrics for it, and Bea Wain's marvelously warm and sensual interpretation with Larry Clinton's band made it a runaway hit.

The Last Time I Saw Paris...The great songwriting team of Jerome Kern and Oscar Hammerstein II did not write this tune for a movie or Broadway play. They were so overcome by Hitler's seizure of Paris in June of 1940, the words and music just flowed: *"The last time I saw Paris, her heart was young and gay. I'll always remember her that way."* Kate Smith introduced this gorgeous tribute to the stricken city, and Ann Sothern then sang it in the 1941 movie, "Lady Be Good."

It won the Academy Award, and Jerome Kern felt he should not receive the Oscar because the song had not been written for the movie. As a result, the Academy changed their rules so that, in the future, only songs that were written specifically for movies could be nominated for the award. It took a big man to tell them he shouldn't receive the Academy's highest honor.

Battle Hymn of the Republic...Stirring patriotic song I've played on every patriotic holiday for over fifty years. As it would be playing over the airways, I would always cry as I listened to the beauty of the music, the swelling sound of the trumpet choir, and the magnificent lyrics beginning with: "Mine eyes have seen the glory of the coming of the Lord." Nothing more glorious have I ever heard.

THE HELLYER SAY

The Stars and Stripes Forever…America's bandmaster John Philip Sousa wrote this for the ages. Can you listen to it without your chest swelling with pride?

Oh! What It Seemed to Be…Elaine and I were courting in 1946. The ride on the Chicago Aurora and Elgin Railroad from Elmhurst, Illinois, to the loop and then on the "El" to The Aragon Ballroom was a long one, and I would croon the words to this, "OUR SONG," into Elaine's lovely shell-like ears. Little did we dream that in a few short years I would be standing on the bandstand introducing dance bands playing our song.

Although I didn't start in Chicago radio until May of 1950, I had one of my fantasies come true. The Trianon and Aragon ballrooms were still doing big band remotes and I got to do some of the last ones. I proudly have the faded copy of one I did on WGN radio at 11:30 p.m. in the fall of 1950, "From Andrew and William Karza's Magnificent Aragon Ballroom on Chicago's far north side, at Lawrence and Broadway, this is music by Eddy Howard and his orchestra. And now here's the maestro opening our dancing program singing his great song, 'My Last Goodbye.'" Life CAN be like the movies. I know.

You'll Never Walk Alone…Richard Rodgers and Oscar Hammerstein II wrote this for a scene in their second musical "Carousel." It is an inspirational song, and when Elaine and I were courting in 1946, she and her all-time closest friend Shirley Grover would stand at the piano and sing it so very beautifully. Elaine's dad, who was the American Conservatory's prize student of the 1930s, accompanied them on the Steinway.

All the Things You Are…Jerome Kern and Oscar Hammerstein

II's poignant song from the 1939 musical "Very Warm for May." A gorgeous song that *Variety* chose for its "Fifty-Year Hit Parade."

The Whiffenpoof Song... "To the tables down at Mory's, to the place we love so well....Sing the Whiffenpoofs assembled with their glasses raised on high." I've always regretted not going to Yale University just to sing that classic song. I can see me gathered around the table with my classmates, at Mory's. George Herbert Walker Bush and I are the same age, and we just might have been together there raising our frosty steins, and perhaps playing together on the Yale baseball team.

Whispering Hope...Gordon MacRae and Jo Stafford recorded a million-seller of this gorgeous hymn in 1949. Gordon was a guest on my WCFL show one morning and he invited me—no mention of "Bring your wife, Art"—to dinner that night in his room at the Ambassador East Hotel. Well, I found out the moment I walked in the door, why Elaine was not invited. He had two nude young women in the living room of his suite when I arrived. One was for him, and one was for me. I turned right around and walked out. He never came on any of my shows again.

Jo Stafford guested on my shows quite a few times. I asked her about formal training and she said she and her sisters sang together as little girls growing up, then auditioned for Los Angeles radio stations when they were teenagers in the mid-thirties. KNX hired the Stafford Trio, and Tommy Dorsey heard them on his car radio. She joined TD in 1937, and soloed with his band, and was the female member of "The Pied Pipers," Dorsey's vocal group. Their recording of "Dream" in 1946 sold over a million copies. In 1947 she went out on her own and recorded "Timtayshun" with Red Ingle and the Natural Seven. You will not see her name on the label, because she billed herself as "Cinderella G. Stump," and had her first solo million-selling record.

Moonlight in Vermont...I recently did an interview with Margaret Whiting. She was the daughter of the great songwriter Richard Whiting, and she talked of her childhood growing up in their mansion in California, never knowing who would stop in and join her dad in song. Everyone from the Gershwins to Johnny Mercer, and as a young child Margaret would sing the new songs they were working on. What a fantastic memory to carry through life. Wow!!!!

Begin the Beguine...My dear buddy Paul Hackert drove us, each seventeen years old, way out north of Chicago in his dad's 1940 faded maroon four-door Dodge to the Rink Ballroom in Waukegan to see Artie Shaw, in person. We wanted to be able to tell our grandchildren we saw Artie Shaw play "When They Begin the Beguine..." Shaw's band was so large, most of the musicians were offstage behind the curtains, but the clarinet master was center stage, and when he slid into our song we were on cloud nine. Yes, and many, many years later I proudly told my grandchildren about that famous night, and one of them looked quizzically at me and asked, "Grandpa...who's Artie Shaw?" GRRRRR!!! The chorale-dance arrangement of this great song by Cole Porter in the original "Cole Porter Story" starring Cary Grant is outstanding.

White Christmas...As mentioned elsewhere in this book, Irving Berlin told me that when he finished writing "White Christmas" he knew he had penned "the most beautiful song ever written." I agree. Every time we GIs in World War Two heard Bing's voice sliding into "I'm dreaming of a White

Christmas, just like the ones I used to know," we broke into tears. And I still do today. What a glorious song!!!!!

My best next-door neighbors in 57 years of home ownership? A tie.....Warren and Diane Green, Naperville, Ill., and Olive and Bob Ryan, Skokie, Ill. And I admire Naperville neighbor Jeff Leston for being a stay-at-home dad while his children were growing up. Also a tip of the hat to my across-the-street neighbors Linda and Dave McElhinny for giving me a gorgeous house and yard view to look at every day.

* * *

Well, the clock on the wall tells me it's time to sign-off. I'm Art Hellyer and I hope you've enjoyed my written trip down memory lane. To paraphrase the close I've used on all my shows since the fifties, "This BOOK has been a work of Art. Bye"........

* * *

THE HELLYER SAY

* * *

 Jeff.....I know other things that happened will pop into my mind from time to time, and older people stop me in parking lots when they see my license plate and recall for me things that happened on my shows....BUT I MUST DRAW THE LINE SOMEWHERE. SO THIS IS IT!!!!!!!!

Thank you for all your help, and Larry, Mike, Debbie and Vickie for your help, too......without which this would have been impossible.

And now that I've written the final words of my tome, I'm off to my favorite vacation spot in all this world—Door County, Wisconsin. Love, Dad

Left to right, back: Mike, Larry
Left to right, front: Vickie, Art, Debbie, Jeff
(Father's Day, June 15, 2008)

THE HELLYER SAY

Key to Cover Photos—Front cover (left to right, top to bottom):

— With Dr. K, WAIT, 1958

— With Irving Berlin and the Lovely Elaine, Irving Berlin's suite, Ambassador East Hotel, Chicago, 1956

— WJOL, 1992

— *Chicago Tribune*, Chief Cartoonist Ed Holland, "A.H. Fanclub"

— "A Tired American Gets Angry," 45 rpm (narrated), 1966, written by Al McIntosh

— With Mayor Richard J. Daley and his wife Eleanor, and their son (background) future Mayor Richard M. Daley, Election night 1959, Morrison Hotel

— WMAW, Milwaukee—"MAW's Matinee," 1948

— WCFL, 1950

— WBBM, 1961

— With Richard Nixon, ABC-TV, 1970

— With Elaine, WJJD, 1982

— With Gloria Swanson, WMAW, Milwaukee, 1948

Key to cover photos—Spine (top, bottom):

— WCFL Morning Show, 1953

— In home/"Studio H," interview for "Wake Up, Chicago! The Art Hellyer Story" documentary, 2001

Key to Cover Photos

Key to Cover Photos—Back cover (left to right, top to bottom):

— Satellite Music Network, 1987
— With Billy Pierce, Comiskey Park, 1954
— With Dr. Robinson, Carmelita Pope, "It's in the Name,"
  WGN-TV, 1958
— Early color TV, People's Pontiac live commercial, WNBQ, 1956
— With Andy Griffith, WCFL, 1953
— Live telecast (Univ. of Illinois Chorale, Christmas),
  WLS-TV, 1976
— With Willie Mays, Comiskey Park, ABC Radio, 1983
— With Les Paul, Mary Ford, Bill O'Connor, WCFL, 1953
— WLS-TV Late Night News, 1964
— Elaine with Sen. Robert F. Kennedy, 1965
— With the Ames Brothers, WCFL, 1953
— Station break slide, A.H. WLS-FM promo, 1967-1972
— With Elaine, Midwest Network Morning Show, from home
  (Skokie), 1958
— With Joe DiMaggio, Comiskey Park, ABC Radio, 1983
— With Peggy Lee, Café de Paris (Chicago), PR shot, 1952
— With Mayor Jane Byrne and Yul Brynner, Grant Park, 1984
— With Casey Stengel and Bob Elson, visitors' dugout,
  Comiskey Park, WCFL, 1953
— With Perry Como, NBC-TV, 1956
— With Mr. & Mrs. Spike Jones in their Hollywood, California,
  home, 1958
— State Street, Chicago, New Year's Eve, WBKB-TV, Channel 7,
  1964

Key to Cover Photos—Back cover (bottom):

— Father, Mother, and son Larry viewing one of the 120
  Chicagoland "Morning Madcap" Art Hellyer WCFL billboards,
  1952—"Wake Up, Chicago! With Art Hellyer"

Index

Index

Howard, Eddy, 260, 274, 331, 377, 378, 382
Hubbard, Eddie, 91, 98, 104, 270, 276
Huckaba, Kate, 274
Hughes, Birdsey, 184
Hull, Bobby, 291

I

Illinois
  Aurora, 10, 52, 55, 60, 69, 84, 85, 91, 92, 124, 140, 143, 192, 225, 294, 342, 382
  Chicago, 5, 10, 17, 19, 22, 26–45, 52–73, 82–98, 104–110, 115–131, 134–168, 172–199, 205–242, 247–248, 256–266, 280, 281, 287–301, 309–327, 331–340, 346, 369, 372–376, 379, 382, 384
  Des Plaines, 155, 259
  Dixon, 28
  Downers Grove, 49, 69
  DuPage County, 34, 37, 38, 49
  El Paso, 46
  Elmhurst, 5, 9, 10, 11, 21, 25, 31, 37, 39, 45, 46, 47, 49, 50, 51, 54, 55, 56, 60, 69, 70, 78, 84, 85, 91, 92, 107, 108, 115, 118, 189, 192, 249, 346, 382
  Evanston, 272
  Galena, 254, 255
  Glen Ellyn, 17, 19, 69
  Hinsdale, 18, 22, 25, 36, 37, 69
  Joliet, 163, 229, 261, 276, 277, 328, 376, 377
  Mokena, 21, 259, 262, 263, 270, 329, 330
  Naperville, 13, 14, 15, 167, 175, 212, 226, 259, 344, 350
  Oak Park, 10, 55, 173, 174, 175, 178, 179, 192
  Rockford, 62, 212, 213, 219
  Skokie, 3, 118, 133, 142, 143, 150, 151, 154, 155, 157, 195, 198, 222, 230, 312, 344, 348
  Waukegan, 384
  Wheaton, 34, 35, 37, 69, 165, 316, 348
Indiana
  Fort Wayne, 75, 76, 91, 124, 188, 189, 190, 191, 192
  Terre Haute, 214, 216, 273
"It's in the Name," 389

J

James, Harry, 54, 260, 311
Jones, Loretta (Hellyer)(sister), 24, 38, 39, 43, 44, 351, 367, 368
Jones, Spike, 144, 231, 233, 332, 389
Jordan, Michael, 373, 374

395

Index

Index

Presley, Elvis, 260
Provence, Bob, 86
Putman, Johnnie, 271–272

Q

Quinlan, Jack, 105
Quinlan, Red, 163, 319

R

Racusin, Leon, 129
Radio Institute of Chicago, i,
  82, 84, 85, 87, 110, 188,
  281
Raila, Andrea, ii
Rapchak, Mike, 104, 183, 377
"Rate Your Mate," 110
Reed, Alan, 30
Reis, Art, 267
Rhodes, Bob, 167
Rivait, Pat, 14
Rivers, Joan, 173
Roberts, Ed, 27
Roberts, Howie, 27, 109, 133,
  148
Robinson, Marty, inside cover
Rodgers, Irene
  (Hellyer)(sister), 11, 22, 23,
  24, 37, 39, 43, 44, 46, 178,
  197, 223, 357
Roorda, Jim, 6, 346
Roosevelt University, 58
Rosenblum, Lya Dym, 328
Ross, Norman, 10, 104, 229
Rosten, Phil, 182
Ruth, Babe, 249, 299, 300,
  301, 302
Ryan, Bob, 288, 350, 385

Ryan, Olive (Ollie), 350, 385

S

SAG, 193, 194, 221
Salk, Jonas, Dr., 25, 101, 316
Sanders, Richie, 346, 348
Salter, Harry, 196
Satellite Music Network, The,
  21, 98, 163, 215, 259, 262,
  263, 269–276, 327–330,
  377, 389
Sawyer, Diane, 212
Sayers, Gayle, 179
Schaden, Chuck, 1, 26, 30,
  49, 125, 233, 280
Schlosser, Len, 161
Schwimmer & Scott
  Advertising, i, 106, 107
Schwimmer, Walter, 106, 112
Sealy Mattress Company, 111
Sears, Roebuck and Co., 35,
  52
Seubold, James, Dr., 221
Shapiro, Howie, 169, 221
Shaw, Artie, 54, 260, 334,
  381, 384
Sheil, Bernard, Bishop, 300
Sherman, Ralph, 98, 163,
  233, 259, 262, 263, 264,
  266, 270, 271, 276, 277,
  278, 331, 377
Shomo, Ernie, 163
Shore, Dinah, 144, 205, 230,
  233, 260, 263, 312, 372,
  377
Sid Schneider, 173
Siegel, Jon, 14

Index